FOUNDATIONS OF EARLY CHILDHOOD EDUCATION

FOUNDATIONS OF EARLY CHILDHOOD EDUCATION

Teaching Three-, Four-, and Five-Year-Old Children

Bernard Spodek
University of Illinois

Olivia N. Saracho
University of Maryland

Michael D. Davis
Virginia Commonwealth University

Prentice-Hall, Inc., Englewood Cliffs, New Jersey 07632

Library of Congress Cataloging-in-Publication Data

Spodek, Bernard.
  Foundations of early childhood education.

  Includes index.
  1. Education, Preschool.   2. Education, Preschool—
United States.   3. Education, Preschool—Curricula.
I. Saracho, Olivia N.   II. Davis, Michael D.   III. Title.
LB1140.2.S733 1987   372′.21′0973   86-12249
ISBN 0-13-329822-1

Editorial/production supervision
  and interior design: Virginia L. McCarthy
Cover design: Bruce Kenselaar
Cover art: Mary Cassatt, *Mother
  Playing with Her Child.* The
  Metropolitan Museum of Art, From
  the Collection of James Stillman,
  Gift of Dr. Ernest G. Stillman, 1922.
Manufacturing buyer: John Hall
Page layout: Peggy Finnerty

Printed in the United States of America

10 9 8 7 6 5 4 3 2

ISBN 0-13-329822-1 01

Prentice-Hall International (UK) Limited, *London*
Prentice-Hall of Australia Pty. Limited, *Sydney*
Prentice-Hall Canada Inc., *Toronto*
Prentice-Hall Hispanoamericana, S.A., *Mexico*
Prentice-Hall of India Private Limited, *New Delhi*
Prentice-Hall of Japan, Inc., *Tokyo*
Prentice-Hall of Southeast Asia Pte. Ltd., *Singapore*
Editora Prentice-Hall do Brasil, Ltda., *Rio de Janeiro*
Whitehall Books Limited, *Wellington, New Zealand*

CONTENTS

14   SOCIAL-PERSONAL LEARNING: The Social Studies and Beyond

PREFACE

Early childhood education has always been an exciting and dynamic field. The increased knowledge we have gained over the past two decades about how children learn and develop, our awareness of the positive results of enrolling young children in early childhood education programs, and the increased acceptance of early childhood education by the American public make this a particularly opportune time to study early childhood education and to prepare to become an early childhood education professional.

Foundations of Early Childhood Education is an introductory text for students preparing to teach children ages three through five. It is intended to provide basic knowledge about the field of early childhood education, about the work that practitioners do with young children, and about the ideas that underlie that work. It can be used in undergraduate courses in four-year colleges and universities as well as in community colleges. Because of the wealth of resources included in this book, students will wish to keep it as a reference as they begin their teaching.

This book presents a realistic view of the field of early childhood education. It integrates theory with practice so that the reader can understand not only what things happen in schools for young children, but why they happen as well. The book is written in a clear, concise style using understandable language. Concepts are carefully explained. Practical examples and appropriate illustrations are provided throughout so that even the most complicated ideas can be understood.

The book describes the historical traditions of the field of early childhood education as well as contemporary early childhood institutions and programs, the types of practitioners in the field, and the requirements for different practitioner roles. It also presents basic theories and knowledge of child development that are so vital to teaching young children. The text provides the basis for planning the physical and social environment for teaching, for using different forms of educational evaluation, and for working with parents. A separate chapter is included for each curriculum area to help the reader focus on the specifics of program planning and implementation.

Within each topic, basic theory and research are related and integrated with practical knowledge gained from classroom teaching. Careful attention is given to provide the most up-to-date research and to address emerging issues in the field. Examples, practical applications, and guidelines for practice as well as verbal and visual illustrations are generously used to help students explore the implications of the concepts, ideas, and theories presented throughout the book.

We wish to acknowledge our debt to the many persons who have contributed to the development of this text. Much of the knowledge we have gained over the years and that is reflected in this book comes from the many contacts we have had with others in the field: teachers, undergraduate and graduate students, and parents and children. We wish especially to thank those who reviewed our manuscript at various stages and provided helpful suggestions, criticism, and comments. These include Dr. Joanne E. Bernstein, Brooklyn College; Dr. Jane Bugnand, Essex County College; Dr. Patricia E. Hanley, University of South Florida; Dr. James Hoot, North Texas State University; Dr. Millicent Savery, University of Nebraska; and Dr. Edith Smith, Alcorn State University.

We also wish to thank the staff, parents, and children of Martin Luther King Jr. and Thomas Paine Elementary Schools in Urbana, Illinois, especially those in Sandra Beak's and Jane Maehr's kindergarten classes, and of Early Learning Children's Center in Champaign, Illinois. The bulk of the photographs of children in school were taken in these classes by Bernard Spodek.

Most important, we wish to acknowledge the support and encouragement we have received from our families during the period we were writing this book. Without the love and support of Connie, Meg, and Sally Davis, of Francisca S., Pablo J., Saul Villareal and Lydia Gonzales, and of Prudence Spodek, this book would not have been possible.

1

INTRODUCTION

OBJECTIVES

After completing this introductory chapter, the student will be able to:

1. Define early childhood education.
2. Describe early childhood programs.
3. Describe the different early childhood settings for children age three to five, including: nursery school, child care center, Head Start program, private kindergarten, and public kindergarten.
4. Identify the social forces that influence the field of early childhood education.
5. Specify the educational effects of preschool programs on children.
6. Describe recent trends in early childhood education.

The early years in children's lives have long been considered among the most important. Children learn a great deal at this age, and what they learn has long-term, significant consequences.

From infancy on, children develop physically, mentally, socially, and emotionally. This development is related to maturation, but it is also influenced by their experiences. Education begins at this early stage. Parents teach children to walk and to talk. They teach children self-caring skills, manners, values, and a host of other things. Parents and other family members become the children's first teachers, stimulating children's physical and mental growth. Parents generally do not study how to teach their children. They naturally and spontaneously interact with children. Their teaching skills grow out of living with their children throughout the day. Although it is informal, the instructional role of parents is critical in the lives of young children.

The child's home provides an important context for learning. In many ways, the school supplements the home. Young children's experiences in school are no less natural than their experiences in their home child-rearing environment, although often, they can be planned with greater care. It is the integration of education in and out of school that is important.

We generally assume that children will be raised in a good home—one that will provide for all the needs of the young child. This is not always the case, however. Many families lack adequate resources to provide all the complex requirements of rearing children within our society. Families are not always able to provide the best conditions for the development of their children. Poverty, isolation, and the demands of earning a living can limit what may be available. Early childhood programs work hand in hand with families to provide the necessary basis for the children's development, supplementing parents' child-rearing efforts and increasing the support to allow children successfully to assume their role in society.

EARLY CHILDHOOD EDUCATION

Early childhood education is generally defined as the education of children from birth to age eight. It includes programs for infants and toddlers, nursery school, child care, and preschool programs, as well as kindergarten and the primary grades. Sometimes the term *early childhood education* is used to refer to those programs serving children under the age of six. Sometimes it is used to refer just to programs for children below kindergarten age. The material in this text will focus only on three-through five-year-old children who are educated and cared for in kindergarten and prekindergarten settings, such as nursery schools and child care centers.

Children in their early childhood years are served by many kinds of institutions. The majority of children from ages five through eight are educated in the kindergarten and primary grades of the public schools. Some are educated in private institutions: religious and parochial schools as well as private secular schools. Most programs for children below age five are in private institutions, operated either for-profit or not-for-profit. These institutions serve fewer children than do the public schools and often enroll groups that are alike in economic status, ethnicity, or some other group trait. Child care centers differ from nursery schools. They have longer daily hours and are concerned with caring for as well as educating children. No one program or setting can meet all the needs of all young children and their families.

Public schooling in the United States usually begins at age five or six, with enrollment in public school kindergarten or first grade. This situation, however, is changing. A number of states are beginning to include four-year-olds in public education. Also while compulsory school attendance is not required in most states until the age of seven, some states are beginning to require attendance as early as age five. Other states are requiring kindergarten attendance for admission to first grade.

As kindergarten became part of the public school system, it was often considered as something different that was grafted on to the elementary grades. Public school educators often seemed unsure as to whether kindergarten really belonged. Early childhood education has become more widely accepted as part of public education.

As was mentioned earlier, most children below age five are not in the public schools. They are educated in nursery schools, day care centers, and Head Start programs as well as private kindergartens. These institutions are similar in many ways. They also differ in some ways, including varied institutional settings, services offered, program goals, and even psychological theories that underlie the programs.

Nursery Schools

The original nursery school, described in Chapter 2, was based on a philosophy of nurturance: a concern for the child's social, physical, emotional, and intellectual needs. The nursery school teacher bathed children, dressed them in clean outfits, provided them with food and rest, saw that they received sufficient fresh air, and also educated them. The children were taught self-caring skills (such as washing oneself and tying one's shoelaces) and taking care of plants, animals, and the school environment. They were involved in music, language, reading readiness, writing, mathematics, and science activities. Play was an important part of the program, which flowed freely indoors and outdoors. The children were provided with opportunities for art construction, water play, playing with sand, and other nonstructured activities.

Nursery schools provide a broad-base education to children below kindergarten age.

Most nursery schools today are concerned *primarily* with children's education. Many colleges and universities also use the nursery school as a laboratory to prepare early childhood teachers and to conduct research. Departments of home economics (or their equivalent) may use nursery schools as laboratories and demonstration centers for education for parenthood and instruction on home management. Parent-cooperative nursery schools, where parents own the school and often participate in the children's programs, offer nursery school education at a reasonable cost and often focus on parent education. This may include child observations, discussions, and meetings on topics such as child development, nutrition, and child-rearing practices.

Presently the emphasis in nursery school is to provide a broad-based education to children below kindergarten age. Nursery educators are concerned with the intellectual learning, but important emphasis is also placed on expression and creativity.

Child Care Centers

The history of child care in the United States consists of sporadic attempts to provide care for workers' children and patchwork legislation to regulate children's centers. A unique feature of a child care center is that it serves the children of parents who cannot be at home full-time to take care of their children. These parents may be working, ill, hospitalized, or not able to care for their children during the day for some other reason.

Presently child care is offered in a variety of settings. Young children are cared for in homes, either by relatives or neighbors, or in child care centers. Licensed or unlicensed family day care homes are run on a small scale in private residences. Child care centers offer care and education on a larger scale. These centers serve three-, four-, and five-year-old children as well as infants and toddlers. Often, they also serve school-age children before and after school and when public schools are closed. The child care center is open for a long period each day, often from 6:00 A.M. until 6:00 P.M. Its hours depend on the needs of the children's parents. The child care center assumes a unique responsibility, supplementing the care of parents who are not available to their children during some part of the day.

Ideally, a good child care center is staffed by teachers who are well prepared in the education and care of young children, contains an adequate amount of equipment and material, and offers a high-quality program of education responsive to the needs of young children. Child care programs can and should be as good as the best nursery school, kindergarten, or Head Start program.

Head Start

It became evident in the 1960s that children from economically impoverished families were failing in school at an alarming rate. Available evidence suggested that early intervention could make a critical difference (e.g., Bloom, 1964; Hunt, 1961). After a variety of research programs were launched, the Department of Health, Education and Welfare funded Project Head Start as part of the war on poverty. Head Start represented a national commitment to provide comprehensive services for children under age six who came from low-income families. When Head Start was conceived, there was a lack of strong research evidence on the effects of early intervention. Significant research to date, however, provides evidence to support Head Start programs.

Head Start is currently administered by the Administration for Children, Youth and Families in the Department of Health and Human Services. It is a compensatory program; 90 percent of the Head Start children come from families with low incomes; 10 percent of the children are handicapped. The purpose of the program is to improve the health and physical ability of poor children, to develop their physical and intellectual skills, to involve parents in their children's program, and to provide appropriate social services for the family. Eighty percent of the funds flow from the federal government, and 20 percent are expected to come from local sources. Sometimes this local support is provided as an in-kind contribution, for example, providing space and maintenance. A community action agency can run the Head Start program directly or can contract for services from public or private nonprofit agencies.

Head Start was created as a unique program for young children. The underlying assumption is that success in school and in life is based on the child's complete growth: what a child knows, how a child feels, how well the child's body functions, the child's social skills, and the child's view of him or herself. Parents play a major role in the Head Start program, attending meetings, participating in the program, and serving on Policy Advisory Committees. Head Start teachers strive to work with parents as a team, to have parents supplement them, support them, and work in the same direction. The teachers work intensively with children and their parents; the parents are included in and feel part of the program.

Kindergarten

Kindergarten programs in the United States serve primarily five-year-old children, although more four-year-old kindergartens are coming into existence and kindergartens in many other countries enroll children ages three through six. Kindergarten programs include crafts and art activities and different types of play activities. The child's present life and its context is often used as a source of learning and is reflected in play. Thus, blocks, dolls, and miniature housekeeping materials are provided to represent the child's life context.

The kindergarten movement began in America as an agent of social and educational reform. As kindergartens were established in public schools they provided an opportunity for greater numbers of children to attend kindergarten.

Kindergarten programs provide a wide range of educational activities.

In earlier kindergartens the teaching of reading was carefully avoided. It is still a major issue as academic skills are being taught in many kindergartens today. Whereas in the past, kindergartens influenced and modified the primary grades, currently the primary grades seem to be influencing kindergartens in the public school (Spodek, 1982).

The kindergarten program has had strong and lasting effects on American education. It has focused on educational issues in a democratic society: the relationship of teachers, parents, and children; whether the kindergarten should be used primarily to prepare children for the primary grades; whether it's more important to develop children's social skills and creativity or train children in academics; and the need to assist low-income children to achieve social mobility. These are all critical issues in early childhood education today, and they are being debated by educators, psychologists, philosophers, sociologists, and politicians.

FORCES THAT AFFECT THE FIELD

In its development, early childhood education has always been responsive to social forces, and these forces continue to shape programs today. One such force has been the increasing number of mothers in the nation's work force. This has had a strong impact on American family life. Women work for a variety of reasons: to raise their standard of living, to adapt to different lifestyles, or to seek greater personal satisfaction. Both home and work had to change as mothers of young children went to work. We have become aware that raising children is a family responsibility rather than only the woman's responsibility. High-quality child care is essential to allow women to achieve career goals outside the home.

A number of employers provide work-site child care centers for their employees as well as for children in the surrounding communities. Others offer a referral service or purchase child care services from existing centers. This development reflects a number of social changes: strides in the education of women; changes in lifestyles and family structure; technological developments in the economy; less time consumed in the management of the household; and the encouragement given to women to employ their strengths and talents in a variety of ways.

Another reason for the need for child care centers is that the increased number of working women has also led to a decline in the availability of traditional baby-sitters. Grandparents and unmarried relatives are no longer at home, known and trusted servants are no longer employed, and neighbors are no longer old family friends. To replace these, child care agencies have expanded.

There are other social conditions that have created a shortage of child care services. Some mothers are returning to college or vocational school to acquire the necessary skills and knowledge to gain meaningful employment. These women need quality care for their children while they attend school. Mothers of young children with handicapping conditions also need special services, as do children of mothers who are ill or themselves handicapped. For these families quality child care may be unavailable or beyond their means.

Another social force affecting young children is the reduced space available for children to play in. High-rise apartments, townhouses, and other multiple family dwellings tend not to have trees, rocks, or large grassy areas. Some homes (rural, urban, affluent, poor) have become simpler and more automated, leaving children with limited opportunities to explore and create. Finally, family planning has reduced the size of families, making it more difficult to find playmates for young children. Previously, children were able to play with their brothers and sisters or with neighbors.

Long-Term Effects

While early childhood programs are used to respond to social problems, they also have pervasive and long-lasting educational effects. The Consortium on Longitudinal Studies report, *Persistence of preschool effects* (Lazar, Hubbell, Murray, Rosche, & Royce, 1977), demonstrates that early intervention programs can provide significant long-term educational benefits to children. Early intervention can help reduce the number of children who are assigned to classes for the handicapped and who are retained in a grade because of low achievement. Early childhood programs have also produced significant increases in IQ and achievement in the early primary grades. Children in these programs are also more likely to give achievement-related reasons for feeling good about themselves.

The High/Scope report *Changed Lives*, (Berrueta-Clement, Schweinhart, Barnett, Epstein, & Weikart, 1984), also demonstrated the long-term effects of early childhood education. The authors suggest that, in terms of both social and economic costs, early childhood education more than pays for itself in relation to money that need not be spent later. Their cost-benefit analysis shows a 7 to 1 return on investment.

It is not enough just to provide programs for young children; the programs must be of high quality. Benjamin Bloom (1964), J. McVicker Hunt (1961), and Robert Hess and Virginia Shipman (1965) all support the importance of environmental factors in the development and education of young children. A study by Jean V. Carew (1980) examined home-reared and day care children in their second and third years of life to record their everyday experiences. She then compared the relationship of these experiences to the children's test performance. Effective caregivers, whether parents or teachers, were successful in integrating a variety of strategies to develop children's intellectual competence. Young children seemed to master important cognitive and social skills and develop positive attitudes about people and situations when they worked alone or interacted with others in a child care setting. The quality of the interactions and the learning experiences were a central factor in the children's cognitive development.

The attributes of effective caregivers found in Carew's study were also found by Marlis Mann (1970), who studied lower socioeconomic parents' use of elaboration and extension to assist their children in describing, labeling, predicting, and defining relationships as well as making associations. The amount and diversity of the mothers' verbal stimulation were important factors in improving children's concept development. Phyllis Levenstein (1970), in her parent education program, focused on improving verbal interaction skills in parents of low-income children. She found that when they were improved, intellectual functioning improved significantly. These studies and one by Ann P. Streissguth and Helen L. Bee (1972) show a relationship between verbal stimulation and the development of intelligence. They suggest that improving the quality of the interactions of caregivers and children can enhance the learning and intellectual development of young children.

The programs described have been designed for low-income children. The impact of early education on the lives of middle-class children is not as clear. Perhaps early childhood programs have emphasized the same types of skills that parents of middle-class children already emphasize, and thus the influence of the educational program is masked for these children.

James Macdonald (1969) describes early childhood education as a form of deliberate social intervention. The need for such intervention has grown out of society's need to prepare children to adjust to the existing social order. School experiences can help children conform to this order or prepare them for a new emerging sociey. Whatever its purpose, however, effective early childhood education programs help children change. The important thing for teachers is to ensure that the change is in a direction we value.

TRENDS IN EARLY CHILDHOOD EDUCATION

Early childhood education has changed significantly since the 1960s. A number of trends have become evident in recent years. One trend is the move to decrease the size of children's groups. In some public schools there may be over 30 children in kindergarten. School personnel are now attempting to make them smaller. In Indiana, for example, the Prime

Time program helped to bring first grades down to an average of 18 children per class in its first year, and similar reductions are being made in second and third grades and in kindergarten.

Another trend has been toward greater parent involvement. As a result of Head Start and various programs for the handicapped, more and more early childhood educators are seeking to include parents in the educational endeavor. Parents can help in identifying children's needs and in advising about program elements. They can also be involved in program design decisions and may have the right to approve or reject program changes as well as make suggestions for its improvement.

Other issues that have recently emerged relate to the education of young handicapped children, especially in classes with normal children, and the expansion of public school kindergarten.

Early Education of the Handicapped

In the past, programs for handicapped children, when available, were provided only for children of school age, often not until they were seven years old. Early intervention programs, however, have shown pervasive and long-lasting effects on children who have educational deficits. Although not all children's disabilities are cured, often children are able to learn to utilize their personal resources and capacities at an early age.

In the past, when handicapped children were educated, they were usually provided separate programs in separate settings. These segregated programs were not necessarily more successful, however, and in many cases they reduced the educational opportunities for children. Handicapped children did not learn to interact with normal people in a normal environment. What they did learn was often difficult to transfer to everyday situations. Furthermore, handicapped children educated in normal settings were shown to achieve at an equal or better level than those in separate programs. As a result, a movement developed to educate children in the least restrictive educational setting and in as normal a situation as possible. Many handicapped children have been integrated with nonhandicapped children in "mainstreamed" classes (Spodek, Saracho, & Lee, 1983).

Unfortunately, the integration of handicapped children into a regular classroom, when appropriate, does not often happen to preschool children. Many public schools do not serve children below age five except for handicapped children. Head Start does provide for the integration of handicapped and nonhandicapped children, since 10 percent of the children enrolled must be handicapped. This number represents a small percentage of those who might be served, however.

Expansion of Kindergarten

Kindergartens have been included in public elementary schools for over one hundred years. However, most kindergartens differ from the rest of the grades in many ways. This is partly the result of the kindergarten children being younger as well as differences in the traditions of kindergarten education and elementary education. Age-grade standards and existing testing procedures for older children place many restrictions on kindergarten teachers and children.

Many early childhood educators believe that the children's classroom should be a miniature society. They focus on the relationship between the children's out-of-school and in-school experiences and value children's active participation as learners. These teachers serve to guide the learning experiences rather than instruct directly.

As kindergartens have been integrated into elementary schools, however, the primary grade curriculum has been imposed on the kindergarten. In many kindergarten classrooms, the educational programs look very much like first-grade programs. Preschools have also been pressured to push for early literacy by parents' anxiety and zeal for their children to learn to read early.

A LOOK AHEAD

These and other issues will be explored in the rest of the book, along with some information about the context of these issues and the implications for teachers. The first chapters will present the historical traditions of early childhood education, a look at early childhood institutions and programs, and a review of the kinds of practitioners found in early childhood education and the preparation necessary to become a practitioner. A brief review of child development concepts and theories is also provided. These represent the foundations of knowledge of early childhood education.

Succeeding chapters discuss the physical and social environment, covering the immediate context in which early childhood education takes place. Following the environment are chapters concerned with ways of working with parents and ways of evaluating programs.

Next are chapters that deal directly with program content: play, creative activities, language and literacy, science and mathematics, and social-personal learning. Since any textbook, course, or program to prepare early childhood practitioners represents only the beginning of professional preparation—a process that continues throughout one's career—the final chapter looks at how early childhood educators can continue to extend their knowledge.

Thus, this book represents a beginning step—a foundation—for those interested in learning about early childhood education. Only by continuously reflecting about practice, seeking additional sources of knowledge, and working together with other early childhood educators can we achieve the level of professional competence necessary for all early childhood teachers.

REFERENCES

BERRUETA-CLEMENT, J. R., L. J. SCHWEINHART, W. S. BARNETT, A. S. EPSTEIN, AND D. P. WEIKART (1984). Changed lives: The effects of the Perry Preschool Program on youths through age 19. *Monographs of the High/Scope Education Research Foundation,* **8.**

BLOOM, B. (1964). *Stability and change in human characteristics.* New York: John Wiley & Sons.

BRICKER, D. D., AND W. A. BRICKER (1971). *Toddler research and intervention project report: Year I.* IMRID Behavioral Science Monograph 20. Institute of Mental Retardation and Intellectual Development. Nashville, TN: George Peabody College.

BUREAU OF THE CENSUS (1978). *Population characteristics: School enrollment...social and economic characteristics of students: October 1977* (Advance report). Washington, DC: U.S. Government Printing Office.

CAREW, J. V. (1980). Experience and the development of intelligence in young children at home and in day care. *Monographs of the Society for Research in Child Development,* **45,** Serial No. 187.

COHEN, S., M. SEMMES, AND M. J. GURALNICK (1979). Public Law 94-142 and the education of preschool handicapped children. *Exceptional Children,* **45,** 270-285.

CONSORTIUM ON DEVELOPMENTAL CONTINUITY (1977). *The persistence of preschool effects.* Department of Health, Education and Welfare Publication #(OHD) 78-30130.

HESS, R., AND V. SHIPMAN, (1965). Early experience and the socialization of cognitive modes in children. *Child Development,* **36,** 869-886.

HUNT, J. M. (1961). *Intelligence and experience.* New York: Ronald.

KEYSERLING, M. (1972). *Windows on day care.* New York: National Council of Jewish Women.

LAZAR, I., V. R. HUBBELL, H. MURRAY, M. ROSCHE, AND J. ROYCE (1977). *Summary report: The persistence of preschool effects: A long-term follow-up of fourteen infant and preschool experiments.* Washington, DC: U.S. Department of Health, Education and Welfare, Administration of Children, Youth and Families, OHDS, #OHDS 78-30129.

LEVENSTEIN, P. (1970). Cognitive growth in preschoolers through verbal interaction with mothers. *American Journal of Orthopsychiatry,* **40,** 426-429.

MACDONALD, J. (1969). A proper curriculum for young children. *Phi Delta Kappan,* **50**(7), 406-409.

MAGID, R. Y. (1983). *Child care initiatives for working parents: Why employers get involved.* New York: AMA Membership Publications Division, American Management Association.

MANN, M. (1970). *The effect of a preschool language program on two-year-old children and their mothers.* Final Report. ERIC Document No. ED 045 224.

SPODEK, B. (1982). The kindergarten: A retrospective and contemporary look. In L. Katz (Ed.), *Current topics in early childhood education,* Vol. 4, pp. 173-191. Norwood, NJ: Ablex Publishing Co.

SPODEK, B., O. N. SARACHO, AND R. C. LEE (1983). Mainstreaming handicapped children in the preschool. In S. Kilmer (Ed.), *Advances in early education and day care,* Vol. 3, pp. 107-132. Greenwich, CT: JAI Press.

STREISSGUTH, A. P., AND H. L. BEE (1972). Mother–child interactions and cognitive development in children. In W. W. Hartup (Ed.), *The young child: Reviews of research,* Vol. 2. Washington, DC: National Association for the Education of Young Children.

UNITED STATES DEPARTMENT OF HEALTH, EDUCATION AND WELFARE, ADMINISTRATION FOR CHILDREN, YOUTH AND FAMILIES (1977). *Day care centers in the United States.* Washington, DC: U.S. Government Printing Office.

UNITED STATES DEPARTMENT OF HEALTH, EDUCATION AND WELFARE (1976). *Statistical highlights from the national childcare consumer study.* Washington, DC: The Department, #OHD 76-31096.

UNITED STATES DEPARTMENT OF LABOR (1977). *Working mothers and their children.* Washington, DC: Women's Bureau, Employment Standards Administration, The Department.

WEBER, E. (1984). *Ideas influencing early childhood education: A theoretical analysis.* New York: Teachers College Press.

WESTHOFF, C. R., AND R. PARKE, JR. (EDS.) (1972). *Demographic and social aspects of population growth and the American future.* U.S. Government Printing Office.

ZIGLER, E. (1972). Paper presented at the Education Commission of the States Meeting, Denver, December 7.

SUGGESTED ACTIVITIES

1. Discuss the ways a good nursery school can help young children, and the value of good child care, Head Start, and kindergarten programs for young children.

2. Visit different early childhood programs as a part of a small group (e.g., child care center, nursery school, Head Start, kindergarten). Compare the similarities and differences in educational setting, educational purposes, goals, philosophy, and types of experiences provided. Allow each group to share its report.

3. Interview an early childhood program director. Inquire about the

purpose of the program, community served, and other related information.

4. Describe an ideal early childhood school for young children. Include descriptions of the building, classrooms, playground, eating facilities, and rest rooms. Use photographs or drawings if possible.

5. Develop a chart comparing the various schedules used in a child care center, Head Start program, nursery school and kindergarten program.

6. Develop a directory of early childhood schools. For each school include a brief description of the settings, fees, requirements for admission, program services, hours, meals (if any), teacher–child ratio, and special services offered.

2

HISTORICAL TRADITIONS

OBJECTIVES

After completing this chapter on historical traditions, the student will be able to:

1. Describe the beginning of early childhood education.
2. Identify the pioneers in the field, including Jean Frederick Oberlin, Robert Owen, Freidrich Froebel, Maria Montessori, and Margaret McMillan.
3. Discuss the philosophy of Owen's infant school, Froebel's kindergarten, Montessori's *Casa dei Bambini,* and McMillan's nursery school.
4. Describe the beginning of Head Start.
5. Explain the relationship between current programs and historical programs.

Young children have always been educated, but only within relatively recent history has this education taken place outside of the home—and only in the last two hundred years have special institutions been designed to educate young children. If we are to understand the field of early childhood education, then we must know something of its historical roots and its development.

This chapter will describe the beginnings of early childhood education in the United States and its roots in European institutions. It will discuss the history of the kindergarten, nursery school, child care center, and Montessori school in relation to the development of contemporary institutions and issues.

EDUCATING YOUNG CHILDREN IN COLONIAL AMERICA

With the establishment of the first colonies in America, even before there was a United States of America, many communities began to provide schools for their children. The American colonies were essentially Protestant. Some were established as religious communities, often to escape religious oppression that particular sects had felt in Europe. In many of these communities each family was responsible for ensuring that their children would learn to read. Since only by being able to read the Bible could each individual achieve salvation, reading ability became a religious imperative. Often the father was the one to teach reading to his young child. In communities with a sizable number of families living close together, the church operated a primary school so that each child would learn to read. In the Massachusetts colony, by 1647 the law required that towns establish schools for young children.

These early schools were not graded by age as our present schools are. All children were educated in the same class and there was no minimum age for school attendance. Often children as young as three and four were enrolled in these schools, spending their day sitting on backless benches, trying to learn to read along with their older brothers and sisters. It was only toward the middle of the nineteenth century that school attendance laws were passed establishing minimum age levels for children to attend school. It was felt that very young children would be better off spending their days at home with their mothers rather than in the primary school. There was also a fear that the pressure of intellectual activity, including learning to read, could cause insanity for younger children who were not quite ready for such learning. In addition, schools would be simpler to manage if the very young were excluded (May & Vinovskis, 1977).

DEVELOPMENT OF EARLY CHILDHOOD EDUCATION

If we wish to find the beginnings of the development of schools for young children, we must look to Europe for these roots.

next final exam   ✗

The Oberlin School

The earliest reported schools designed especially for young children were developed about 1767 by Jean Frederick Oberlin, a Protestant minister who lived in Alsace, an eastern province in France. Although Oberlin was responsible for founding the school, he did not teach in it. That responsibility rested with his wife, Madame Madeleine Oberlin, until her death in 1784, as well as with Sarah Banzet and Louise Scheppler, who also managed the Oberlin household.

The Oberlin school enrolled children as young as two or three. The school program included teaching handicrafts as well as exercise and play. The children gathered in a circle around Louise Scheppler, who would talk to the children as she knitted. Later, older children took on some of her responsibilities. Pictures of subjects taken from nature and history were shown to the children. At first they were shown the pictures alone. When the children were familiar with the pictures, they were told the names of the objects in their regional dialect. Later, the names of the objects were spoken in proper French while the picture was shown. Thus, the children learned to speak and read French as well as the dialect spoken in their home, while they learned about the world (Deasey, 1978).

This "knitting school" was so popular that it expanded to five neighboring village centers before Oberlin's death. Oberlin's methods were not adopted more generally in other sections in France, however. With the coming of the French Revolution, religious clerics and their work became suspect. Since Oberlin was a minister, French citizens were concerned that his teaching would be both religious and anti-revolutionary. Although Oberlin was respected both during and after the revolution, the "knitting school" remained an isolated phenomenon in France and the idea never expanded in Europe. Perhaps the time was not yet ripe for a major effort in support of education for young children.

Robert Owen Creates the Infant School

Another early childhood institution that began in Europe was the *infant school*, established by Robert Owen in 1816. Owen was an English industrialist and social reformer. When he took over the management of a textile mill in New Lanark, Scotland, he became concerned about the working and living conditions of his employees. Children as young as six worked in the mills, where conditions were poor. The conditions under which the workers lived were like those described in Charles Dickens' novels; working people all over England at that time lived poorly. This situation led Owen to seek social reforms, at least in his mill community. He raised the minimum working age in his mill from six to ten years and provided better housing for his workers. He also started a company store where merchandise was sold to the workers at lower prices. He worked at making the town cleaner and at convincing the people who lived there to remain sober. In addition, he started schools for both children and adults. All these reforms were to prepare for the creation of a newer society that would improve the lives of all people.

Owen called his school the *Institute for the Formation of Character.* The part of the school set aside for the youngest was called the *infant school.* The children enrolled in this school were taught reading, writing, arithmetic, sewing, geography, natural history, modern and ancient history, dance, and music. Often children were taken on field trips to observe things as they existed in the real world. Objects and models were also brought into class for children to observe. The youngest children spent a great deal of time out-of-doors and were not forced to attend to lessons. Most important, children were not physically punished and were not restrained more than was necessary. Children were taught only what they could understand. The teachers wanted to help the children, as a result of instruction, to form good habits and learn to treat each other with kindness.

Robert Owen, father of the infant school.

Owen's ideas about a school for poor and working-class children spread well beyond his mill town in Scotland. Owen's books about his new view of society and the schools that would prepare children for it were read throughout Europe and the United States. Infant schools were established in many American cities in the 1820s. Robert Owen himself came to the United States during this time to lecture and to establish a community based upon his new view of society. He purchased a town, New Harmony, Indiana, from a religious group as a base for establishing his new society. The settlement at New Harmony lasted for only two years, and by the mid-1830s the infant school movement had faded in the United States (Harrison, 1968).

Although they did not last a long time, the infant schools served an important function. They represented a movement to provide a humane form of education for young children. They also represented a type of social reform through education. Many of these infant schools served poor children. While the children were given moral instruction and taught to read, their mothers were freed from child care so that they could find work outside their homes.

The Beginning of the Kindergarten

Freidrich Froebel established the first *kindergarten* in Blankenburg, Germany, in 1837. In its view of children and in its educational purpose, it was different from any school that had been designed before. It had an influence on the education of young children throughout the world.

Froebel viewed education as an extension of his view of the world and his understanding of the relationship between the individual, God, and nature. Each individual, he felt, reflects the whole of his or her culture, just as each tree reflects the whole of nature. Froebel saw education as fostering the natural development of children. He used the garden as a symbol of childhood education. Just as young plants and animals grow naturally according to their own laws if cared for properly, so would children grow according to their laws. Thus, kindergarten education would follow the nature of the child. Play was seen as a method of education and a way for children to copy the natural life of man.

Froebel thought of education as knowledge being transmitted through symbols. He developed a set of activities and materials that would teach young children the important concepts of the unity of the individual, God, and nature. The *gifts* that he designed included ten sets of manipulative materials. The first gift consisted of six woolen balls, each symbolizing unity. The second gift consisted of a wooden ball, cube, and cylinder, representing unity, diversity, and the combination of the two ideas. The next four gifts were sets of small wooden blocks made up of different shaped elements that formed a cube when put together. The seventh gift consisted of sets of wooden tablets, one of squares and the other of

Freidrich Froebel, creator of the kindergarten.

triangles. The eighth gift included lines made of wooden strips. The ninth gift was circles or parts of circles. The tenth and final gift was soft peas or wax pellets and sharpened sticks or straws. Each gift was to be used to make specific constructions according to specific instructions given by the kindergarten teacher.

The curriculum also included *occupations,* or arts and craft activities and constructions. These included work with clay, wood, and cardboard as well as paper cutting, paper weaving, paper folding, and paper pricking. Bead stringing, drawing, embroidering, and weaving were also included. The games and songs used in the Froebelian kindergarten were taken from Froebel's *Mutter and Kose-Leider.* In addition to these, the kindergarten program also included nature study and work in language and arithmetic (Lilley, 1967).

Froebel's kindergarten program soon became popular in Germany. The kindergarten concept expanded as young women were trained to be kindergarten teachers by Froebel and his followers. With the wave of German migration into the United States in the mid-nineteenth century, which brought many of these trained women into the country, the kindergarten idea came to America just as it had come to other countries. The first American kindergarten was established in Watertown, Wisconsin, in 1856 by Margarethe Schurz. She invited the children of her relatives into the kindergarten she had created in her home for her own children. Other German language kindergartens were established at about this time in various cities throughout the United States.

FIGURE 2-1

ABSTRACT FROM: SYLLABUS OF FROEBEL'S *EDUCATION OF MAN*

Education defined by the law of divine unity.

Free self-activity the essential method in education.

Unity, individuality, and diversity the phases of human development.

The several stages of childhood, boyhood, and manhood to be duly respected in their order.

The various powers of the human being to be developed by means of suitable external work.

Nature and value of the child's play.

The family is the type of true life and the source of active interest in all surroundings.

The games of boyhood educate for life by awakening and cultivating many civil and moral virtues.

The true remedy for any evil is to find the original good quality that has been repressed or misled, and then to foster and guide it aright.

The purpose of the school and of its work is to give to the child the inner relations and meanings of what was before merely external and unrelated.

The essential work of the school is to associate facts into principles, not to teach isolated facts.

Mathematics should be treated physically, and mathematical forms and figures should be considered as the necessary outcome of an inner force acting from a center.

Writing and reading grow out of the self-active desire for expression and should be taught with special reference to this fact.

In the study of plants, animals, etc., the work proceeds from particulars to generals, and again from generals to particulars in varied succession.

From natural objects and the products of man's effort, the study should proceed to include the relations of mankind.

The prime purpose throughout is not to impart knowledge to the child, but to lead the child to observe and to think.

The general purpose of family and school instruction is to advance the all-sided development of the child and the complete unfolding of his nature.

F. Froebel, *The Education of Man*. W. H. Hailmann, Trans. (New York: D. Appleton, 1887).

5. **Embroidering.**
— For Girls and Boys —
Worsted, of 12 different colors, and 3 Worsted-Needles, 1 Perforating-Needle, 10 pieces of Bristol Board, 1 piece of Blotting Paper, 10 leaves of white paper, 136 Designs on 12 plates, and Instructions.   Price $0.75.

Designed to teach the elements of fancy-work, to convey correct ideas as to number and form, and to still further educate the eye in the selection and combination of colors. — The objects produced (like those of most of the other Occupations) look pretty, and may be used as presents.

6. **Cork- (or Peas-) Work.**
— For Boys and Girls —
60 Cork Cubes, 60 pieces of Wire, 1, 2, 3, and 4 inches long, respectively, 1 Piercing-Pin, 108 Designs on 12 plates, and Instructions.   Price $0.75.

Designed to instruct in the proportions of geometrical figures and in the production of outlines of solids and of real objects, while teaching also accuracy of measurement and the elements of perspective, etc.

7. **Plaiting (Slat-interlacing).**
— For Girls and Boys —
30 Wooden Slats, 9 inches long by ¼ inch wide, and 30 Slats, 6 inches long by ¼ inch wide, 93 Designs on 12 plates, and Instructions.   Price $0.75.

Designed to teach precision and nicety of adjustment, to instruct in geometrical form, and to stimulate the invention of fancy figures.

Children's occupations in a Froebelian kindergarten.

The first English-speaking kindergarten was founded in Boston in 1860 by Elizabeth Peabody. For many years she traveled throughout the United States, speaking about the purpose of kindergartens and their benefits to children. She helped establish kindergartens wherever she went. The first public school kindergarten was established in 1873 in St. Louis. Susan Blow, the teacher, lectured and taught kindergarten education, continuing to be a champion of Froebelian kindergarten education throughout her life.

During the rest of the nineteenth century kindergartens were sponsored by many different agencies. Churches, settlement houses, factories, and trade unions all sponsored kindergartens. A number of private kindergartens for which fees were charged were also established. Kindergartens were seen as particularly important for the children of the poor. They served to make life better for those children growing up in a slum. In each case, kindergarten teachers worked not just with the young children in their classes: parents were also served by the programs. Mother's clubs were organized so that the kindergarten program could be brought into the homes of children as well.

Reform in the Kindergarten

By the beginning of the twentieth century, ideas about kindergarten were beginning to change. A liberal group of kindergarten educators, who continued to support Froebel's views on the importance of childhood, suggested that we were learning things about the nature of childhood that were making Froebelian kindergarten education obsolete. Kindergartens were paying too much attention to symbols and not enough to the child's life. The child study movement had emerged. The study of children through observation suggested new ideas about what was considered educational for children. In addition, the progressive education movement was developing. This movement emphasized freedom and activity in the classroom and suggested a form of kindergarten education that would reflect the everyday life of the child. Under the leadership of the younger kindergarten educators like Patty Smith Hill and Alice Temple, the kindergarten program was modernized and Americanized. The *occupations* of Froebel were considered too tedious for children, and different arts and crafts activities were substituted. The *gifts* were supplanted by building blocks and dramatic play areas. American songs and games were included in the program as the kindergarten was transformed.

By the middle of the 1920's the reform of the kindergarten that had begun at the turn of the century was essentially completed. Kindergarten education was still not available to all children. There were some public schools that supported kindergartens, but not a great many. Even as late as the mid 1960s less than half of the five-year-olds in the United States were attending kindergarten (Spodek, 1982).

Today the picture is quite different. By the beginning of the 1980s, almost 90 percent of five-year-olds were in kindergarten, and by 1986 all states were providing support for public kindergartens within the elementary schools.

The Child Care Center Develops

There seems to be some disagreement as to when child care centers first appeared in the United States. Some say the first day nursery, as these centers were called, was established in Philadelphia during the Civil War, to free women for work in war factories and as nurses in hospitals for the war wounded (Whipple, 1929). Others say that the first day nursery was established some years earlier, in 1854, in the New York Nursery and Child's Hospital (Forest, 1927). In any event, the American day nurseries were modeled after the French *crèche*, which translates into English as "crib." These crèches were established in Paris as early as 1844 to care for children of working mothers, to fight infant mortality, and to teach hygiene to parents.

The day nurseries were primarily custodial agencies. They were more concerned with *caring* for children than with educating them. When the factory system was established in the 1800s, women were forced to look for work outside of their homes. Handicraft activities that could be done at home were becoming obsolete. Goods began to be manufactured by large machines that needed to be tended by relatively unskilled workers, and women and children were often hired. Women tending to the machines for long periods of time during the day could not care for their young at the same time, and day nurseries were established to serve the needs of the children of these women.

In the first day nurseries, children were cared for, cleaned, and fed by matrons who might also cook and clean in the centers. In the better day nurseries, trained kindergarten teachers might be hired to provide educational activities during part of the day. It was not until the 1920s, however, that day nursries began to offer early educational programs on a regular basis. The image of the day nursery as a purely custodial agency gave way to that of a child care center in which children are cared for and educated by formally prepared nursery school teachers and child care workers as well as by more informally prepared caregivers.

Final exam ☆

The Montessori Method

Maria Montessori was the first woman to graduate as a physician from an Italian medical school. After her graduation at the turn of the century, she worked at the psychiatric clinic of the University of Rome, where she came in contact with "idiot children." She came to believe that it ought to be possible to train these mentally defective children to be more competent and lead fuller lives rather than to simply keep them safe. Dr. Montessori sought out the ideas of others to find the key to an appropriate education for handicapped children. She read the works of Froebel as well as those of Edouard Sequin, a French physician who had developed innovative methods of working with handicapped children. Building on what she found, she experimented with new methods and materials that proved successful in the education of these children.

When Maria Montessori was asked by the Rome Association for Good Building to establish a school, she was able to transfer her success from handicapped to normal children. This association was creating new houses for poor families in a slum neighborhood and wished to provide for the children. For two years Maria Montessori worked to develop her innovative program in the *Casa Dei Bambini,* or children's house, as she called her school. To help her, she hired a young woman who had not been trained as a teacher. Montessori brought materials she developed into the school and observed how the children used them. On the basis of these observations, Montessori then modified the materials as needed and established procedures for their use.

Maria Montessori with a child studying shapes.

News of the success of the program spread. People from all over Italy and throughout the world came to observe her work and report on it. Many came to be trained in the new method by Dr. Montessori. As word spread, her method became popular and soon Montessori schools were established worldwide.

Montessori, like Froebel, saw the development of the young child as a process of unfolding. She also conceived of education as self-activity, leading to self-discipline, independence, and self-direction. Unlike Froebel, who was interested in abstract ideas, Montessori viewed the child's perceptions of the world as the basis for knowledge. The senses had to be trained for the child to become more knowledgeable. Thus, she developed a set of materials and procedures that allowed each sensory element to be separated out. With the use of these self-correcting materials, children learn to become aware of different sensations and organize them in their minds.

To help children to learn about sounds, Maria Montessori created a set of boxes. All the boxes looked alike, but each contained a different kind of material. By shaking each box, a child would produce a unique sound. The sound made by one box could be compared with the sounds made by other boxes. The boxes could be ordered on the basis of the loudness of the sound. They could also be matched with boxes in another set. Similar activities were devised to train the other senses: touch, sight, smell, and taste. Each activity was matched with a set of special materials to be used by children in specific ways. Children could use the self-corrective materials independently.

Children in a Montessori class in sensory activities and
exercises in practical life.

Muscular education, gardening, and nature study were also included in the Montessori program. Emphasis was also placed upon
teaching academic skills through the Montessori materials. Materials used
for counting led the children to learn arithmetic. Reading and writing
were taught simultaneously, with children first feeling sandpaper letters
against a smooth background, forming letters with a finger in a basin of
sand, then placing wooden or cardboard letters together to form words.
The reading method taught was a phonetic one, since in Italian each letter
form corresponds to a specific sound. Montessori was concerned that
reading be taught early. She felt there was a sensitive period for learning to
read between the ages of two and six. Instruction before that period would
not be effective and children would have a more difficult time learning to
read once the sensitive period was past (Montessori, 1965).

The Montessori program also included Exercises in Practical Life.
These were activities that would help children function independently.
They include dressing oneself, as well as cleaning and caring for oneself
and one's surroundings. Each practical skill was taught with a prescribed
sequence of activities.

The Montessori method arrived in the United States before World
War I. Montessori education continued to grow from that time until about
1930. Each year during this period saw more Montessori schools established, primarily private ones which depended upon tuition payments for
survival. With the stock market crash of 1929 and the depression that
followed, many of these schools were forced to close. The Montessori
movement faded in the United States during this time even though it

continued to survive in other countries. Maria Montessori helped establish new schools in Spain, Italy, and other European countries during the 1920s and 1930s. She spent the World War II years in India, where she trained teachers and helped to create new Montessori schools. After World War II she returned to Europe, where she remained active professionally until her death. Not only did she train Montessori Directresses, as these teachers are called, but she also worked to maintain the integrity of the Montessori method.

There was a resurgence of interest in Montessori education in the United States in the late 1950s. Montessori education has again become popular in our country, though differences have surfaced among Montessori educators. There are two groups that currently support Montessori education. One, the Association Montessori Internationale (AMI), strives to maintain the purity of the Montessori method. The other group, the American Montessori Society (AMS), is less concerned with preserving the purity of the method. This group recognizes that other child development specialists have had insights about the education of children similar to those of Maria Montessori. They also feel that new knowledge has been created about children and about education since Montessori's time. The AMS schools are willing to modify the Montessori method and to include activities that were not a part of the original *Casa Dei Bambini*.

The Nursery School

Rachel and Margaret McMillan created the first nursery school in London in 1911. Although they were both born in the United States, the McMillan sisters came to Britain during childhood, after their father had died and their mother returned to her family home. Margaret was the speaker and writer for the two sisters. She had studied music and acting during her formative years. While spending much of her young adult life as a governess and companion, she gained personal satisfaction by pursuing social causes and engaging in political activities. In 1894 she was elected to the school board of Bradford, England, and became an advocate for the needs of poor children in school. She fought to provide children with medical examinations, school lunches, and school baths. She became convinced that the medical and social problems she saw in these children could be corrected or prevented by proper care before the children's entrance to school.

In 1902 Margaret left Bradford and joined her sister in London, where the two sisters opened a medical clinic for children. Soon they expanded the clinic's activities and an open air children's camp was established. A daytime nursery was a logical extension of these activities, and the entire operation was moved to the Depthford area of London, which was then a slum. There a college to prepare nursery school personnel soon took its place alongside the nursery school.

Margaret McMillan, founder of the
nursery school.

Rachel McMillan died in 1917, but her sister continued the work until her own death in 1931. Together they conceived of the nursery school as an institution for the education and nurturance of children from two to seven years of age. The nursery school was to provide to children of the poor the same advantages in growing up that were available to children in wealthier homes. Good health practices, medical examinations, adequate nutrition, cleanliness, fresh air, and proper exercise were all elements of the nursery school. These, combined with a worthwhile educational program, would support the total development of the child.

Unlike the Montessori school, the nursery school placed a high value on creativity and play. It was felt that imagination grows naturally in young children and could help the children advance in all areas of human development. Creativity would serve the needs of workers as well as managers, scientists, and artists. School programs could support the development of creativity in children by providing expressive activity, play, art, and movement. Along with these, the nursery school provided activities to teach self-caring skills and to support perceptual-motor learning. Gardening and nature study were also a part of the program, as were academically oriented readiness activities (McMillan, 1919).

The work of the McMillans and of others who joined in the nursery school movement drew considerable attention in England. The government there passed the Fisher Act of 1918, which allowed for the establishment of nursery schools within the public school system of

England. Unfortunately, adequate funds to make them universal were never forthcoming. In the 1920s English-trained nursery school educators came to the United States to demonstrate their program while a number of Americans went to England to study nursery school education. Nursery schools were established in many colleges and universities throughout our country. A number of private and welfare-oriented independent nursery schools were also established during this decade.

FEDERAL INVOLVEMENT IN EARLY CHILDHOOD EDUCATION

The 1930s depression had its impact on early childhood education as it had on other forms of human services. The nation's economy was in trouble. Tax collections slowed dramatically and many public school systems had to limit their activities because they lacked funds. Some kindergartens that had become part of public schools were closed. Other classes at various levels were also closed and class sizes were increased. Teachers were released by school boards who could no longer pay their salaries. The federal government, under the New Deal policies of President Franklin D. Roosevelt, established a number of work relief programs. Nursery schools were established to provide work for unemployed teachers. Training workshops were established to orient teachers who came from many grade levels to work in these nursery schools. These workshops would provide them with an understanding of child development and early childhood education.

Thus nursery schools were introduced into many communities in the United States, not primarily as a service to children, but as a service to adults. However, the children were well served by these programs, which continued until work relief was no longer needed.

The end of the depression saw the beginning of World War II. Whereas there had not been enough jobs for those seeking work during the depression, the country soon felt a need for increased numbers of workers. Young people were going into the armed forces, and war-related industries were expanding. As in past emergencies, the call went out for women to join the war effort by joining the work force. To accommodate the needs of children of war workers, the federal government, under the Lanham Act, established child care centers in war industry areas. Education and care were provided for young children in these centers, which sometimes operated on a 24-hour basis while their mothers were at work. Unfortunately, the Lanham Act called for the withdrawal of these day care funds shortly after the end of the war. With peace came the withdrawal of government involvement in early childhood education.

It was not until the mid-1960s that the government again became involved in early childhood education. At this time there developed an increased concern for the status of poor people. There was also a belief that poverty was a social problem that could be solved. It was felt that the federal government should use its resources to aid in the solution of these problems. Working along with foundations, the government funded research studies on the effects of early experience on the development and academic achievement of poor children. A number of experimental programs in preschool education were established and a variety of educational programs tested. Growing out of this effort came the Head Start program, which has offered massive support of early childhood education. Although only about 20 percent of the eligible preschool children have been served by Head Start, it still remains one of the largest and most popular programs of early childhood education in existence.

CONTEMPORARY DEVELOPMENTS

The institutions described in this chapter have all influenced early childhood education as it exists today. Those still in existence have changed in some way from the original, since all must respond to contemporary concerns. The kindergarten is no longer a separate institution. In America it is a class serving five-year-olds primarily as part of an elementary school. Kindergartens are part of public education in all states, although not all five-year-old children attend kindergarten. In addition, a number of states are adding classes for four-year-olds to the public schools.

Nursery schools are no longer designed to serve children of the poor. They have become half-day programs and are primarily educational in their orientation. Child care programs have become the fastest growing element in the early childhood education field. To a great extent this development reflects the changing family structure and the changing role of women in our society. As more women work, there is a greater need for child care services. As nuclear families become more dominant and single-parent families increase, that care must be provided outside the home. Day care for the youngest is often provided in individual homes, with child care centers serving children from the age of three up.

Montessori schools still exist and seem to be thriving. They are not all as pure in their adherence to the Montessori method as they once were. There is still a search for what is essentially Montessorian in the method. While still predominantly a form of private education, Montessori education is an alternative program in some public schools. Head Start continues to survive and it remains a popular government program for young children. In 1972 the Head Start concept was expanded to include service for handicapped children. In addition, special programs for preschool handicapped children have been evolving over the past fifteen years.

In the last several years we have seen an increase in the acceptance of early childhood education as an essential service for our society. Positive long-term effects have been shown for both Head Start and other programs for poor children (Collins, 1983; Consortium for Longitudinal Studies, 1983). In addition, positive effects of good day care programs for young children have also been demonstrated (Caldwell & Freyer, 1982). While the field continues to grow and evolve, it is becoming stable in relation to the kinds of early childhood institutions that have been created and the kinds of services provided by each. These will be discussed in greater detail in the next chapter.

REFERENCES

CALDWELL, B. M., AND M. FREYER (1982).   Day care and early education. In B. Spodek (Ed.), *Handbook of research in early childhood education*, pp. 341-374. New York: Free Press.

COLLINS, R. C. (1983).   Headstart: An update on program effects. *Newsletter of the Society for Research in Child Development*, Summer.

CONSORTIUM FOR LONGITUDINAL STUDIES (1983).   Lasting effects of early education. *Monographs of the Society for Research in Child Development*.

DEASEY, D. (1978).   *Education under six*. New York: St. Martin's Press.

FOREST, I. (1927).   *Preschool education: A historical and critical analysis*. New York: Macmillan.

HARRISON, J. F. C. (1968).   *Utopianism and education: Robert Owen and the Owenites*. New York: Teachers College Press.

LILLEY, I. (1967).   *Freidrich Froebel: A selection from his writing*. Cambridge, England: Cambridge University Press.

MAY, D., AND M. A. VINOVSKIS (1977).   A ray of millennial light: Early education and social reform in the infant school movement in Massachusetts, 1826-1840. In T. Harevan (Ed.). *Family and kin in urban communities 1700-1930*. New York: New Viewpoints.

McMILLAN, M. (1919).   *The nursery school*. London: J. M. Dent and Sons.

MONTESSORI, M. (1965).   *Dr. Montessori's own handbook*. New York: Schocken Books.

SPODEK, B. (1982).   The kindergarten: A retrospective and contemporary view. In L. Katz (Ed.), *Current topics in early childhood education, Vol. IV*, pp. 173-191. Norwood, NJ: Ablex.

STEINFELS, M. O. (1973).   *Who's minding the children? The history and politics of day care in America*. New York: Simon & Schuster.

WHIPPLE, G. (1929).   *Preschool and parental education*. 28th Yearbook of the National Society for the Study of Education.

SUGGESTED ACTIVITIES

1. Talk to directors of local nursery schools and child care centers in the community. Find out which is the oldest nursery school and the oldest child care center. Learn why and how these programs were originally established. Compare the original goals of the center with their current goals. Prepare a report to share with the class.

2. Interview the curriculum director of a local school district. Find out when kindergartens were first offered in the public schools. See if they have some of the original curriculum guides or photographs of early classes to share with the class.

3. Visit a Montessori program. Observe there for a morning. Compare the activities and equipment you observe with those originally suggested by Dr. Montessori.

4. Search through your college and local libraries. See if you can find books written before 1900 on kindergarten education. Compare these books with current early childhood textbooks you know.

3

EARLY CHILDHOOD INSTITUTIONS AND PROGRAMS

OBJECTIVES

After completing this chapter on early childhood institutions and programs, you should be able to:

1. Define child care, child care home, and industrial child care.
2. Distinguish between licensing and accreditation of centers.
3. Describe Head Start, Home Start, kindergarten, and Montessori programs.
4. Compare public with private centers; profit with not-for-profit centers; church-related with secular; and fee-oriented with tax-supported centers.
5. Explain the relationship of early childhood centers to social services agencies.
6. Describe the use of "purchase of service" to provide child care services.

If you were to walk into ten different early childhood programs at 9:30 on a Wednesday morning, there's a good possibility that you would see children participating in very similar activities. Whether they are in large groups with the teacher, in small groups, or working individually, they may be using similar materials.

If you stayed awhile, however, differences among the programs would become apparent. Some programs have half-day sessions; others last a full day. Some programs provide meals; others do not. Some involve parents as volunteers in the classroom or may even be owned and operated by parents; others provide no role for parents. Some have teachers who act as guides for learning; others have teachers who use direct instruction throughout the day. You would also notice differences in class size, adult/child ratio, and physical settings.

Even though all early childhood programs provide similar experiences for children, there are differences among programs. Some differences are more apparent than others. Programs may differ in philosophy, goals, and purposes, but they all exist to meet the needs of children and their families.

Early childhood programs have been gaining more acceptance in the United States in recent years. Kindergarten programs have expanded, Head Start remains a strongly supported federal program, and income tax credits for child care have become acceptable. A growing number of parents are making use of child care programs (Almy, 1975).

In 1981 about 90 percent of all five-year-olds were enrolled in kindergarten programs. In addition, about 36 percent of all three-year-olds were enrolled in programs. At the kindergarten level about 88 percent of the children were enrolled in public programs, with 12 percent enrolled in private schools. For the threes and fours, enrollment was 52 percent in private schools and 48 percent in public programs (Grant & Snyder, 1984). In addition, by 1985 there was a trend toward more five-year-olds attending all-day kindergarten programs and four-year-olds enrolled in public school programs.

As was noted in the previous chapter, programs for young children have a long and varied history. However, it was not until the mid 1960s with the advent of President Lyndon Johnson's "Great Society" initiative that early childhood programs were seen as relevant to our economic and social needs (Decker & Decker, 1984). Head Start began in the summer of 1965 as a way to help break the cycle of poverty for children, provide comprehensive support for their development, and improve their chances for success in public schools. The Head Start movement was only one of a number of catalysts that hastened the growth of early childhood education programs in the United States. Changes in the roles of women, in family structures, and in the economy all have influenced the development of the field.

In this chapter we will explore the various types of early childhood programs that are available and the ways in which they differ from one another. Institutional sponsorship, relationships with social service agencies, and important issues such as day care standards and licensing will also be discussed. It may be interesting to compare some of the historical forerunners of these programs as described in Chapter 2 with those that exist today.

INSTITUTIONS IN EARLY CHILDHOOD EDUCATION

Many different institutions provide programs for young children. Federal, state, and local governments, industry, religious groups, parent groups, and private entrepreneurs all sponsor early childhood programs. However, these programs are not all offered for the same reasons. Governments have attempted to improve the quality of life for families; industry has provided child care for workers to lower worker absenteeism, to keep them on the job longer, or as a fringe benefit; religious groups often wish to provide a service to parishioners and increase church membership; and so on. Regardless of the sponsorship or the purpose, the quality of care should be the most important concern for everyone involved.

According to Bettye M. Caldwell (1984), a former president of the National Association for the Education of Young Children:

> Professional child care is a comprehensive service to children and families which functions as a sub-system of the child rearing system and which supplements the care children receive from their families.... Professional child care is not a substitute or a competitor for parental care.... Professional child care programs vary in quality, just as family experiences vary in quality. Program quality depends upon the characteristics and training of the staff, the physical setting, and the support for such service provided by the society at large. (p. 4)

Caldwell's statement can be applied to *all* early childhood programs regardless of sponsorship or philosophy.

Child Care Centers *final exam*

Child care is usually an extended day program with children being cared for up to 12 hours daily. It may take place in the child's home, in another person's home, or in a child care center. Child care programs fall into one of three categories: (1) *custodial care,* where care is primary and no attempt is made to educate the child; (2) *developmental care,* where psychomotor development, cognitive development, language, self-concept, and social development are primary concerns; and (3) *comprehensive child care,* where developmental care is provided along with a full range of support services (Decker & Decker, 1984).

Early childhood programs can be found in many settings.

A public elementary school contains a kindergarten program.

This community child care center functions in a building specifically designed for young children.

This former elementary school houses the community's Head Start program.

A child care center operates in a private residence.

This church operates a weekday child care center.

Contemporary child care centers have at least two components: child care and education. The primary purpose of child care, however, is the *care* of the child. The care component can include providing hot meals, adequate rest, and a safe environment under the supervision of trained personnel. The education component may include large-group, small-group, and individual activities that teach children and are developmentally appropriate.

Child care is normally provided in one of two settings: a child care center, or a child care home. Child care centers may be housed in community buildings, public schools, factories, hospitals, and just about any place else where a space is available that can be modified to meet health and safety regulations and serve the needs of children. Sunday school classrooms or church halls, for example, are used as child care centers during the week. Regardless of where programs are housed, there are a number of factors that seem to influence the quality of child care. Among these are staff/child ratio, group size, and staff qualifications.

Bettye M. Caldwell and Marjorie Freyer (1982), reporting on the National Day Care Study, stated that the highest quality programs were those that had a high staff/child ratio. The report suggests a ratio of one adult for every seven children as being optimum for three-to-five-year-olds, 1:6 for two-to-three-year-olds, and 1:4 for children under two. These ratios allow each child to be cared for as an individual and to be provided with quality care and educational experiences.

The second and most important variable that affects the quality of child care is group size. The group should be no larger than twice the number of children allowed per adult in the staff/child ratio (Caldwell & Freyer, 1982). In other words, in a center using a 1:7 adult/child ratio for three-to-five-year-old children, the maximum size of the group should be 14 children with two adults.

The third variable affecting the quality of child care is the qualifications of the teaching staff. Those centers that had staff members with child development or early childhood education training tended to have higher quality programs.

Child Care Homes

When caregivers open their homes to serve small groups of children, they create child care homes. Many parents who are uncomfortable with having their children placed in a child care center value the warm, family atomsphere that may be available in a child care home. Many people believe that a home is the proper place to care for young children. This attitude is reflected in the fact that care for very young children is more often provided in homes than in centers (Almy, 1975).

Child care homes tend to serve toddlers more than other age groups. However, infants, preschool, and school-age children are also served in this setting (Stevens, 1982). A day care home can be beneficial because of the small number of children served in each setting, the flexibility that parents have in dealing with one person, and the fact that parents can choose a home that has a value orientation similar to their own (Almy, 1975). Finally, day care homes serve a wide range of ages, and children can benefit from playing with those both older and younger.

One problem is that a great number of child care homes are unregulated. Thus, there are no legal controls over the environment or the caregiver. The National Day Care Home Study found that, regardless of regulatory status, homes tended not to exceed the recommended group size limit of six children per home, but caregivers spend more time interacting with children in regulated homes that in unregulated homes (Stevens, 1982).

Often child care has been viewed as a need of low-income families. Actually child care is used by families at all socioeconomic levels. In a study done in Shaker Heights, Ohio, an affluent suburban community, Davis and Solomon (1980) found that of the 423 families using child care, the most common arrangement was to have a baby-sitter come into their own home. Twenty-one percent of those surveyed reported that their child care needs were unmet and 40 percent felt that the cost of child care was a problem. The major reason that people used child care was employment related, and centers were the least used or desired choice of care.

Regardless of the type of center or program that a child participates in, it is important to note that no consistent negative effects of out-of-home child care have been found in over a dozen child development investigations (O'Connell, 1983). Good child care is not harmful to children. Since in many cases it allows people to improve their standard of living and to more effectively provide for their children, it is a benefit to both families and society.

Kindergarten

With Mississippi beginning to provide kindergarten classes for all children in 1986, all fifty states for the first time have kindergarten included as part of the public school experience. This is over 100 years after the first public school kindergarten was established in St. Louis in 1873.

Most adults who attended kindergarten vaguely remember a time of circle games, sand, water, blocks, housekeeping centers, and other activities that were enjoyable while allowing for their interaction with teachers, children, and materials. The memory reflects the valuing of the social, emotional, physical, and intellectual development of the child.

Recently there has been increased concern that kindergarten programs should focus on the acquisition of specific learning goals (Spodek, 1982). Many educators feel that kindergarten should be a time for beginning instruction in reading, arithmetic, and language skills and that experiences that detract from gaining these competencies have no place in the program. Often the pressure to offer academics in the kindergarten comes from people who know little about young children and how they learn. The unfortunate result of such pressure can be that first grade work may be expected of kindergarten children.

Another concern has been whether children should attend all-day or half-day kindergartens. Current research studies, though neither consistent nor conclusive, suggest that all-day kindergarten programs have some advantage in regard to increasing children's academic achievement. Too little evidence is available to draw any conclusions regarding children's socio-emotional development (Stinard, 1982). Although only a minority of children attend all-day kindergarten at present, the number is growing as states move to provide funding for kindergartens on the same basis as for other elementary grades.

No matter what the structure and focus of kindergarten programs, teachers must recognize that for most children today kindergarten is not their first experience with schools. More than half the children who come to kindergarten have had prior experience in a nursery school or child care center.

Head Start

Head Start began in 1965 as an eight-week summer program for children from low socioeconomic-status families. The intent was to give children an early experience that would help them prepare for their school careers. During the first summer, 500,000 children were enrolled in 11,000 centers (Hodges & Cooper, 1981). Over 8 million children have since been enrolled in Head Start and approximately one out of five eligible children is currently being served (Decker & Decker, 1984).

In the beginning, Head Start had seven objectives: (1) improving the child's physical health and abilities, (2) helping the social and emotional development of the child, (3) improving the child's mental processes and skills, (4) establishing patterns and expectations of success, (5) increasing the child's capacity to relate positively to family members while at the same time strengthening the family's stability and capacity to relate positively to the child, (6) developing a positive attitude toward society in the child and his or her family and fostering constructive opportunities for society to work together with the poor in solving their problems, and (7) increasing the sense of dignity and self-worth within the child and his or her family (Hodges & Cooper, 1981). The program was child and family oriented and was seen as both an educational and a social endeavor.

Head Start soon grew into a full-year program, and in the years of its existence it has been responsible for many educational innovations. Although the initial program was similar to that of a good traditional nursery school, later modifications incorporated many contemporary theories and practices.

Home Start was developed as an offshoot of the Head Start program and was designed to take place within the child's home. It was primarily for poor children and their families. Its objective was to strengthen the parents' ability to facilitate their children's development. Home Start made use of personnel who regularly visited homes and trained parents in appropriate ways of working with children (Almy, 1975).

Head Start has been one of the most studied early childhood programs, and the results have been encouraging. To date, researchers have found that Head Start (1) produces substantial gains in children's cognitive and language development, (2) provides the greatest amount of benefits to the most needy children, (3) allows participants to perform equal to or superior to their peers when regular school begins, (4) provides positive contributions to the development of socially mature behavior, (5) supports generally better health and nutritional practices in children, and (6) lessens the likelihood of children being retained in grade or assigned to special education classes (Calhoun & Collins, 1981; Hodges & Cooper, 1981; Collins & Delaria, 1983).

Researchers have also found an improvement in parenting abilities and an enhancement of positive reactions between mothers and their children as a consequence of Head Start enrollment (Calhoun & Collins, 1981). Over 95 percent of Head Start parents have favorably endorsed it and a large percentage of parents have actually participated in the program (Zigler & Lang, 1983).

Edward F. Zigler and Mary E. Lang (1983) feel that Head Start should begin expanding into (1) full-day child care for children of working parents, (2) programs to fight child abuse and neglect, (3) parent education and teenage pregnancy programs, and (4) childhood injury prevention programs. These are critical needs in our society and Head Start may be the proper place to address them.

Montessori Programs

After the resurgence of Montessori education in the late 1950s and early 1960s, Montessori education has established itself as a small, respected, though controversial approach to early childhood education. While much remains constant among Montessori programs, there is also significant variation from program to program.

The teacher's role in a traditional Montessori school is different from that of the teacher in other preschool programs. The teacher prepares a learning environment, then intervenes only when a child needs help, when new material is introduced, or when the child is being abusive to materials or children. Conversing with children, participating in activities, and helping to stimulate a child's interest are not considered appropriate for the teacher.

Within the Montessori movement there has been debate over whether or not the traditional program should be modified. This has resulted in two separate approaches to Montessori education: one organized within the Association Montessori Internationale which believes in the strict interpretation of Maria Montessori's writing, and the other within the American Montessori Society which has a more liberal view. Even within each of these associations, programs and educators may differ with one another on philosophy or methodology (see Chapter 2).

American Montessori schools include creative art, dramatic play, science activities, and large muscle play along with the traditional Montessori activities. Teachers in these schools take a more active role. An additional change that David Elkind (1983) has described is that children are allowed to experiment with the Montessori materials after they have learned how to use them correctly.

Regardless of the approach, research on Montessori education has proved it to be effective in a number of areas. Montessori preschools have been shown to have positive effects on general verbal intelligence, perceptual and motor performance, IQ development, and the development of attention and concentration (Chatlin-McNichols, 1981).

INSTITUTIONAL SPONSORSHIP

Early childhood programs are sponsored by many different institutions. Social agencies, parent groups, school districts, corporations, and private individuals may each assume the responsibility for providing programs to young children and families. It is helpful to understand the distinctions among the various types of institutional sponsorships.

Final exam ✱

Public vs. Private Programs

One of the major distinctions made between programs is whether they are publicly owned or privately owned. Public programs are those that are operated by governmental bodies such as school districts or departments of social services. Sometimes programs are sponsored by nongovernmental agencies but are funded through public monies. Many Head Start and Home Start programs are examples of such sponsorship.

Private programs are those that are offered by an individual, a group, or a corporation. They do not receive public funding directly. Such programs rely on fees, contributions, or purchases of service by government agencies to generate operating income. Montessori schools, most nursery schools, parent cooperatives, United Way-sponsored programs, and owner-operated day care centers are examples of private sponsorship. Even privately operated centers may receive some public support, since about 20 percent of the children in private centers receive some public subsidy.

For-Profit vs. Not-For-Profit Programs

A second distinction that can be made is between programs that are operated "for profit" and those that are "not for profit." Those that are for profit are run as businesses with the purpose of making money, providing their owners with a return or profit on their financial investment. According to Celia A. Decker and John R. Decker (1984), the majority of day care centers in the United States are privately owned and operated for profit. Those centers are also called *proprietary centers.*

All public centers operate on a not-for-profit basis. They operate within a fixed budget. Their income usually contains a combination of funds from an agency or foundation, along with fees paid by parents, and they hope that the income generated by such a center will equal its expenses. Most church-sponsored and agency-sponsored programs are in the private, not-for-profit category.

Church-Related vs. Secular Programs

Early childhood programs in the United States have always made use of church-owned facilities. Sometimes the space for the center is rented or it may be donated by the church. Often early childhood programs make use on Monday through Friday of Sunday school classrooms, kitchens, and meeting halls. Programs that operate in church facilities are not necessarily religious but may be independent of the churches in which they are housed. A study done by the National Council of Churches found that of 14,589 church-housed programs, 56 percent were operated by the church and 44 percent were operated independently. Only 9.3 percent of the centers used the preschool program to further Christian education (Lindner, 1983). Ninety-nine percent of the programs surveyed did not restrict enrollment in the center to church members.

Secular programs do not represent any religious orientation. All programs with public sponsorship are secular even with such a program is housed in a church facility. In fact, many government-sponsored programs make use of church buildings.

Fee-Supported vs. Tax-Supported Programs

Fee-supported programs are those that depend on fees charged for services. Some centers require fees but also receive funds from sources such as the United Way or a private foundation to supplement their income. Often these centers base tuition upon parents' ability to pay for services. In other centers the fees charged are the only revenue available to the operators. The fees in these programs tend to be higher than in subsidized programs unless the cost of the program is deliberately kept low.

Tax-supported programs are those that receive financial support from state, local, or federal governments. They may or may not charge fees to their clients, depending on the level of funding received from government sources and upon the program's policy.

Industrial Child Care

According to Sandra L. Burud, Raymond C. Collins, and Patricia Devine-Hawkins (1983), the fastest growing type of child care is employer-sponsored or industry-based child care. These increased from 105 employer-sponsored programs in 1978 to 415 programs in 1982. Industry-based child care can take many different forms, but basically it is child care that is sponsored by an employer for the benefit of the workers.

Industry-based child care is not a new concept. The federal Lanham Act provided $51 million during World War II for the establishment of 3,100 child care centers to care for children while their mothers worked in war-related industries (Hicks & Powell, 1983).

Employer interest in day care has been generated as a consequence of a changing labor force. There are a great many more women with families working today, and women tend to return to work sooner after having a child (Burud et al., 1983). Employers are sometimes interested in sponsoring child care to (1) reduce employee turnover, (2) reduce absenteeism, (3) increase worker productivity and concentration on the job, (4) improve employee recruitment, (5) enhance worker morale, and (6) enhance company image (Burud et al., 1983; Hicks & Powell, 1983). Employer-sponsored day care can increase the opportunity for families to spend time together, since parents can spend lunch, breaks, and travel time with their children. Employees also benefit financially when child care is offered as a fringe benefit. Parents may save time by bringing their children to a center at work rather than having to drop them off at a different destination (Hicks & Powell, 1983).

An industry may own a day care center, it may indirectly support centers through in-kind donations, or it may agree to purchase day care services in existing centers. Industries may also work in the community to support public policy that affects child care (Verzaro-Lawrence, LeBlanc, & Hennon, 1982; Burud et al., 1983; Hicks & Powell, 1983). Some industrial child care programs provide supplemental services such as meals, parent counseling, medical services, and parent discussion groups.

Currently, hospitals sponsor most employer child care programs in civilian life. Child care centers in military bases have been in operation the longest and have the highest enrollment (Perry, 1978).

As there are more single-parent families, the need for industrial child care is sure to grow. While most businesses are competent in their own field, they often lack knowledge about the developmental needs of young children. Employers entering into child care must hire a director and staff members who have appropriate background, education, and experience to work with young children (Hicks & Powell, 1983).

Purchase of Service

Purchase of service refers to an agency's paying for services for a child in a child care center. The responsible agency, whether government, community, or corporate, contracts with an independent center to provide an appropriate early childhood program for particular children.

Some companies that provide day care for their employees are not large enough or are not willing to take the responsibility to sponsor their own child care center. These companies often purchase space for their employees' children in a setting that is convenient to the employees' home or work place. Service may also be purchased for handicapped children when a public-school-based program isn't available but an appropriate private center is; in this case the local school board assumes financial responsibility.

RELATIONSHIPS WITH SOCIAL SERVICE AGENCIES

As increasing numbers of children enroll in child care programs, there has been a corresponding increase in the number and range of services they require in order to have an optimal educational experience. While in many centers the staff is adequately trained to present educational programs, few centers can provide the comprehensive social, psychological, and medical services that may be needed. In many cases this need has led to preschool programs becoming closely affiliated with local social services agencies that can provide these services.

Medical assistance can take the form of free physical examinations, immunization, and general health care. Often physicians and nurses from a local clinic visit the center on a regular basis to provide services to children. Some centers have a nurse or doctor on call for emergencies, while others make use of local hospitals or medical and dental schools.

Psychological services may include counseling for children, parents, or families, and testing in the event of suspected handicapping conditions. In many cases parents seek advice from the center staff for direct help or knowledge of where they can go for assistance. Knowing how to make referrals is a necessary part of the early childhood educator's skills.

Social service agencies may help parents obtain welfare or food stamps. They may also be involved in substance abuse counseling. In many states social service agencies have responsibility for handling child abuse and neglect cases.

People who work in early childhood programs cannot be all things to all people. Often teachers can help parents deal with simple family problems. However, it is important that teachers recognize the limits of their expertise and be aware of the community agencies that are available to serve the parents and children.

ISSUES RELATED TO EARLY CHILDHOOD INSTITUTIONS

In dealing with issues related to early childhood education, we always seem to come back to one set of questions: "What are reasonable standards for early childhood centers and for the people who work in them?" and "How can we ensure that these standards are met?" There are many views as to which standards would most likely result in quality programs. The important point to remember is that all standards are designed to protect children.

Standards for Child Care Services

In order to arrive at a set of standards for early childhood programs, it is first necessary to establish goals. The Child Welfare League of America states that all early childhood programs should have the same essential components: the children in all programs should benefit from the knowledge and professional skills available in the fields of child development, early education, medicine, and social work; the preschool education experience should be good for children; the program should support and enhance the parental role; and the program should be appropriate for the particular needs of child and parent (Almy, 1975).

These broad goals are concerned with children, parents, and, indirectly, staff. However, they are not standards for programs. They do not tell us what is required.

Licensing

Licensing is a way for a government agency to protect children by ensuring that a center has met minimum standards. While each state establishes its own requirements, there are some common areas that seem to be a part of all licensing procedures.

Decker and Decker (1984) refer to the following components for licensing:

1. regulations for organization and administration
2. regulations for staffing
3. regulations for plant and equipment

4. health and safety regulations
5. program regulations, including content, scheduling, and planning and guidance of children

Regulations concerning content are generally minimal and do not specify objectives or goals for learning.

At one time licensing standards for day care were also established by the federal government. The Federal Interagency Day Care Regulations were passed in 1968 and were incorporated into Title XX of the Social Security Act of 1975. These requirements applied only to centers receiving federal assistance. Presently, if a center is receiving federal funding, it must meet state and local licensing requirements, but there are no longer any federal requirements to be met (Collins, 1983).

NAEYC (1984) has taken the following position regarding child care licensing:

> The National Association for the Education of Young Children affirms the importance of child care licensing as a vehicle for controlling the quality of care for children in settings outside their own homes. NAEYC supports licensing standards that:
>
> - take into account the nature of the child care setting and the number of children to be served
> - set standards for centers, group homes, and family homes
> - include care of children from infancy through school age
> - cover full-time, part-time, and drop-in care arrangements
> - include facilities serving children with disabilities
> - reflect current research demonstrating the relationship between the quality of care provided and such factors as group size, staff/child ratio, and staff knowledge and training in early childhood education or child development
> - are clearly written, enforceable, and vigorously enforced
> - are administered by agencies which are known about and accessible to parents and the individuals providing care for children
> - include written policies describing processes for initial licensing, renewal inspections, revocation, and appeals
>
> Because licensing requirements stipulate the basic necessary conditions for protecting children's well-being, NAEYC firmly believes that all forms of supplementary care for young children should be licensed and that exemptions from licensing standards should not be permitted. Whenever a single program or group of programs is exempted or given special treatment, the entire fabric of licensing is weakened.
>
> It is a public responsibility to ensure that child care programs promote optimal development in a safe and healthy environment. All parents who need child care have the right to choose from settings which will protect and educate their children in a nurturing environment. (Passed by the NAEYC Governing Board, November 2, 1983.)

The National Day Care Study findings provide guidelines for selecting high-quality child care: small groups, supervised by caregivers with career preparation in child development and early childhood education (Collins, 1983). While there is much we still do not know about the relationship of program elements to young children's learning and development, there exists a good deal of accepted professional knowledge to guide regulators of early childhood programs.

While 90 to 95 percent of early childhood centers are licensed and all states provide at least minimal standards, only 5 to 10 percent of child care homes are licensed. This situation concerns many since this setting serves the greatest number of very young children (Class & Orton, 1980). In spite of the difficulty in locating and evaluating the thousands of child care homes in the United States, the effort should be undertaken for the protection of children.

Accreditation

Because licensing addresses *minimum* standards for early childhood programs, a license does not provide a judgment of quality. In order to identify high-quality centers that meet standards beyond those of licensing, NAEYC has developed a program of center accreditation through the establishment of the National Academy of Early Childhood Programs. It is hoped that, through the Academy, the quality of programs serving young children will improve with the evaluation of these programs based upon the established criteria.

The NAEYC accreditation program is based upon a self-study by a center, using the accrediting criteria. These criteria are related to:

- interactions among staff and children
- curriculum
- staff-parent interactions
- staff qualifications and development
- administrative procedures
- staffing patterns
- physical environment
- provisions for health and safety
- provision of nutrition and food services
- assessment of program effectiveness

On the basis of the self-study, the center submits a written program description. If the Academy staff determines that the description is complete and that standards seem to have been met, it arranges for an on-site visit by an early childhood specialist to validate that the information provided is an accurate reflection of the center's program. On the basis of the center's and the validator's reports, a commission may accredit the center. This accreditation is valid for three years (NAEYC, 1984). Accreditation does not have the force of law, but it does carry the backing of an organization with over 40,000 members who are interested in quality experiences for young children.

The Center Accreditation Program is new. It has within it the potential for establishing and maintaining standards of quality in early childhood programs and of recognizing centers that meet these standards. It is hoped that this process will stimulate recognition of the need for high-quality programs in early childhood education and will, directly and indirectly, improve the education and care of young children in the United States.

Making Child Care More Accessible

Another continuing issue in the field of early childhood education relates to making education and child care accessible to the growing number of young children and families that require it. One way this might be done is through an expanded Head Start program, serving a wider population of children and including a full-day child care component. A second possibility that has been suggested is to include extended child care as part of public school programs (Morgan, 1980). This approach has been endorsed by the American Federation of Teachers. There are some, however, who feel that the lack of flexibility in traditional elementary schools would limit the chance of success of child care programs (Grumman, 1978).

Regardless of the setting, societal needs require more early childhood centers to educate and care for young children. The establishment of standards, licensing procedures, and accreditation will help determine whether or not they are good places for children and families. Our concern should be not only to make early childhood education programs more readily available, but to ensure that all programs are of the highest quality possible.

SUMMARY

Early childhood programs provide a wide range of services to families. Programs vary in purpose, philosophy, size, sponsorship, and standards. Within this diversity, however, there are certain elements such as adult/child ratio, group size, and staff qualifications that seem to be universal conditions for a high-quality program. These are embedded in licensing and accreditation standards.

People in the field of early childhood education and those anticipating entering it have the responsibility of ensuring that the concern for standards of quality programs will continue and that reasonable conditions and appropriate programs are available for all children.

REFERENCES

ALMY, M. (1975). *The early childhood educator at work.* New York: McGraw-Hill.

BURUD, S. L., R. C. COLLINS, AND P. DEVINE-HAWKINS (1983). Employer supported child care: Everybody benefits. *Children Today,* **12**(3), 2-7.

CALDWELL, B. M. (1984). What is quality child care? *Young Children,* **39**(3), 3-12.

CALDWELL, B. M., AND M. FREYER (1982). Day care and early education. In B. Spodek (Ed.), *Handbook of research in early childhood education,* pp. 341-347. New York: Free Press.

CALHOUN, J. A., AND R. C. COLLINS (1981). A positive view of programs for early childhood intervention. *Theory into Practice,* **20**, 135-140.

CHATLIN-MCNICHOLS, J. P. (1981). The effects of Montessori school experience. *Young Children,* **36**(5), 49-66.

CHILD CARE LICENSING: POSITION OF THE NATIONAL ASSOCIATION FOR THE EDUCATION OF YOUNG CHILDREN (1984). *YOUNG CHILDREN,* **39**(2), 50-51.

CLASS, N., AND R. ORTON (1980). Day care regulations: The limits of licensing. *Young Children,* **35**(6), 12-17.

COLLINS, R. C. (1983). Child care and the states: The comparative licensing study. *Young Children,* **38**(5), 3-11.

COLLINS, R. C., AND D. DELARIA (1983). Head Start research: A new chapter. *Children Today,* **12**(4), 15-19.

DAVIS, J., AND P. SOLOMON Day care needs among the upper middle classes. *Child Welfare,* **41**(8), 497-499.

DECKER, C. A., AND J. R. DECKER (1984). *Planning and administering early childhood programs* (3rd ed.). Columbus, OH: Merrill.

ELKIND, D. (1983). Montessori education: Abiding contributions and contemporary challenges. *Young Children,* **38**(2), 3-10.

GRANT, W. V., AND T. D. SNYDER (1984). *Digest of education statistics: 1983-1984.* Washington, DC: U.S. Government Printing Office.

GRUMMAN, J. (1978). Day care in the schools? A response to the position of the AFT. *Young Children,* **33**(4), 4-13.

HICKS, M., AND J. POWELL (1983). Corporate day care, 1980's: A responsible choice. *Dimensions,* **11** (4), 4-10.

HODGES, W., AND M. COOPER (1981). Head Start and follow through: Influences on intellectual development. *Journal of Special Education,* **15**(2), 221-237.

LINDNER, E. W. [LETTER TO THE EDITOR] (1983). *Young Children,* **38**(6), 2.

MERRO, J., ET AL. (1976).   Options in education, radio program #45 broadcast the week of September 20. ERIC Document Reproduction Service No. ED 133082.

MORGAN, G. (1980).   The politics of day care. *Day Care and Early Education,* **8**(1), 29-31.

NATIONAL ASSOCIATION FOR THE EDUCATION OF YOUNG CHILDREN. (1984).   *Accreditation criteria and procedures of the National Academy of Early Childhood Programs.* Washington, DC: National Association for the Education of Young Children.

O'CONNELL, J. C. (1983).   Research in review. Children of working mothers: What the research tells us. *Young Children,* **38**(2), 63-70.

PERRY, K. (1978).   *Survey and analysis of employer sponsored day care in the United States.* Unpublished Doctoral dissertation, University of Wisconsin, Milwaukee.

RASHID, H. M. (1984).   Some make it, some don't. *Dimensions,* **12**(2), 11-14.

SPODEK, B. (1982).   The kindergarten: A retrospective and contemporary view. In L. Katz (Ed.), *Current topics in early childhood education,* Vol. 4, pp. 173-191. Norwood, NJ: Ablex.

STEVENS, J. H., JR. (1982).   Research in review. The National Day Care Homes Study: Family day care in the United States. *Young Children,* **37**(4), 59-66.

STINARD, T. A. (1982).   *Synopsis of research on kindergarten scheduling: Half-day, everyday; full-day, alternate day; and full-day, everyday.* (ERIC Document Reproduction Service No. Ed 219151.

ULREY, C. L., K. ALEXANDER, B. BENDER, AND H. GILLIS (1982).   Effects of length of school day on kindergarten school performance and parent satisfaction. *Psychology in the Schools,* **19,** 238-242.

VERZARO-LAWRENCE, M., D. LEBLANC, AND C. HENNON (1982).   Industry-related day care: Trends and options. *Young Children,* **37**(3), 4-9.

WHITEBOOK, M. (1981).   Problems in day care—Millie Almy. *Day Care and Early Education,* **8**(3), 29-30.

ZIGLER, E. F., AND M. E. LANG (1983).   Head Start: Looking toward the future. *Young Children,* **38**(6), 3-5.

SUGGESTED ACTIVITIES

1. Visit a Montessori program and interview the director. Find out if the program is accredited by the American Montessori Society or the Association Montessori Internationale. Ask the director about the reasons for choosing that particular accreditation.

2. Locate and read your state's regulations for reporting child abuse and neglect. Identify your legal responsibility as an early childhood educator.

3. Interview a parent who has a child in a child care program. Find out why that parent enrolled the child in that program.

4. Obtain a copy of your state's licensing regulations for child care centers. Compare their requirements with NAEYC's center accreditation standards.

5. Observe a Head Start center for a day. Describe how the activities are related to the seven Head Start objectives.

6. Interview a child in a child care program. Find out what he or she likes best and likes least in the center.

4

BECOMING AN EARLY CHILDHOOD PRACTITIONER

OBJECTIVES

After completing this chapter on becoming an early childhood practitioner, the student should be able to:

1. Describe the roles and responsibilities of a center director, teacher, caregiver, assistant, and aide.
2. Compare certification with credentialing.
3. Discuss the qualifications and responsibilities related to early childhood educational careers.
4. Identify the nature of early childhood education professionalism.
5. Discuss the role of males in early childhood education.
6. Identify ways to increase the social status of early childhood educators.

Saul began his career in early childhood education as an aide in a Head Start program. He had a high school degree and an interest in working with young children. Head Start sponsored him over a period of years to take continuing education classes that led to a two-year degree. He then continued through a Bachelor's degree in early childhood education. Saul is now beginning his fifth year as a first-grade teacher in a Follow-Through class.

Elise graduated from college in 1970 with a Bachelor's degree in elementary education. She began teaching second grade in a large urban city. After three years her husband was transferred to Europe. There she helped establish a parent cooperative nursery school. On returning to the United States, she completed a Master's degree in early childhood and became the director of a nursery school. From there Elise became director of a large community-supported day care center. Today she is affiliated with a junior college as a CDA trainer.

Mark graduated with a two-year degree in electronics. He quickly discovered he was more comfortable in a "people-oriented" setting. Since he had worked as a baby-sitter while in school, he decided to become a child care aide. Mark applied for and obtained a job at the center at his church. As his interest in children and in the field grew, he began taking courses at night for a degree in child development. After a year at the center he was promoted to teacher. He received his degree after five years of part-time study. He has now decided to begin work on a Master's degree in social work. He wants to continue working with children and families but not in the classroom. He felt that he was beginning to burn out after 6 years, 50 weeks a year, 9 hours a day of working with two- and three-year-old children.

Mary Jo graduated with an early childhood degree. She taught kindergarten for five years. Now she works for a major publisher as a specialist in literature for young children.

Susan received a Bachelor's degree and Master's degree in child development. She was a teacher and director in a franchised day care center for 15 years. She is now a licensing supervisor for her state's Department of Children and Family Services.

Martha received a vocational school certificate as a child care aide and went to work in a small neighborhood center upon graduation. After six months she decided she liked working with children but only in a one-to-one relationship. She went back to school and became a licensed practical nurse, specializing in pediatric care.

All of the people mentioned have a long-term relationship to the field of early childhood education, but only Saul has been working in a classroom with children for his entire career. This is a classic "good news/bad news" situation for early childhood education. The good news for people entering the field is that it is exciting to think of the large number of career possibilities that are available. The bad news is that as the field has developed, many fine teachers have been leaving the classroom to move into other positions.

Twenty years ago a degree in child development or early childhood education allowed you to spend your career as a classroom teacher of young children, possibly moving into a director's position after a period of time. Today, career opportunities for people who specialize in early childhood are available in hospitals, community centers, publishing houses, computer companies, retail businesses, and recreation. As the field continues to expand, the possibilities for people with early childhood backgrounds will be endless.

In this chapter we will present issues related to becoming an early childhood practitioner and discuss how they may affect your career in early childhood education. We will also provide information about the traditional careers and some of the newer career paths available to those interested in working with young children.

ROLES

The traditional careers in early childhood education have been in five job categories: director, teacher, caregiver, assistant and aide. Each of these positions requires different competencies; each may have a role in a quality program. Positions may differ from one another in the kinds of duties performed. There may also be different entry-level expectations for each. For example, a director needs all of the skill, knowledge, abilities, and experience that a teacher needs but must also have additional training in administration and supervision to run a center. A brief description of each of the job categories may be useful to illustrate this point.

Final exam

Center Director

A director has the ultimate responsibility for what happens in that center during the day. To be a successful director, one must have knowledge of both children and teaching as well as knowledge of administrative methods (Davis, 1982).

Administering a center takes specialized skill and knowledge. It requires expertise in budgeting procedures, licensing regulations, payroll and benefit procedures, and hiring, due process, and firing procedures. Directors must also know about health, safety, and fire regulations, nutritional needs of children, and ways to evaluate both children and staff.

Teacher

Teachers of young children have an enormous responsibility to children and families because they provide both care and learning. What does it take to be a teacher of young children? Lillian Weber (1982) feels that

Teachers of young children must possess important personal qualities.

teachers must trust parents and that they have an obligation to know the content that is part of their teaching role. Millie Almy and Agnes Snyder (1947) suggest that teachers should have the personal characteristics of physical stamina, world mindedness, understanding of human develop-ment, and respect for personality, and that they should be imbued with scientific spirit. Sarah Lou Leeper (1968) adds the importance of a love of children, patience, kindness, warmth, outgoingness, and security.

The personal characteristics of a teacher become more meaningful when they are applied to the following tasks for which teachers are responsible each day. These include:

- establishing the learning environment
- selecting and developing goals
- managing a classroom
- acting as go-between for parent and school
- choosing appropriate content
- choosing appropriate instructional materials
- evaluating children's progress
- reporting on the special needs of children to the appropriate authorities (e.g., suspected child abuse or neglect, suspected handicapping conditions)
- working as a faculty member and as part of an instructional team.

In addition, in some centers teachers may be called upon to do other things. They might teach religious education, work as part of a child screening team, speak to parent groups, or help in the recruiting of new children.

*Final exam = *

Caregiver

Caregivers function in child care centers and day care homes. They are primarily responsible for the health, care, and safety of the children in their group. While there is no doubt that their interaction with children results in the children's intellectual, physical, emotional, and social growth, their primary concern is to see that the children are healthy, happy, and safe. Caregivers feed, change, protect, empathize with, and care for those in their charge. Giving children a sense of well-being, a sense of security, and a sense of trust are goals the caregiver strives to meet. Christine Cataldo (1983) feels that infant caregiving requires emotional responsiveness, a high level of initiative and energy, and skills in managing groups of babies. Other important traits for all caregivers to possess include patience, sensitivity to changing needs, and good observational skills.

Assistant Teacher

Assistant teachers may do many of the things that a teacher or caregiver does. However, they are generally not responsible for planning or evaluating activities. Assistants take directions from the teacher and implement those directions to the best of their ability. The assistant teacher may work with large groups, small groups, or individual children and may supervise indoor or outdoor activities. However, the assistant is always working under the direction of the teacher or caregiver.

In many instances, assistant teachers are part-time people. Often they work as assistants while attending school to become teachers.

Teacher Aide

Teacher aides see that all of the little tasks that make a center or classroom run are done well and on time. They may be responsible for mixing paint, filing records, setting up activities, supervising nap time, fixing snacks, and any other of the hundreds of jobs that are necessary for a center to function. Aides also may have to assist in the kitchen, drive the bus to pick up children, or comfort children who become ill during the day. The aides make it possible for teachers and caregivers to spend most of their time with children.

PROFESSIONALIZING THE FIELD

Bernard Spodek and Olivia N. Saracho (1982) reported the following, illustrating the wide range of preparation for practitioners in the field:

> The National Day Care Study (Roup, Travers, & Goodrich, 1980) does provide a profile of caregivers. Interestingly, 20 percent of the head teachers and 13.5 percent of the teachers surveyed had degrees or certificates in elementary education, 5.7 percent of the head teachers and 4.3 percent of the teachers were qualified to teach secondary education, and 17.1 percent of the head teachers and 20.7 percent of the teachers were degreed or certified in preschool education. Caregivers were overwhelmingly female (93.7 percent), and about two-thirds of them were between eighteen and thirty-five years of age. Of the classroom staff, 66 percent were white, 28 percent black, and 7 percent members of other minority groups. As far as educational attainment is concerned, 31.4 percent of the head teachers and 29.3 percent of the teachers held Bachelor's degrees, 11.4 percent of the head teachers and 8.2 percent of the teachers held advanced degrees, while 20.0 percent of the head teachers and 12.5 percent of the teachers held associate degrees. Interestingly, 8.6 percent of the head teachers and 15.9 percent of the teachers held no degree at all including a high school diploma. The educational attainment of directors was somewhat higher while that of assistant teachers and aides was lower. (p. 405)

The problem with making job distinctions within the early childhood education field is that we have relatively little status in the eyes of society. Lana Hostetler and Edward Klugman (1982) state that while child care programs are expanding, the status of workers in those programs has not risen. They refer to the Department of Labor *Dictionary of Occupational Titles,* which assigned a low skill level rating to "day care workers and nursery school attendants" as recently as 1977.

One reason for low status is the lack of entry-level requirements for positions in the field. The fact that there is a general lack of certification or credential requirements for directors, teachers, caregivers, assistant teachers, and teacher aides in early childhood programs makes it possible for almost anyone to enter the field (Davis, 1982; Spodek & Saracho, 1982). When little is required of practitioners in a field, then little status is given to those practitioners.

It is hoped that we will come to a time when specific expectations will be established for each position and those applying will be screened to ensure that they are qualified. The field must be able to guarantee to the public that those working with young children have the necessary skills and are competent practitioners (Davis, 1982). We need to establish standards for the different levels of knowledge and skills necessary for aides, assistants, caregivers, teachers, and directors to perform their jobs well (Davis & Alexander, 1982).

Early Childhood Professional Path

NAEYC has recommended an early childhood professional path that consists of four levels. The following is a description of the knowledge and skills required for each level and the ways in which these can be acquired:

Level 1. Early Childhood Teacher Assistant

Level 1 is an entry-level position. People at this level are preprofessionals who implement program activities under direct supervision of the professional staff. Such supervision occurs directly in the classroom by an Early Childhood Associate Teacher or Early Childhood Teacher who is in charge of the group of children and who models professional skills and contributes to the growth of the individual serving in the assistant role.

This level requires basic and minimal personal qualities which include a potential for and willingness to improve one's skills in working with young children, mental and physical health, a genuine liking of children, ability to get along with other adults, and general dependability.

The basic educational requirement for entry at this level is a high school diploma or equivalent. No specialized Early Childhood preparation is required for entry at this level, but once employed, the individual should participate in professional development programs.

Level 2. Early Childhood Associate Teacher

Level 2 consists of Early Childhood Associate Teachers, professionals who independently implement program activities and who may be responsible for the care and education of a group of children.

To be qualified as an Early Childhood Associate Teacher, the individual must be able to demonstrate competency in six basic areas as defined by the National Child Development Associate (CDA) Credentialing Program:

—to establish and maintain a safe, healthy learning environment

—to advance physical and intellectual competence of children

—to support social and emotional development and provide positive guidance and discipline

—to establish positive and productive relationships with families

—to ensure a well-run, purposeful program responsive to participant needs

—to maintain a commitment to professionalism

These qualifications can be achieved by successfully completing either a system of competency evaluation such as the one implemented by the CDA National Credentialing Program or an associate degree in Early Childhood Education or Child Development. The attainment of these competencies requires supervised field experiences in appropriate settings with young children.

Level 3. Early Childhood Teacher

Level 3 consists of Early Childhood Teachers, professionals who are responsible for the care and education of a group of children. Individuals at Levels 2 and 3 may perform similar roles and functions. The different titles reflect the different patterns of formal education received and the extent of background knowledge of child development.

The qualifications of an Early Childhood Teacher are presented in NAEYC's *Teacher Education Guidelines for Four- and Five-Year Programs* (1982). To be qualified as an Early Childhood Teacher, the individual must demonstrate all Level 1 and 2 competencies and also possess theoretical knowledge and practical skills in:

—human development through the life span, with special emphasis on cognitive, language, physical, social, and emotional development, both typical and atypical, from birth through age eight

—historical, philosophical, psychological, and social foundations of Early Childhood Education

—curriculum for young children, including goal setting and developmentally appropriate content and methodology

—observation and recording of children's behavior for purposes of assistance in achieving goals, providing for individual needs, and appropriately guiding children

—preparation for working in settings that include atypical children: understanding the needs of developmentally diverse children, and recognizing conditions requiring assistance from other professionals

—communication and conference techniques, interpersonal and intergroup relations, and techniques for working with staff as an instructional team

—family and community relations, including communication with parents and parent involvement

—awareness of value issues and the existence of codes of ethics in professional life

—comprehension of cultural diversity and its implications

—legislation and public policy as it affects children, families, and programs for children

Completion of a baccalaureate degree in Early Childhood Education or Child Development from an accredited college or university is used to predict the existence of the competencies required of an Early Childhood Teacher. The attainment of these competencies requires supervised field experiences in appropriate settings with young children. The requirements specified for this level do not exclude people who wish to enter Level 3 primarily on the basis of experience in the field, as colleges are increasingly accepting relevant experience as evidence of partial fulfillment of degree requirements.

Level 4. Early Childhood Specialist

Level 4 consists of professionals who supervise and train staff, design curriculum and/or administer programs. Every Childhood program should have at least one qualified Early Childhood Specialist, who in small programs may also be the Director or Master Teacher. Larger programs should have more than one Early Childhood Specialist.

To qualify as an Early Childhood Specialist, an individual must be able to demonstrate all Level 1, Level 2, and Level 3 competencies as well as competency in the following areas:

—designing and supervising the implementation of developmentally appropriate program content and curriculum

—designing and implementing appropriate staff development activities and adequate supervision of personnel and volunteers

Completion of the following education and experience is used to predict the existence of the qualifications required of an Early Childhood Specialist: baccalaureate degree in Early Childhood Education or Child Development from an accredited college or university plus successful completion of at least three years of full-time teaching experience with young children, and/or an advanced degree.

The Early Childhood Specialist role requires expertise in the areas of curriculum design, supervision of adults, and staff development. This expertise may be obtained through specific administrative coursework within the baccalaureate program or may require additional training and experience beyond the baccalaureate degree (NAEYC, 1984).

Alternative Careers Related to Young Children

Most students going into early childhood education want to become teachers. A few students look beyond the classroom and think of becoming a center director, a parent counselor, a university teacher, or a supervisor. Those who enter early childhood generally want to teach children and can see themselves doing it for a long time.

However, Lana Hostetler (1984) stated, "Not everyone can (or should) work with young children in group care. Although mothers and grandmothers have cared for children for generations without training, group care of young children is not the same as mothering, nor is it baby-sitting or substitute care" (p. 77). Some students who begin a program in early childhood education will find they are not suited as *teachers* of young children and may choose to work with children in other ways. Majoring in Early Childhood can provide a background for a career in a related field that can still provide contact with children and families.

Recently, the increased interest in early education, the increased need for child care, the continuing societal pressures on children and families, and the growing field of high-technology teaching tools have helped to open up a wide range of career opportunities for people with backgrounds in early childhood education or child development.

Publishers of children's books, learning materials, and computer software need people who can develop and present materials to teachers and who understand the specific learning and instructional needs of young children. Producers of children's television programs also need people with knowledge of young children to assist in the development of programming.

New laws protecting the rights of children and laws against child abuse and neglect have fostered the development of a group of social workers who have an understanding of young children and who can assist both parents and children during difficult times. While such a position requires added preparation, a background in early childhood education can provide a solid base.

Managing toy stores, merchandising children's clothes, books, and furniture, and representing firms that sell school equipment and supplies are sales-oriented professions in which an early childhood background can be particularly helpful.

For those interested in staying within the field of education but not in a classroom, there are a number of career possibilities. School psychologists, visiting teachers, and school librarians are professionals who work with individuals or small groups of children. Each of these requires training beyond early childhood education. How many hours of preparation and what specific types of courses will be required will vary from state to state, depending on certification requirements. Most of these positions require some classroom experience as well.

Another area that has a growing number of opportunities is health care. Hospital teachers, home teachers, and child-life specialists are three roles that enable early childhood majors to apply their expertise in health-related areas.

Judith Seaver, Carole A. Cartwright, Cecilia B. Ward, and C. Annette Heasley (1979) have organized careers with young children into five different patterns: those that serve children directly, those that serve families directly, those that organize services for children and families, those that provide information to professionals that work with or for children and families, and those that provide to the general public goods and services affecting children and families. Figure 4-1 lists available careers in each of the five patterns.

FIGURE   4-1

CAREERS WITH YOUNG CHILDREN

Pattern	Examples of Careers
1. Serving children directly	Teacher, child care worker, school nurse, physical therapist, hospital play aide
2. Serving families directly	Social worker, family therapist, parent educator, public health nurse
3. Organizing services for children and families	School administrator or supervisor, college teacher, recreation director
4. Providing information to professionals who work with children and families	Researcher, evaluation specialist, librarian, author, editor
5. Providing goods and services affecting children and families	Department store buyer, newspaper reporter, toy designer, children's book author, architect, legislative aide.

J. W. Seaver et al., *Careers with Young Children* (Washington, DC: NAEYC, 1979).

While the growth of career possibilities in early childhood education has been a positive development, it has also brought with it a number of concerns. These concerns for professionalism, certification or credentialing, entry requirements, and working conditions are all "growing pains" that the field is currently working through. It is to be hoped that they will be resolved in a manner that will be equitable for everyone and that will ensure quality programs for children.

If you find working with young children inspiring but feel you are not a match for day-to-day classroom contact, these alternatives may be worth pursuing. A visit to your college or university counseling center can provide further information about careers that require and value knowledge of young children.

PREPARING TO BE AN EARLY CHILDHOOD PRACTITIONER

In 1982 James L. Hymes, Jr., stated that one major accomplishment of the past fifteen years in the field of early childhood education was an increase in junior college, four-year college, and graduate programs and the advent of the Child Development Associate Credential to train people to work with young children. This means that more people are entering the field of early childhood education. It also means that those who do enter the field are more likely to have adequate preparation.

Programs that Prepare Practitioners

There are a number of programs that prepare early childhood practitioners. Some train aides, others educate teachers, but all are dedicated to improving the level of competence of those in the field.

The students who are in these preparation programs are almost always people who are planning to enter the field. They have little or no experience with young children and are relying on their education to provide them with the expertise necessary to be successful. Preparation programs can be found in high schools, vocational-technical schools, community colleges, and four-year colleges and universities. High school and vocational-technical schools usually prepare students to be aides or caregivers in child care centers. Community college programs may prepare students to be teacher aides in elementary schools or teachers in child care centers or nursery schools. Most four-year programs enable students to become certified teachers. Students in these programs can complete all the requirements to receive state certification and become qualified to teach in kindergarten or the primary grades.

Most of the four-year programs are relatively young. They generally offer Bachelor's degrees and in many cases are closely related to elementary education programs (Spodek, Davis, & Saracho, 1983).

An important trend in teacher education is the addition of a testing requirement and the demonstration of competency before a candidate can be awarded a permanent certificate. Many states require teachers to complete a college program and take a standardized test such as the National Teacher Examination in order to receive a provisional teaching certificate. To qualify for a permanent certificate, the candidate then has to demonstrate mastery of specified teaching skills such as questioning, classroom management, and the evaluation of learning. The final judgment as to whether a teacher is competent may be made by a building administrator or by an outside evaluation team. In some cases, teachers receive feedback on their strengths and weaknesses and are provided with in-service assistance to help them improve before they are observed a second time.

All programs, those preparing aides as well as teachers, include some form of teaching practice or field experience. This practice gives students an opportunity to work with children in a realistic setting and allows them to gain a better understanding of what children are like. These experiences also allow students to discover if they are suited for teaching. Regardless of the purpose of the preparation program, the goal is to ensure that those who work with young children have the skills, knowledge, and ability to do it well.

Credentialing and Certification

Final exam

A *teaching certificate* is a license to teach. It is granted by a state to everyone who has successfully completed the necessary requirements. Usually certification is based at least partly on the completion of a Bachelor's or Master's degree teacher education program, though there may be other requirements. Certification offers legal permission to teach a certain grade level or in a certain subject area. While certification is required to teach in public schools, it is often not required in private schools or in nursery schools or child care centers.

A *teaching credential* is usually offered by an agency or association upon completion of a specialized training program rather than by a state. Although some certified teachers take additional training to receive a specialized credential, normally one need not be certified to earn the credential.

Two of the best-known credentials in early childhood education are the Montessori Credential, offered by the Association Montessori Internationale (AMI) or the American Montessori Society (AMS), and the Child Development Associate (CDA) credential. It is not necessary to be a certified teacher to obtain these credentials. In fact, CDA was set up to offer a credential to people working in early childhood education who did not have a college degree or formal teacher preparation.

The Child Development Associate credential came into being in 1970. Dr. Edward Zigler, then director of the Office of Child Development, recognized a need for a system to ensure that those working with young children had the skills, knowledge, and values necessary to provide quality educational programs. A task force was commissioned to determine the scope of the program, and the Child Development Associate Consortium was funded in 1972 (Campbell & Reed, 1976). There are six CDA competency areas (see Figure 4-2). A CDA candidate must demonstrate competence in each of these areas in order to qualify for the credential. Each candidate's ability is assessed by an evaluation team.

Whereas certification is necessary to teach in the public schools and the Montessori credential is necessary to teach in a Montessori school, the CDA credential is usually earned by people who have already entered the field and are working with children. It is a requirement for employment for some roles in Head Start and in some child care programs.

FIGURE 4-2

CDA COMPETENCIES AND RELATED FUNCTIONAL AREAS

Compentency Area I:

Setting Up and Maintaining a Safe and Healthy Learning Environment.

Functional Areas:

1. **Safe:** Candidate provides a safe environment by taking necessary measures to reduce or prevent accidents.
2. **Healthy:** Candidate provides an environment that is free of factors which may contribute to or cause illness.
3. **Environment:** Candidate selects materials and equipment and arranges the room to the developmental level of the children.

Competency Area II:

Advancing Physical and Intellectual Competence of Children.

Functional Areas:

1. **Physical:** Candidate provides a variety of appropriate equipment, activities, and opportunities to promote the physical development of children.
2. **Cognitive:** Candidate provides activities and experiences which encourage questioning, probing, and problem-solving skills appropriate to the developmental level of the child.
3. **Language:** Candidate helps children acquire and use language as a means of communicating their thoughts, feelings, and understanding.
4. **Creative:** Candidate provides a variety of experiences and media that stimulate children to explore and express their creative abilities.

Competency Area III:

Building Positive Self-Concept and Individual Strength in Children.

Functional Areas:

1. **Self-Concept:** Candidate helps each child to know, accept, and appreciate him- or herself as an individual.
2. **Individual Strength:** Candidate helps each child develop a sense of independence and acquire the ability to express, understand, and control his or her feelings.

Competency Area IV:

Organizing and Sustaining the Positive Functioning of Children and Adults in a Group in a Learning Environment.

Functional Areas:

1. **Social:** Candidate helps the children learn to get along with others and encourages feelings of mutual respect among the children in the group.
2. **Group Management:** Candidate provides a positive routine and establishes simple rules with the group that are understood and accepted by children and adults.

Competency Area V:

Bringing About Optimal Coordination of Home and Center Child-Rearing Practices and Expectations.

Functional Areas:

1. **Home/Center:** Candidate establishes positive and productive relationships with parents and encourages them to participate in the center's activities.

Competency Area VI:

Carrying Out Supplementary Responsibilities Related to the Children's Programs.

Functional Area:

1. **Staff:** Candidate works cooperatively with other staff members concerning plans, activities, policies, and rules of the center.

(Child Development Associate Consortium, *Competency Standards* (Washington, DC: The Consortium, 1977).

Professionalism

No single issue in the field of early childhood has attracted as much attention during the 1980s as the concern for professionalism. Professional status normally suggests specialized knowledge, a desirable service, and effectiveness. While there is some specialized knowledge necessary to be a successful early childhood teacher, there has been no systematic way of ensuring that practitioners have that knowledge. There is also no systematic way of ensuring that children are receiving quality, dependability, and effectiveness in the programs they attend.

Different levels of professional status may need to be established for different roles in the field. The highest levels of professional status and the highest set of requirements might be required of those who have the responsibility for planning and supervising programs. Lesser professional status can be sought for those trained personnel who assist the professionals and work under their guidance. This approach is represented in the

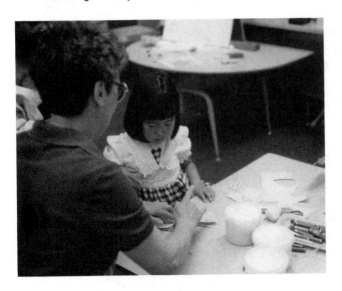

Professionalism means doing the right thing at the right time for the right reasons.

NAEYC levels of professional status, where different expectations are appropriate for different positions.

Finally, professionalism in teaching has to do with doing the *right* thing at the *right* time for the *right* reasons. Arthur W. Combs (1982) feels that what distinguishes a profession like counseling, social work, medicine, law, pastoral care, or teaching from some mechanical operations is the necessity for the professional worker to act as an immediate problem solver. In the helping professions there are no cut-and-dried decisions about what acts to perform or words to say. What teachers do at any given moment is based on a judgment about what is appropriate to the hundreds of factors in any situation. These actions must be justified. It is the justification that separates the professional from the others.

Ethical Considerations

Ethics are guidelines that help early childhood educators to determine how they should conduct themselves. Such guidelines can assist us in distinguishing between good and bad practice. Lilian Katz (1977) feels that ethics help us to act in terms of what is right rather than merely on what is expedient. They keep us from taking shortcuts in the way we approach children.

One set of ethical guidelines has been developed by the Minnesota Association for the Education of Young Children. The "Code of Ethical Conduct Responsibilities for the MnAEYC Members" includes eleven general principles for everyone working with children (see Figure 4-3).

A code of ethics affirms to the public that there are standards of practice that all early childhood educators are expected to follow in their

FIGURE 4-3

CODE OF ETHICAL CONDUCT RESPONSIBILITIES FOR MnAEYC MEMBERS

We, as workers and parents within the early childhood educational profession, declare our commitment to promote the developmental growth of each young child in cooperative relationships with the family and the community. We want each child, regardless of race, sex, religion, creed, or economic situation, to learn, develop, and fulfill his/her talents because it gives pleasure, purpose, and meaning for his/her own self. We believe each child is a valued member of society.

General Principles for All MnAEYC Members

Principle 1. General

A member should be primarily responsible to the child viewed within the context of the family.

Principle 2. Regulations

A member should know and be familiar with federal, state, and local regulations pertaining to the care and education of young children.

Principle 3. Compliance

A member should know that any program in which he/she works must comply with the state and local regulations as mentioned above. He/she ought to report instances of noncompliance to the director, board, or other responsible persons for the program. A member who finds that compliance with these standards is not accomplished through this process and within a reasonable time has a responsibility to the child and the community for reporting such violations to the appropriate authority in state or local government.

Principle 4. Legal Rights

A member should know basic laws pertaining to the legal rights of parents and children with respect to the service he/she provides and is obligated to act in accord with that knowledge and its ethical implications. The member must respect the child's and parent's right to privacy and confidentiality.

Principle 5 Reporting Child Abuse

A member should know the reporting law pertaining to child abuse and take the responsibility to report any suspected cases of child abuse or neglect to the police or to the Protective Services Office of the county welfare agency. This responsibility includes reports in which the alleged abuse or neglect is caused by a child care worker, a parent, a guardian, or any other persons.

Principle 6.   Grievance Procedures

A member should know and follow or foster the establishment of procedures for resolving grievances, and these procedures should be available to children and parents as well as staff.

Principle 7.   Exploitations

A member should refuse to take part in or condone the exploitation of any child, any parent, or any staff member.

Principle 8.   Atmosphere

A member who provides services for children ought to strive to create an atmosphere in which children become secure, grow toward their potential, and have opportunities for successful experiences.

Principle 9.   Continuing Education

A member should behave in ways which reflect knowledge and understanding of children and be committed to continuing to acquire and update his/her knowledge in the field of early childhood education.

Principle 10.   Misrepresentation

A member should avoid misrepresentations of his/her own professional competencies/qualifications, affiliation, and purposes, and those of institutions and organizations with which he/she is associated.

Principle 11.   Human Relations

A member should interact with all persons he/she comes in contact with, regardless of race, sex, or age, in a humane manner, regarding each as an individual with strengths and weaknesses. It is important to notify authorities of any child suspected of being a victim of substance abuse.

work with children. When a child is accepted into a center, the parent has the right to assume that the staff will serve the child's interests. Standards of ethics provide the caregiver with rules to ensure that only acceptable behavior is practiced.

Dealing with Social Issues

Increasingly early childhood educators have been expected to deal with a wide range of social problems including child abuse and neglect, substance abuse (drugs or alcohol), and sex education. Whether or not sex education is included as part of the curriculum may depend on the value orientation of the parents. Substance abuse and child abuse, however, must be every practitioner's concern.

In many states a teacher who knows or suspects that a child is being abused or neglected is required by law to report that suspicion to the authorities. Usually there is a statewide toll-free number that can be called. The information is passed on to a social service agency for investigation and action. The caller is protected from legal suit as long as there is no malice involved in the report.

Whether or not there is a legal requirement to report suspected cases of substance abuse, early childhood practitioners have an ethical responsibility to protect the children who are left in their care.

Males in Early Childhood Education

There are many more females than males in early childhood education. Most males who enter education tend toward the higher age levels; few work with young children. The field of early childhood education has been traditionally female oriented.

Recently, there has been an increase in the number of males entering the field. One cause of this trend is a better understanding of the qualities necessary to work successfully with young children. Many males have those qualities. Another reason has been the blurring of boundaries between male and female roles in our society. It is acceptable for males to assume what were traditionally female roles just as it is acceptable for females to assume what were traditionally male roles. In addition, the growth of the field of early childhood education is providing numerous opportunities for well-trained males and females.

Seifert (1983) reported a study with the following findings about the male teacher in early childhood education:

—He likes children as well as any other teacher who works with young children.
—He likes children enough to ignore the distractions of other careers.
—He may sometimes experience discrimination against males, but not necessarily.
—He sees relationships between his teaching and other related work.
—He expects to act on those relationships eventually, and possible move out of the classroom.

The stigma against males working with young children is lessening. In addition, support groups are making the field a more comfortable place for males to enter and to remain.

SUMMARY

There never has been a better time to enter the field of early childhood education. The field is growing. Jobs with children within the field and in related fields are plentiful. Society is beginning to recognize the importance of caring for and educating young children. However, this growth has raised a number of issues that have affected the field. We will have to come to grips with concerns for credentialing, certification, status, and professionalism in order for the field to focus on providing quality experiences for children. The fact that these issues have been raised is an indication of the vitality of the field. We have recognized many of the problems facing the field and we are moving to correct them.

In her book *The Early Childhood Educator at Work,* Millie Almy (1975) reflected on the fact that the early childhood educator is a double specialist in a number of ways. Early childhood educators teach and evaluate learning, work with children and adults, and think concretely and formally. Almy's description of the role identifies the complexity of being a practitioner in early childhood education. There are always at least two things to do at one time in order to meet the needs of the children.

REFERENCES

ADE, W. (1982). Professionalization and its implications for the field of early childhood education. *Young Children,* **37**(3), 25-32.

ALMY, M. (1976). *The early childhood educator at work.* New York: McGraw-Hill.

ALMY, M. C., AND A. SNYDER, (1947). The staff and its preparation. In *Early Childhood Education,* 46th Yearbook of the National Society for the Study of Education. Part II. Chicago: University of Chicago Press.

BROMAN, B. (1982). *The early years in childhood education* (2nd ed.). Boston: Houghton Mifflin.

CAMPBELL, D. M., AND I. B. REED (1976). *Traveling toward competence: The California State College Child Development Associate project.* ERIC Document Reproduction Service No. ED 138359.

CATALDO, C. (1983). *Infant and toddler programs.* Reading, PA: Addison-Wesley.

CHILD DEVELOPMENT ASSOCIATE CONSORTIUM (1977). *Competency Standards.* Washington, DC: Child Development Associate Consortium.

COMBS, A. W. (1982). *A personal approach to teaching: Beliefs that make a difference.* Boston: Allyn & Bacon.

DAVIS, M. D. (1982). The Preparation of administrators, teachers, and caregivers. In M. Dickerson, M. Davis, and G. Rose (Eds.), *Young Children: Issues for the 80's.* Little Rock, AR: Southern Association on Children Under Six.

DAVIS, M. D., AND N. L. ALEXANDER (1982). Quality teaching and professional role responsibilities: Concerns for early childhood education. *Reading Improvement,* **19**(3), 232-235.

DECKER, C. A., AND J. R. DECKER. *Planning and administering early childhood programs* (3rd ed.) Columbus, OH: Merrill.

HOSTETLER, L. (1984). The nanny trap: Child care work today. *Young Children,* **39**(2), 76-79.

HOSTETLER, L., AND E. KLUGMAN (1982). Early childhood job titles: One step toward professional status. *Young Children,* **37**(6), 13-22.

HYMES, J. L., JR. (1982). Young children: Past accomplishments—future priorities. In M. Dickerson, M. Davis, and G. Rose (Eds.), *Young children: Issues for the 80's.* Little Rock, AR: Southern Association on Children Under Six.

KATZ, L. G. (1977). *Ethical considerations for working with young children.* ERIC Document Reproduction Service No. ED 144681.

LEEPER, S. H. (1968). *Nursery school and kindergarten.* Washington, DC: National Education Association.

MINNESOTA ASSOCIATION FOR THE EDUCATION OF YOUNG CHILDREN (N.D.) *Code of ethical conduct responsibilities for MnAEYC members.* Minneapolis: MnAEYC.

NATIONAL ASSOCIATION FOR THE EDUCATION OF YOUNG CHILDREN (1982). *Early childhood teacher education guidelines for four- and five-year programs.* Washington, DC: National Association for the Education of Young Children.

————(1984). *NAEYC position statement on nomenclature, salaries, benefits and the status of the early childhood profession.* Washington, DC: National Association for the Education of Young Children.

ROBISON, H. F. (1977). *Exploring teaching in early childhood education.* Boston: Allyn & Bacon.

ROUP, R., J. TRAVERS, AND C. GOODRICH (1980). *Report of the National Day Care Study,* Cambridge, MA: Abt Associates.

SEAVER, J. W., C. A. CARTWRIGHT, C. B. WARD, AND C. A. HEASLEY (1979). *Careers with young children: Making your decision.* Washington, DC: National Association for the Education of Young Children.

SEIFERT, K. (1983). *The achievement of care: Men who teach young children.* ERIC Document Reproduction Service No. ED 231542.

SPODEK, B., AND M. D. DAVIS (1982). A study of programs to prepare early childhood personnel. *Journal of Teacher Education,* **33**(2), 42-44.

SPODEK, B., M. D. DAVIS, AND O. N. SARACHO (1983). Early childhood teacher education and certification. *Journal of Teacher Education,* **34**(5), 50-52.

SPODEK, B., AND O. N. SARACHO (1982). The preparation and certification of early childhood personnel. In B. Spodek (Ed.), *Handbook of research in early childhood education,* pp. 399-425. New York: Free Press.

U.S. DEPARTMENT OF EDUCATION (1983). *National Center for Education Statistics Bulletin.* Washington, DC: U.S. Department of Education.

WASHINGTON ASSOCIATE FOR EDUCATORS OF PERSONNEL IN EARLY CHILDHOOD PROGRAMS (1978). *The preparation and certification of early childhood personnel: A position statement.* ERIC Document Reproduction Service No. ED 221288.

WEBER, L. (1982). Education: Issues for the 80's. In M. Dickerson, M. Davis, and G. Rose (Eds.), *Young children: Issues for the 80's.* Little Rock, AR: Southern Association on Children Under Six.

SUGGESTED ACTIVITIES

1. Visit the career placement center on your campus and find out about related careers for people with early childhood backgrounds.

2. Compare and contrast the requirements of your program with those in secondary education. Where do the differences come from?

3. Write to the American Montessori Association or the Child Development Associate Consortium for information on their credentials. Compare their requirements with the requirements of the program in which you are currently enrolled.

4. Interview both a male and a female teacher of young children using the same set of questions. How are their answers similar? How are they different?

5. For one week keep a record of all the child-related references you see or hear on TV or radio, in magazines and newspapers, and from people. How many different careers are featured in your references? Choose one of the careers that particularly interests you and collect information about it.

5

THE CHILD
IN THE EARLY
CHILDHOOD
PROGRAM

OBJECTIVES

After completing this chapter on the child in the early childhood program, the student will be able to:

1. Describe six developmental theories and their contributions to early childhood education.
2. Relate developmental theories to the nature and nurture of children's development.
3. Identify the general characteristics of children three through five years of age.
4. Describe physical development, cognitive development, language development, emotional development, social development, and the development of values.
5. Discuss the basic influences in language development.
6. Describe individual and group differences in children's development.

Throughout this century the field of early childhood education has been influenced by the concepts and theories of the field of child development. Many of the most prominent theories about children's psychological development and behavior continue to influence the field today. These are presented in this chapter, along with information about their originators.

DEVELOPMENTAL THEORIES AND THEORISTS

Up to about one hundred years ago there was no field of child development or child psychology. What we knew about how children grew and learned came from the introspection of adults who wrote down what they remembered of their own childhood, or from the journals and diaries of parents who recorded their impressions of their own children. These sources provided an interesting basis for understanding young children, but the information was often of questionable validity. Before the beginning of the twentieth century the pioneering work of G. Stanley Hall led to the establishment of the child study movement out of which grew the scientific field of child development.

Final exam

G. Stanley Hall: The Child Study Movement

G. Stanley Hall contributed several original theories to the field of child development. One of the most significant was his evolutionary development or recapitulation theory. This theory reflected the theory of evolution, which suggests that humans evolved from lower animals. Hall speculated that children's behavior was a reflection of primitive aspects of those species from which humans evolved. Since these primitive aspects were no longer adaptive or necessary, they needed to be eliminated. Hall believed that children could lose these primitive behavior patterns through play. Children's water play, for example, can be traced to the play of fish, and their climbing and swinging can be associated with the play of anthropoids. These activities allow children to role-play some facets of their evolutionary past so they can work through their primitive needs and move on to more appropriate forms of behavior.

Hall, who lived during the latter nineteenth and early twentieth century, sent questionnaires to teachers asking them to identify children's interests and activities. These questionnaires provided him with a great deal of information from many sources in a simple, quick, and inexpensive way. He conducted more than 100 questionnaire studies on a variety of topics (Kessen, 1965). According to today's research standards, these questionnaires would be considered a crude and inadequate research technique. However, his work stimulated many of the current interests of today's child developmentalists.

Hall's most enduring contribution was his focus on child study. His work stimulated psychologists to study children as a way to understanding the development of adult behavior. He believed that the study of children provides insight into adult behavior and that those who work in child-oriented institutions need to know more about children and their development. Hall believed that the educational system should be adapted to children's patterns of development.

Hall's work changed child study research. It led the field to use more sources of information than adult memory or parents' records. Researchers began to base their studies on information gathered on large numbers of children to understand general patterns of development.

Some of Hall's other contributions included bringing Sigmund Freud to the United States and assisting in the introduction of Freudian psychoanalysis to American psychologists. Hall, along with John Dewey, was influential in moving early childhood programs toward more progressive, developmentally appropriate forms.

final exam

Arnold Gesell: Developmental Ages and Stages

Arnold Gesell developed detailed descriptions of the changes in children throughout the period of childhood. These descriptions were integrated to provide norms or characteristic pictures of development for infants and children through ten years of age. He organized these norms into a series of stages.

For over forty years Gesell studied the development of children's motor behavior, language, visual capacities, adaptive functions, and personal and social relations. By 1950 he had studied more than 3,000 behavioral elements which he described in detail at 34 stages or levels of maturity from birth to ten years of age (Gesell, 1952). For example, Gesell describes 18-month-old children as able to scribble if they are given a paper and crayon. At two years of age they can draw vertical marks. Six months later they are able to include horizontal strokes to their drawing.

In addition to integrating and norming information about the development of children, Gesell proposed a theoretical model of development. He believed that children's development depends on maturation. He strongly maintained that infants' minds evolve through the growth process. He felt that childhood represents a unitary action structure of behavior evolving in a consistent sequence. Behavioral tests could be used to assess children's development and thus determine their maturity and the status of their nervous system (Gesell, 1952). This maturational view of development supported a noninterventionist approach to early childhood education. Teachers are able to support development, but they are not able to influence it in a significant way.

Final exam

Sigmund Freud: Personality Development

Sigmund Freud originated the psychoanalytic theory of personality development. His purpose was to understand the adult personality as it developed from childhood, beginning in the earliest periods of life through maturity. Although Freud's major interest was the adult personality, his psychoanalytic theory identified the importance of early childhood experiences in the development of that personality.

Freud felt that it is essential to know the child in order to understand the emerging adult. He believed that individuals develop through a series of conflicts derived from within their own nature. He thought that the roots of mature emotional life are developed in the early years.

Freud's theoretical explanation of behavior emphasizes the interaction of physical development and maturation with the early life experiences. Behavior is affected by biological drives, instincts, and unconscious motives interacting with early family experiences. He believed that almost every experience is stored in the mind. While we are not consciously aware of these memories, they influence our behavior.

Freud believed that a person's essential psychological nature depends on biologically based desire rather than reason. The emphasis in psychoanalysis was primarily on individuals' passions or emotions and secondarily on their rational abilities or intellect. The person was born with basic animal instincts functioning at the unconscious level of thought. Such instincts, or irrational needs, demand instant rewards. An individual's development relies in part on the transformation of these desires into socially acceptable, rational behavior (Langer, 1969).

Freud identified three elements of the human personality: the *id*, *superego*, and *ego*. The *id* is an inborn factor which includes the basic instinctive drive to seek pleasure. The *superego* develops through society's influence, as an individual's conscience strives to differentiate right from wrong. In seeking pleasure, the *id* and the *superego* (which does not permit pleasure) conflict. The *ego*, the rational or reasoning factor, functions to resolve this conflict. It develops socially acceptable ways to meet the pleasures of the *id*. For example, when a child gets angry with another child, he or she may feel the urge to hit out but has been taught that hitting others is not permitted. The child strives to decrease the conflict and handles the anger in a socially acceptable manner. The child may verbalize the anger or reduce the pent-up emotional energy by punching a bag or pounding clay.

Freud's psychoanalytic theory suggested a somewhat more active role for early childhood educators. Teachers still were not expected to intervene in the child's development to any great extent. They were, however, expected to provide a warm and nurturant environment. At the same time they could offer activities that would allow children to rid

TABLE 5-1 Freud's Psychosexual Stages

AGE	STAGE	CHARACTERISTICS
0-1 year	oral	Mouth and upper digestive tract is the center of sensual stimulation and pleasure.
1-3 years	anal	Anus and lower digestive tract is focal; pleasure in withholding or eliminating feces.
3-6 years	phallic	Pleasure focused in genital area, creation of Oedipal or Electra attachment, identification with parents.
6-12 years	latency	Focus on industriousness, suppression of sexual interest.
12 years and beyond	genital period	More mature sexual interests develop.

themselves of feelings they could not express at home. Teachers were also expected to help children find socially acceptable ways of expressing their emotional needs.

final exam

Erik Erikson: Psychosocial Development

Erik Erikson, like Freud, felt that a healthy adult is one who satisfies personal needs and desires while learning to meet the demands of society. In his early adulthood Erikson studied teaching and received a Montessori teaching certificate. He also studied psychotherapy with Anna Freud. He incorporated these two interests by applying psychoanalytic theory to educational issues. Later he conducted research in the area of children's play and child-rearing practices. He also became a long-term student of the growth and development of the ego.

Erikson transformed Freud's psychosexual-stage theory of development to one of psychosocial stages, theorizing that people develop throughout their lives as they interact with their social environment, and that all individuals go through eight unique stages during the course of their lives. Each stage features a specific crisis. Individuals who are unable to resolve that crisis may move on to the next stage, but they are not capable of resolving the crisis of the new stage until the earlier ones are resolved. The crisis in each stage is related to the ego strengths which begin to form at birth and accumulate throughout development (Erikson, 1963). The epigenetic principle, that development is predetermined by genetic principles, is another important aspect of Erikson's theory. Erikson, like Freud and Piaget, felt that growth develops along a discontinuous or age/stage route (Erikson, 1968).

Whereas Freud focused on the importance of sexual or biological pleasure in development, Erikson has emphasized the social, historical, and cultural influences on development. Like Sigmund and Anna Freud, Erikson was interested in the development of the ego. Although he was aware that the individuals' instinctual drives and interest in various parts of the body evolve in a prescribed sequence, he has focused on children's interactions with their surroundings. He perceives the ego, not the id, as the main driving behavioral force.

In developing his theories, Erikson studied healthy personalities instead of analyzing neurotic people, as Freud did (Maier, 1978). He disagreed with Freud's concept of infantile sexuality, believing that society provides the major influences in developing children's behavior. He also believed that the developmental course can be reversed to the point that the later events can modify elements of children's personality that were developed during earlier periods. Freud, like Erikson, believed that the basic personality system is established by five years of age. For both Freud

TABLE 5-2   Erikson's Stages of Psychosocial Development

AGE	STAGE	CHARACTERISTICS
0-1½ years	trust vs. mistrust	Reliance on caregiver, predictability leads to trust in environment; or lack of care leads to basic mistrust.
1½-3 years	autonomy vs. shame and doubt	Environment encourages independence, pride, and sense of self-worth; or doubt and lack of self-esteem result from overcontrol.
3-6 years	initiative vs. guilt	Ability to learn and to enjoy mastery; or fear of failure and of punishment leads to guilt.
6 years-puberty	industry vs. inferiority	Valuing work, skill, and competence; or feelings of inadequacy and inferiority.
Adolescence	identity vs. role confusion	Development of individuality; or confusion related to self.
Young adulthood	intimacy vs. isolation	Commitment to personal relations; or withdrawal from others and self-absorption.
Middle age	generativity vs. stagnation	Care of next generation, widening interests; or self-indulgence.
Old age	ego identity vs. despair	Gaining the meaning of one's existence; or disappointment with life and fear of death.

and Erikson, stages are linked to ages in the sense that the ego leads the transition to a new stage regardless of experience and reorganization at the previous stages.

Erikson's work suggests an even more active role for early childhood education. Teachers can help children cope with the essential crisis of their developmental stage. They can also help children develop competencies that will strengthen each individual's ego.

Final exam

B. F. Skinner: Operant Conditioning

In the 1950s B. F. Skinner advanced the behaviorist school of thought in learning and development. He focused on exploring the nature of reinforcement and reinforcing stimuli in relation to learning. Skinner developed problem boxes to experiment with animals. The Skinner box dispensed a reward (food pellet) to an animal if it correctly manipulated a lever or button. Trial and error were linked to rewards for correct behavior. The animals learned to operate the mechanisms in the box as a result of being rewarded.

Skinner's theory of learning has been referred to as *operant conditioning* or *instrumental learning*. According to Skinner, consequences (either negative or positive) that follow a behavior control that behavior. Operant conditioning concentrates primarily on positive reinforcement because of the negative effects punishment can have. A correct response must provide a reward to encourage that behavior to occur again in a similar circumstance. Such instrumentally conditioned responses are referred to as *operants* because they operate on the environment. The nature of the consequences can be critical, because they determine the future behavior of the organism.

The role of early childhood education on an individual's development is considered to be a major one from a behaviorist point of view. The child's development can never be considered as separate from the events in the child's environment. The early childhood teacher can design an environment that will elicit appropriate, desirable behaviors from the child. The teacher can also increase the chances of these behaviors appearing and being sustained by purposely reinforcing only those behaviors. Children increase their range of behaviors as they go through development, but there are no specific stages related to specific kinds of behavior.

Jean Piaget: Intellectual Development

Cognitive-developmental theory has been most completely elaborated on and described by Jean Piaget. He did not study children's emotions or their personality development, although he considered them important. Rather, his interest in examining thought processes and their developmental changes led Piaget to study changes in how children process information as they mature. Piaget believed that children's thinking differed in profound and significant ways from adult thinking and that children's thought processes are modified as they grow. He described their thought processes at different levels and demonstrated that they were active and self-motivated in the creation of their own knowledge. For Piaget, children's thinking abilities follow a consistent developmental pattern beginning early in their life and continuing until maturity.

Most of young children's play behavior reflects the child's important work of *equilibration,* that is, by assimilating new information and accomodating existing intellectual structures, the child develops a balance of understanding while investigating people and their environment (Piaget, 1962). Mental activity and parallel physical activity are essential as children construct their systems of knowledge in more and more mature ways and become effective, competent, thinking adults.

Piaget identified four major stages of cognitive development: (1) the sensorimotor stage (birth to two years), (2) the preoperational stage (two to seven years), (3) the concrete operational stage (seven to eleven years), and (4) the formal operational stage (from eleven or twelve through adulthood). Children progress through these stages in a regular sequence but at their own rate of development, which is influenced by their experiences and their own maturing abilities.

While Piaget believed that children regulate their own thinking, his theory suggests an active role for early childhood education. The teacher should not tell children what they should know, either directly or indirectly through audiovisual techniques. Instead, the teacher should

TABLE 5-3   Piaget's Stages of Intellectual Development

AGE	STAGE	CHARACTERISTICS
Birth–1½ or 2 years	sensorimotor	Children develop schemas based on sensory input and bodily motion.
2–7 years	preoperational	Children develop language and other symbolic representations. Intuitive thought is not systematic or sustained.
7–11 years	concrete operational	Children deal with logical processes, can deal with only one form of classification at a time; logical thought requires actual physical objects or events.
11 years and beyond	formal operational	Children reason logically; formulate and test hypotheses; think abstractly.

design developmentally appropriate activities which allow children to act upon concrete materials and develop conceptual skills. Teachers also can ask questions to develop a degree of cognitive conflict, posing issues that force children to think in more mature ways. This approach represents a major shift in theories about what schools can do for young children.

NATURE AND NURTURE IN CHILDREN'S DEVELOPMENT

The concepts that have been set forth by these developmental theorists vary from one another in considerable ways. One way relates to the areas of development each theory addresses. Some theories deal with all areas of development, while others address only a narrow range of development—for example, intellectual development or socioemotional development.

Another way in which they differ is in how they consider the individual's genetic makeup (nature) or the experiences of growing up (nurture) as being critical to each child's development. Some theorists suggest that an individual's development is primarily determined by nature; while a poor environment might limit any individual's ultimate development, it cannot be considered the prime cause of development. Other theories suggest that human development is more plastic and that ultimately it is the child's experiences that determine what the individual will finally become. Most child development specialists avoid either of these two extremes, believing in the importance of both these influences and feeling that the environmental influences should never be ignored. Although the family serves as the major environmental influence for the young child, early childhood education is also important. Thus, the teacher of young children can have a significant impact on the life of each child in a class.

It should also be noted that developmental research has provided us with a picture of the normal development of children. While this picture represents the central tendencies of development, with half the children developing at a somewhat faster rate and the other half at a somewhat slower rate, it does represent the characteristics of most children at particular points in their lives. Teachers can plan for appropriate activities knowing about how most children mature, then making modifications for the individual differences that are found in a particular class. General characteristics of children age three to six that are considered important to teachers are presented in Table 5-4.

Any chart of developmental expectations should be used only as a general guide. Not all children will show the same characteristics at the same point in their development, though many do. This chart merely illustrates the order of development and provides you with a general sense of what to expect.

TABLE 5-4   Characteristics of Early Childhood Development

	THREE-YEAR-OLDS	
Socioemotional Behavior	*Perceptual-Motor Behaviors*	*Cognitive Behaviors*
Knows self as an individual	Climbs stairs unassisted	Likes to talk with adults
Plays by self and with others	Learns to hop	Talks to self in monolog
Learns to share toys	Jumps, walks, runs with	Asks questions
Cannot share work space	music	Has 250–900 word
Feels sympathetic	Rolls ball with direction	vocabulary
Rests for 10 minutes	Throws underhand	Says full name
Waits and takes turns	Catches large ball	Tells action in picture
Enjoys dress-up clothes	Walks on tiptoe	Listens longer to stories
Enjoys simple humor	Sits with feet crossed at	Sings, laughs
Enjoys praise	ankles	Says simple nursery rhymes
Enjoys floor play	Turns wide corner with	Speaks in 6-word sentences
Is proud of what he or she	tricycle	Repeats 3 numerals
makes	Stops or goes on slide	Counts to 5 in imitation
Helps with adult house	Walks a walking board	Identifies own drawing
activities	holding adult hand	Works puzzles with as many
Separates from mother to	Buttons and unbuttons	as 7 pieces
go to preschool	Enjoys easel paint	Builds tower of 5 graduated
Invents people and objects	Holds crayon with fingers	blocks
	Copies a cross on paper	Builds 3-block bridge
	Cuts with scissors	Understands prepositions
	Toilets self during the day	(on, under, inside)
		Can point to parts of body
		Can point to smaller of 2
		squares
		Identifies big and little

	FOUR-YEAR-OLDS	
Socioemotional Behaviors	*Perceptual-Motor Behaviors*	*Cognitive Behaviors*
Plays with small group	Walks alone up and down	Can identify and point to
Likes birthday parties	stairs, one foot per stair	pictures described
Talks about inviting or not	Climbs ladder and trees	Matches and names 4 basic
inviting someone	Runs on tiptoe	colors
Learns to express sympathy	Gallops to music	"Reads" pictures
Shows off in dress-up	Hops on one foot	Counts and touches 4 or
clothes	Bounces large ball	more objects
Likes to brag	Cuts with scissors on line	Gives home address and age
Likes to go on (field) trips	Eats with fork and spoon	Can tell what material
Runs ahead but waits at	Dresses self except tying	objects are made of
corner	shoe laces	Asks for explanations
Is interested in rules	Builds building with blocks	Is interested in death
Plans ahead with adults	Builds tower of 10 or more	Makes up words and rhymes
Acts silly if tired	blocks	Learns to distinguish
Answers telephone	Balances on walking board	between fact and fancy
efficiently	Draws man with 2 or more	Likes to finish activities
Aware of sexual differences	parts	Can compare 3 pictures
Is courteous without verbal	Adds 3 parts to incomplete	Can tell likenesses and
clues	man	differences in 3 out of 6

	Draws and paints recognizable objects	pictures
	Folds and creases paper 3 times	Carries out a series of 3 directions
	Copies square	

FIVE-YEAR-OLDS

Socioemotional Behaviors	Perceptual-Motor Behaviors	Cognitive Behaviors
Pleased and conscious of new maturity	Is able to sit longer	Identifies pennies, nickels, dimes
Has more cooperative play	Explores neighborhood	Is interested in clock and time
Likes to play house and baby	Has more hand-eye control	Draws what he or she has in mind at the moment
Gets along well in small group	Prints first name	Recognizes some numerals and letters
Conforms to adult ideas	Prints numerals 1-5	Tells what numeral follows another through 10
Asks adult help as needed	Can trace around a diamond	Listens and takes turn in group discussions
Likes to have rules	Draws a triangle	Knows agent (producer) of 15 of 20 actions
Begins to show respect for group property and rights of others	Studies for reality in drawing and painting	Works with several children to lay out simple "maps" with blocks, showing streets and buildings and their locations
Has poise and control	Is self-sufficient in personal care	Learns left from right
Is proud of what he or she has and does	Does simple errands	Speaks fluently and correctly except s/f/h
Chooses owns friends	Can roller skate	Loves stories and acts them out
Begins to distinguish masculine and feminine roles	Skips on alternate feet	Asks meaning of words
Is irritable and cross only when tired and hungry	Can jump rope	Places 10 or more pieces to complete puzzle
	Like to eat simple food	Can tell how a crayon and pencil are the same and how they are different
	Runs, skips, and dances in response to music	
	Catches a ball 5″ in diameter	
	Learns to use overhead ladder	
	Uses knife and fork	
	Washes and dries face and hands without getting clothes wet	
	Draws person with major body parts and features	

Missouri State Department of Elementary and Secondary Education, *Focus on Early Childhood Education: Resource Guide for the Education of Children Ages 3-6.*

DEVELOPMENTAL AREAS

Physical Development

Physical development is a long-range process which is influenced by many elements. Some of the influences are related to an individual's internal characteristics, while other elements are related to the general environment, independent of the individual. Each of these sources plays an important role in the overall development of every child (Gardner, 1973). Sex, race, nutritional state, and general physical condition all affect children's physical growth, including their stature and body proportions. Although physical growth is genetically determined, environmental influences (such as nutrition, health, and exercise) significantly influence development.

Motor development proceeds in predictable patterns. Children (including infants) who are provided with adequate environmental stimulation and practice gradually acquire the capacity to control their bodily movements. Their brains process information from the environment and coordinate actions and interactions with the environment.

Physical development influences personality development in several ways. Physical appearance affects the way children act and how they think about themselves and others. Children's rates of maturity especially influence the personality development of handicapped children (McCandless & Trotter, 1977).

Children need time to develop, opportunities to explore, and freedom to experiment and test ideas and actions. Their personal drive to learn will motivate them but they must be allowed to develop at their own rate. Teachers need to provide the space and materials, allow the time, and accept the children's idiosyncratic developmental rate.

Final exam

Cognitive Development

Cognition refers to an individual's intellect or thinking. The development of thinking skills is based on changes in the child's mental structures. The ability of a child to coordinate various ways of thinking in order to solve problems is a good measure of intellectual growth.

Mature thinking and reasoning begin to develop with the discriminations and regular pattern of actions found in infancy and toddlerhood. Toward the end of their first year most infants are able to distinguish their mother from others in their environment, to understand simple relationships, to point to an object, and to develop fundamental attention and memory skills. As infants' memories are refined, they begin to consider themselves as unique individuals, separated from their environment. Children's limited memory capacities increase with age. Children begin to explore the world around them, developing a sense of object permanence. Toddlers also begin to use language as a vehicle for expression, substituting words for sounds or actions. Thus they develop mental processes that enable them to understand simple problem-solving situations.

Infants and toddlers can make rather fine sensory discriminations. Researchers have found that infants as early as their crawling stage show a high degree of sensory awareness. Perceptual development also takes place as the sense of hearing, taste, smell, and touch develop. Extraordinary developments during infancy and toddlerhood include progressively finer perceptions of shape and form, space, class, and time (Helms & Turner, 1981).

Infants' perceptions are soon transformed into *concepts.* A concept is an individual's mental construction of a class of things. Concepts change to a large extent from early childhood into late adolescence, when socially accepted meanings become stabilized (Klausmeier & Allen, 1978). Such changes are obvious even in the early years. Barry J. Wadsworth (1971) describes the changes in early childhood from preconceptual to intuitive thought.

Preconceptual thought characterizes children ages 2-4 and is especially important to those working with young children. Like Piaget's stage of sensorimotor development, preconceptual thought provides a basis for the appearance of later mature cognition.

During the stage of intuitive thought (4-7 years), children's thinking is marked by immediate perceptions of experiences rather than mental functions. The high degree of egocentrism tends to change with the cognitive change taking place at this time. The mental system which arises at each developmental stage does not have a lower form of egocentrism but conceals it in a higher form of the same thinking style. The form in this stage is an egocentrism of symbols represented by its objects.

Symbolic functioning produces mental images and develops the child's capacity to distinguish signifiers (words, images) from significates (the objects or situations to which signifiers refer). The meanings of words and other symbols accepted by social groups speaking the same language are also word concepts or mental constructs. Mental constructs are a critical element of a maturing individual's continuously modifying and amplifying cognitive structure. Individuals' own concepts guide them in interpreting and organizing incoming information and to develop principles and other complex relationships among concepts. Maturing individuals acquire concepts based on their unique informal learning activities and their maturational patterns (Kagan, 1966).

Concepts are the underlying executors of intellectual work. The theoretical importance of cognitive concepts for symbolic mediators in psychological theory is similar to the fundamental role that genes play in biology or energy plays in physics. Concepts are perceived as the concentration of sensory experience and the crucial relationship between external inputs and overt behaviors.

Language Development

As children grow, their language production increases in quantity, range, and complexity. Studies of language development have focused on sequence and rate of development as well as on those factors influencing language acquisition from infancy throughout life. In a discussion of language development, three basic points need to be made:

1. *There is a difference between language and speech.* Language is usually conceived as a complex system of grammatical and semantic properties, while speech consists of actual utterances. Although language and speech are closely related, they are not the same.

2. *Two areas of language growth are receptive (understanding) and expressive (producing) language.* Receptive language (such as listening or reading) refers to the children's capacity to understand and act on the language communications they process. Expressive language (speaking and writing) refers to the creation of language which is being communicated.

3. *Self-communication or inner speech must also be considered.* Children employ internal language when they daydream, plan ways to solve problems, provide directions, and coordinate their movements. This language component increasingly controls learning. (McCandless & Evans, 1973)

Children gradually make the transition from using sounds to communicate emotional expression, and from using movements and gestures to communicate personal purposes or desires, to communicating through appropriate elaborated language. The children's change in language relates to the development in their perception of the world around them. Two-year-olds have an intense interest in the names of things. Such interest continues to be strong for several years and helps children to quickly increase their vocabulary. In a sense, children construct their own world as they are able to name and/or describe their surroundings. Without this language ability, their surroundings would be a confusing set of vague and unidentified entities with no pattern. The elements in their surroundings come to have meaning when children know their names; experiences and situations become meaningful when children are able to use words to describe them. Using words to name objects or describe events helps children to construct an objective world they can share with others. Through language the listener can perceive the world as the speaker views it. Young children can use language with other forms of expression, such as role playing, expressive gestures, and art forms. Such expressions provide clues as to the children's perceptions of their world in relation to themselves and others.

Emotional Development

Emotional development is related to children's overall development. Individuals adapt to the existence of emotions—joy, anger, pain—through everyday experiences (i.e., as they feel, as they know they feel, and they know what they feel). Beyond this everyday knowledge, experts in emotional development have provided elaborate systems to categorize the various kinds of emotions. There has been a lack of agreement, however, on the definition of emotion and emotional development. Children employ unique but specific sets of behaviors which are observed and from which emotional states are inferred. Fear, like other emotions, is a highly complex phenomenon requiring an understanding of the child's behavior, the circumstances in which the behavior takes place, and the attribution that the caregiver and society provide to that coherence of behaviors and circumstances (Lewis & Michaelson, 1983).

Individual differences in emotion can be considered by one's focusing on those emotional stages and experiences that are enduring. For example, an individual's mood is affected by differences in personality development and personality structure (Lewis & Michaelson, 1983).

Social Development

Social development usually refers to the child's developing ways of adapting to society's rules of behavior. With young children this means learning about cooperating and taking turns. Children first respond to other persons (usually their parents) using a recognizable, consistent, and predictable sign (such as a smile). Even crying is an early sign of socialization. These are social responses. Social development encompasses social controls as well as responsiveness. For example, children stop what they are doing when an adult says "No." Children follow such directions regardless of their desires.

The interchange of the total development is illustrated in the interplay of social and emotional behavior. It is important to understand the elements that create optimum socialization. Socialization is learned, it does not simply result from maturation. Social development requires maturity and the opportunity to learn individual responses. It is promoted in an early childhood classroom through the availability of interested, accepting, and communicative adults. A healthy social setting also facilitates the development of a positive self-concept, of social skills, and of readiness for formal learning. Play serves an important function in the social development of young children.

Development of Values

Attitudes and values are significant aspects of early childhood learning which is partly nonintellectual. To some extent, values are learned the same way that general concepts are learned. A learner has expectations, experiences events, and seeks confirmation for set expectations. Most prejudices, loyalties, and preferences are learned from others. The significant people in a child's life usually guide the children's testing of expectations, serving as models that children imitate. Since young children tend to view their teachers as models, we need to provide children with positive examples to follow. In learning the school's and community's values, young children imitate the models that are available. Teachers should encourage young children to adopt the desirable behavioral patterns which they and others present. Children need to learn to distinguish socially appropriate values while taking into consideration the feelings of others.

The subsystems of development described above continuously work together to affect behavior and development. They do not function independently but are integrated. In attempting to understand the children's behavior, one must take into account their development and the relationship of their whole system. For example, when a child is being administered an intelligence test, the results will be affected by that child's physical, language, emotional, and social state as well as by his or her intelligence.

REGULARITIES AND IRREGULARITIES IN YOUNG CHILDREN'S DEVELOPMENT

Teachers have a tendency to treat all children as average or slightly above average. Although this might be a reasonable approach most of the time, there are occasions when it is totally inappropriate. There are many children who differ from the average in profound and significant ways, and programs for them need to be specially designed to be responsive to those differences. Among the differences that are especially important in the development of early childhood education programs are cultural differences, language differences, social class differences, and differences that result in identifiable exceptionalities.

Children differ from one another by age, sex, culture, language, and social class.

Cultural Differences

Culture has been defined as a set of attitudes and behaviors that have been learned and shared by a group of people. Each group of people live and function within a society that has specific cultural values and cultural techniques that are meaningful to the group.

American society has been characterized by cultural pluralism, with a number of groups having their own, somewhat isolated culture within the larger American culture. Cultural pluralism means that the values, attitudes, and behaviors that children acquire as they interact with persons closest to them may be different from those of other people they will meet throughout their lives. Our society requires that we help children learn to develop the flexibility they need to understand and accept cultural differences.

Early childhood education programs socialize children by exposing them to the dominant values, customs, and habits of the culture. This exposure creates a cultural frame of reference that will become part of them and serve as a vital force in determining their behavior. Educators need to acquire a clear perspective on the role of culture in child development. Many of the children in our schools come from families that share a different culture. Teachers must be sensitive to the cultural roots of the children in their classes as well as those as others in our society. Teachers should keep in mind that there are some cultural values we all accept, but there are others that we must respect as being important to others, even though we may not accept them personally. Teachers need to use a variety of resources, including children, parents, and experts on culture, to help the children share the different cultures in the classroom. This approach communicates respect for cultural difference and shows that every culture is valued.

Language Differences

Just as children differ in their cultural roots, they may differ in their dominant language. Some children use words, grammar, and speech patterns that are different from the standard pattern. Within American society, children learn many different dialects and native languages. The grammar of children from rural New England, Appalachia, and parts of the South (for example, where Creole and black English are spoken) will be strikingly different from standard formal American English. Although children from these areas may not speak the established standard English, they may have achieved language competence in their own dialects.

There are also groups of people who have a first language other than English and who may incorporate rules of the first language into the standard English. These children may come from native-American tribes or immigrant families. They may be French-speaking, Chinese-speaking, or Spanish-speaking. Migrant children, regardless of their ethnic group, also speak differently since they move from place to place, becoming exposed to a variety of language patterns and meanings.

Teachers need to be careful that children are not demeaned or embarrassed because they do not speak standard English or because they speak a language other than English. Children need to feel proud of their own language and heritage. Teachers can provide opportunities in the classroom for children to share diverse languages and heritages and can provide meaningful learning experiences that enable children to learn to speak standard English.

Social Class Differences

Social class membership has been identified as one of the major causes for academic failure in schools. For several decades research has examined group differences in intellectual and academic tasks between low-income and middle-income children. Psychologists such as J. McVicker Hunt (1961) believed that these differences were not genetically determined and that changes in the environment could serve as a major stimulus to increase intellectual development. Since development is most heavily influenced in a child's early years, he suggested that preschool enrichment, preferably initiated at age two, be used as an effective "antidote" or compensation to enhance cognitive growth in low-income children.

A number of experimental early childhood education programs developed in the 1960s led to the creation of Head Start, an early childhood program for low-income children (see Chapter 3). Head Start has been characterized as a comprehensive child development program, providing health, nutrition, and social services along with education. Parent involvement is an important part of the program, extending children's learning beyond the classroom and ensuring that the program is responsive to the needs of the children, their parents, and their community.

Exceptional Children

Most schools now enroll some handicapped children in regular classes. These children deviate in one or more ways from normal children; they may have behavior disorders, learning or developmental disabilities, mental retardation, visual or hearing impairment, communication disorders, and/or physical health impairments. Often these children are multiply handicapped, complicating diagnosis and remediation. Both the child's disability and strength must be taken into account when one designs or modifies an educational program. Each child's total developmental condition needs to be understood.

Handicapped children are usually assigned labels which may become stigmas. Such labeling can create low expectations of their learning, leading to a self-fulfilling prophecy. Once children are associated with a narrow educational path, it becomes difficult to change them to a different path (Spodek, Saracho, & Lee, 1984).

Teachers who work with exceptional children usually require special assistance. While severely or profoundly handicapped children should be educated in segregated settings, it is recommended that, whenever possible, exceptional children be "mainstreamed" or integrated in the regular class program so they can be educated in the least restrictive environment possible. The responsibility of identifying exceptional children and providing appropriate education in the classroom falls primarily on the classroom teacher with the help of special education teachers, psychologists, parents, and others who serve together as a team.

All children, regardless of whether they are handicapped or nonhandicapped, have special educational needs that require individualized educational programs. However, some groups of children have specific educational needs that require the modification of teaching techniques. *Mainstreaming Young Children* (Spodek, Saracho, & Lee, 1984) is a rich source of material for teachers who work with handicapped young children.

SUMMARY

Since the beginning of the child study movement, the field of child development has been closely related to early childhood education. Its theories have provided the foundations for early childhood curriculum practices. These theories have related to physical development, intellectual development, language development, and socioemotional development.

Child development research has also given us a clear picture of what children are like at various age levels. This knowledge has helped teachers establish expectations for how children will function and what they will accomplish at any particular age level. These norms, or expectations, are helpful, but they can also be harmful. Because a norm represents an average of everyone's characteristics, they cannot be used to characterize any single child. Each child at any age will be different from the average in important ways. Teachers must look at individual children and see how each one differs from the average before planning a program and establishing an expectation.

REFERENCES

ERIKSON, E. H. (1963). *Childhood and society.* New York: Norton.

————(1968). *Identity: Youth and crisis.* New York: Norton.

FLAKE-HOBSON, C., B. E. ROBINSON AND P. SKEEN (1983). *Child development and relationships.* Menlo Park, NJ: Addison-Wesley.

GARDNER, D. B. (1973). *Development in early childhood.* New York: Harper & Row.

GESSEL, A. (1952). *Infant development: The embryology of early human behavior.* New York: Harper & Row.

HALL, G. S. (1906). *Youth.* New York: Appleton-Century-Crofts.

HELMS, D. B., AND J. S. TURNER (1981). *Exploring child behavior.* New York: CBS College Publishing.

HUNT, J. McV. (1961). *Intelligence and experience.* New York: Ronald Press.

ILG, F. L., L. B. BATES, AND S. M. BAKER (1981). *Child behavior: Specific advice on problems of child behavior.* New York: Barnes and Noble Books.

KAGAN, J. (1966). *A developmental approach to conceptual growth.* In H. J. Klausmeier and C. W. Harris (Eds.), *Analysis of concept learning,* pp. 97-116. New York: Academic Press.

KESSEN, W. (1965). *The Child.* New York: John Wiley & Sons.

KLAUSMEIER, H. J., AND P. S. ALLEN (1978). *Cognitive development of children and youth: A longitudinal study.* New York: Academic Press.

LANGER, J. (1969) *Theories of development.* New York: Holt, Rinehart & Winston.

LEWIS, M., AND L. MICHAELSON (1983). *Children's emotions and moods: Developmental theory and measurement.* New York: Plenum Press.

MAIER, H. W. (1978). *Three theories of child development* (3rd ed.). New York: Harper & Row.

McCANDLESS, B. R., AND E. D. EVANS (1973). *Children and youth: Psychosocial development.* Hinsdale, IL: The Dryden Press.

McCANDLESS, B. R., AND R. J. TROTTER (1977). *Children: Behavior and development.* New York: Holt, Rinehart & Winston.

PIAGET, J. (1962). *Play, dreams, and imitation in children.* New York: Norton.

SCHIMDT, W. H. O. (1973). *Child development: The human, cultural, and educational context.* New York: Harper & Row.

SPODEK, B., O. N. SARACHO, AND R. C. LEE (1984). *Mainstreaming young children.* Belmont, CA.: Wadsworth Publishing Company.

THOMPSON, G. G. (1952). *Child psychology: Growth trends in psychological adjustment.* New York: Houghton Mifflin.

WADSWORTH, B. J. (1971). *Piaget's theory of cognitive development: An introduction for students of psychology and education.* New York: McKay.

SUGGESTED ACTIVITIES

1. Collect a set of photographs of a six-year-old child that had been taken at intervals since infancy. Compare the different photos. Describe the changes in weight, appearance, and body proportions.

2. Observe a pair of young children of different ages and record how they perform tasks such as holding a cup, painting a picture, and building with blocks.

3. Observe a three- to five-year-old child during the self-selected play period. Describe the social contacts the child has. Compare your observations with those of other students who observed children who are different in age, culture, social class, and/or who are handicapped.

4. Follow a child for a full school day in order to see him or her in a variety of environments and situations. Describe the consistencies as well as the differences in the behavior observed in these settings.

5. Interview parents of two infants of the same age. Ask them to describe their child's sleeping, eating, and toileting habits.

6

PLANNING AND ORGANIZING THE PHYSICAL ENVIRONMENT

OBJECTIVES

After completing this chapter on planning and organizing the physical environment, the student should be able to:

1. Define activity centers and identify ways to use centers.
2. Describe safety guidelines for organizing a room, for designing an outdoor play area, and for choosing materials for young children.
3. Schedule daily activities for an early childhood class.
4. Develop a plan to arrange activity centers in a classroom.
5. Discuss the importance of the outdoor play area as a vehicle for fostering development.
6. Identify the relationship between classroom materials and physical, social, emotional, and intellectual development.

Early childhood settings are not all the same. Some programs are in new buildings that have been especially designed for educating young children. There are also programs in church Sunday school classrooms in which teachers need to put everything away on Friday afternoon and then set up again on Monday morning. There are even programs in places that were never originally conceived to serve young children: former stores, warehouses, and lofts, for example. Within these settings there may be fully furnished learning centers or centers containing only a bare minimum of resources, sometimes little more furniture than tables and chairs. Open-ended materials may be provided in the setting, such as manipulative and constructive materials, or the program might rely primarily on pencil and paper activities. Regardless of what resources are provided for a teacher at the beginning, all learning environments need to be extended and the most effective use possible made of resources.

In this chapter ideas will be presented to help teachers plan and implement a physical environment that will be an inviting and stimulating place for children. The physical organization of the room will be discussed, with attention given to activity centers, furniture, equipment, and materials. The outdoor play area will be discussed as well. Ideas for scheduling the day are also included.

SETTING THE STAGE

Ideally, all early childhood classrooms should be provided with an adequate supply of equipment and materials to serve the children assigned to the group. Realistically, few teachers are given everything they would like to have in their classroom. Teachers need to supplement what is provided as well as modify the setting in ways that will make it more useful. As teachers consider their physical setting and develop plans for their classrooms, they must ask, "How can I make this setting the best possible place for young children to live and to learn in?" The question should first be asked before the school year starts, but it should also be asked repeatedly during the year, for what works at one time may become stale and be less useful as time goes by.

Teachers begin the year with limited knowledge of the children who will be with them. They set up their rooms, hoping the arrangement, materials, and equipment provided will continue to be suitable for most of the school year. However, arranging a room with only a limited sense of what you want to accomplish and with only limited knowledge of the children who will live and work in the room may lead to error. An arrangement may be created that gets in the way of the program's goals rather than helping the children achieve them.

The first thing that must be considered in planning the classroom

Teachers begin their planning even before children enter school.

environment is the children involved. Although a teacher knows little about them, there may be sources of information. There may be records and reports written by the previous year's teacher. There may be an information form such as many preschools collect before a child is enrolled (see Figure 6-1). The children may have visited the class individually and a parent intake interview may have been held. All these are helpful in giving a teacher a sense of the class. These sources are limited, however. What a teacher thinks about the children and class at the beginning of the year will have to be modified as the teacher sees each child interacting with others and with the materials available. In addition, every group has a life of its own. A class represents more than a sum of its parts. The group is a growing organism that develops and changes just as each child develops and changes. Yet the knowledge gained from first impressions is important in getting teaching started at the beginning of the year.

The second question to ask is, "What do I want my children to accomplish?" If you expect children to accomplish a specific goal, you must develop a room arrangement that will support that goal. If you want to support socialization, you need to plan areas where children can work together. If you want children to be creative, then materials like blocks, wood and woodworking tools, and a range of arts and crafts material should be provided for them. The support of physical development requires space and equipment for both large-scale and small-scale activity. You must also recognize that many materials allow children to be working on two or more goals at one time. For example, children playing with Lego's may be sorting and classifying, which are intellectual tasks, while they are learning to share, a social task. Table 6-1 shows the relationship between specific developmental areas and materials and equipment provided in a classroom.

FIGURE 6-1

CHILD ENROLLMENT INFORMATION

Name _____ Age _____

Address _____ Phone _____

Mother's name _____ Phone _____

Mother's address _____

Mother's work place _____ Phone _____

Father's name _____ Phone _____

Father's address _____

Father's work place _____ Phone _____

Person responsible for child's transportation _____

_____ Phone _____

Name of doctor _____ Phone _____

Physical conditions that may affect the child's participation _____

_____

Required medications _____

_____

Sibling's name _____ Age _____

_____

_____

_____

In case of emergency who should be contacted?

Name _____ Phone _____

In the space below please list any other information you wish us to know:

_____

_____

_____

TABLE 6-1 The Relationship Between Developmental Areas and Early Childhood Materials and Equipment

AREAS OF DEVELOPMENT	MATERIALS AND EQUIPMENT
Physical Development	Climbers, wheel toys, blocks, tires, balls, button frames, shoes for lacing, beads for stringing, pattern cards, balance beams, ladders, scissors, woodworking tools, sand tools, puzzles and any other equipment or materials that allow a child to develop large- or small-muscle coordination.
Social Development	Prop boxes, including materials related to the child's experience, such as post office, fire department, or grocery; housekeeping materials, activities or experiences that allow for two or more children to work together.
Intellectual Development	Animals, plants, manipulative materials, sand, water, wood, blocks, pan balance, magnifying glass, matching games, block props (stop sign, toy trucks, etc.), books, records, cassette players, leaves, stones, twigs, flowers, pictures, puzzles, cooking activities, other materials that allow a child to reflect on, act on, and learn from.
Creative Development	Varied kinds of paints, varied sizes, shapes, and textures of paper, markers, clay, "junk," beans, rice, macaroni, paste, wire, cloth, yarn, weaving frames, straight edges, scissors, crayons, brushes, materials for making prints, blocks, dress-up clothes, straws, wood, and any other materials children can use to represent their world.
Language Development	Books, records, materials for language experience charts, stories, finger plays, puppets, child-made books, dress-up clothes for make-believe, social situations, field trips, opportunities to interact with children and adults.
Emotional Development	Any materials that allow for success, that challenge but do not frustrate, that leave a child with a sense of accomplishment.

Another concern is for the number of children that will be in the group. Generally the minimum indoor space requirement for a preschool class is 35 square feet per child, although some authorities recommend 100 square feet. This includes space for equipment as well as room for children to move. No matter how large a room, however, there should be limits placed on the number of children in a group as well as the ratio of children to adults.

The National Day Care Study (Roup et al., 1979) found that differences in program quality related to group size and staff/child ratio.

They found the ratio of one adult to seven children to be the best for preschoolers ages three to five. They recommended that the size of the group be limited to twice the number of children recommended per adult. They also recommended group size and ratios for toddlers: an adult/child ratio of 1:4 for children under three years of age, with groups no larger than 8 for children under two, and no larger than 12 for children between two and three.

Teachers often break the class into smaller groups for particular activities, such as cooking or block building. The size of these groups should be determined by the activity, the amount of supervision required, the space available for the activity, the amount of materials and equipment available, and the ability of the teacher to provide supervision.

ORGANIZING THE CLASSROOM

The classroom should be designed to support a flexible educational program. Floors can be carpeted or covered with resilient tiles. Walls should be pleasantly but unobtrusively colored and there should be enough display space, including bulletin boards and a display shelf or table. A small chalkboard mounted on the walls may be useful. Window shades or blinds that both reduce glare and darken the room completely are helpful for resting as well as for controlling light. A drinking fountain and a sink for various activities and for cleaning should be readily available. Bathrooms should be immediately adjacent or close to the classroom.

The teacher needs to be aware of what elements can be arranged to accommodate the children and the program and what elements cannot be changed and must be adjusted to. Doors, windows, lighting fixtures, electrical outlets, plumbing fixtures, radiators, and heat registers are the kinds of elements that are built into a room and can seldom be changed. They can be modified, though. While windows cannot be shifted to another wall, they can be covered. Similarly, extension cords can be used to allow better placement of equipment as long as they are placed carefully and safely. In this way the best use can be made of a room's physical structure.

As teachers plan their room, they must consider the amount of usable floor space that is available and how it can best be allocated to meet the program's needs. How much space is needed for the movement of traffic, for large-group activities, for large-muscle activity, and for any special projects a teacher might have in mind needs to be considered. The room should be arranged so that a teacher can see students in all areas of the room and so that the teacher can be seen. The placement of blackboards, bulletin boards, film screens, and windows must be considered.

Bulletin boards provide opportunities to teach through displays.

The location of electrical outlets may determine where the record player, aquarium, or other equipment that needs electricity is placed. Electrical cords must be kept along the wall and off the floor. Extension cords should not be used unless absolutely necessary, and then only when they can be placed safely along baseboards. Loose wires left on the floor are sure to be tripped over.

Teachers must always be sure to check that the physical arrangement of the room is safe in other ways as well. Furniture and equipment should have no sharp edges. Worn and unsafe equipment should be repaired or removed from the class. Traffic patterns should be designed to avoid unnecessary conflict. Climbing equipment should be installed over soft surfaces. When handicapped children are in a class, additional modifications may need to be made. Furniture might have to be rearranged or crutch tips placed on the legs of tables so they will not slip. In addition, teachers and children should establish and enforce safety rules for functioning in the classroom.

The aesthetic climate of the classroom should also be considered. Colors should be soft, not distracting. Attractive pictures and fabrics, fresh flowers, and pleasing displays all add to the children's learning experience. The teacher should regularly monitor the room temperature, noise level, and lighting. All of these can affect the way children behave and how well they learn.

Storage should be carefully planned. A classroom should have enough storage and locker facilities for children's coats, boots, extra

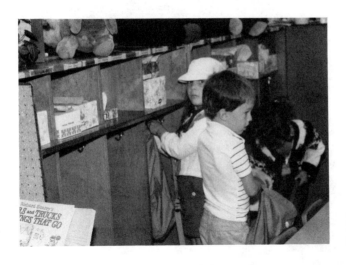

A classroom should have lockers for the children's clothing and personal belongings.

clothing, and personal belongings, as well as for the teacher's needs. Providing a locker or cubby for each child's use is desirable. Teachers also need their own storage space. In addition, considerable and varied storage space should be provided for materials and equipment. Large wheel toys, paper, art supplies, and materials for different learning units all need different kinds of storage facilities. The room should be arranged so that children know where materials go, and the children should help with cleanup. Having the children responsible for putting things away is a way of helping to develop autonomy. The children should know what is expected of them and expectations should be related to what they can do.

It is important to keep the room neat and pleasing. Messy shelves, broken equipment, and careless displays all give the same message to

The classroom should be an attractive, inviting place for children to learn.

children: that sloppiness is acceptable and that their activities are not valued. The materials in the classroom are tools for children's learning and should be treated with respect.

The room should be ready when the children walk in each day. The teacher should be at the door to greet them and invite them to participate in a carefully arranged, well-organized room. The physical setting should extend a personal invitation to learn.

Activity Centers

Early childhood classrooms are best organized into activity centers, each center supporting some portion of the program. Though the centers can be modified to serve the changing needs of the program, made larger or smaller, or even merged with other centers, most should be available as separate areas throughout the activity period. Activity centers allow rooms to become child centered rather than teacher centered. They help programs become more individualized and allow children to participate more actively and be more independent of the teacher (Blake, 1977). Figure 6-2 provides a floor plan for an early childhood classroom and demonstrates how activity centers might be arranged.

Early childhood programs generally include arts and crafts activity centers, dramatic play centers, block-building centers, manipulative materials centers, library centers, music centers, and display centers. Temporary centers can also be organized around specific themes, such as an environmental studies center or a transportation center. Materials and activities related to the theme would be organized and the center would remain for as long as the theme holds the children's interest.

Centers should include materials related to their purposes. All supplies and equipment should be readily accessible to the children. Table 6-2 provides examples of equipment to be included in various activity centers. The boundaries of a center should be clearly defined. Children should also know the acceptable limits for use of materials. Centers should be designed to be easily supervised, and their contents should support independent activity. Place the art center and water play center near the source of water, to avoid the need to carry buckets of water across the room. Centers should be arranged so that children have room to move around without disturbing the activities of others. Teachers should be sure that children have easy access to materials without climbing on chairs or tables. In addition, doors, water fountains, and restrooms should not be blocked. A child who has to use the bathroom is not going to wait while the easel is moved away from the door. A well-thought-out traffic pattern can eliminate many behavior problems, because children will not interfere with each other as they move from one activity to another.

Ample supplies should be available for the number of children who are going to participate in each activity. Nothing is more frustrating to

Figure 6-2 Floor plan of an early childhood classroom.

TABLE 6-2 Provisions for Activity Centers

CENTER	EQUIPMENT
Arts and Crafts	Easels, tables and chairs, a drying rack for pictures, a place to store children's products, and a place for material storage.
Woodworking	A sturdy workbench, an adequate number and variety of tools, a scrap box for wood, and a tool board.
Housekeeping	A play sink, refrigerator, cupboards, stove, bed, table, and chairs; storage for cups, saucers, and utensils as well as a place to hang dress-up clothes.
Music	A board for hanging rhythm instruments, a record player, a listening center, and storage for records; a cassette player, cassettes, and piano are excellent additions to the music area.
Blocks	Storage for unit and hollow blocks, adequate floor space for building, and adequate storage for props.
Water/Sand	A table that can be used for water or sand, a plastic sheet to cover the floor, and a place to store the water/sand play props.
Reading/Language	A rocker, pillows, rug; and storage and display for books.
Science/Math	A pan balance, aquarium, plants, tables, chairs, display space, and storage.

a child than to run out of material when the child has been waiting all morning to participate. Materials that children can use should be separated from those that they are not supposed to use. Books, resources, and materials that are not for children's use should be stored out of sight and out of reach.

A quiet area should be available for children who need time away from the group. This may be a rocker, a large pillow in the corner of the room, a cardboard box with the side cut out, or a loft. Quiet activities should be grouped away from those that are noisier and more active. Reading or listening areas, for example, should not be next to the blocks or woodworking areas.

There should be enough space for the activities. For example block building or other constructive activities can require considerable floor space. Good building space can be as important to block building as an adequate supply of blocks.

Each center should be analyzed to determine how many children can comfortably be involved at one time. The number of children that are allowed to use a center might need to be limited. The children should know what the limit is.

All activities, materials, or centers in a classroom do not have to be out at the same time. Too many things in a room may make it difficult for children to make choices. It is also helpful to rotate centers or materials throughout the year. If children begin to lose interest in a center, the materials can be put away for a few months. Bringing it back will make it seem as if the activities and materials are new. It will rekindle interest and will often turn the center into a desirable learning setting once more.

Furniture and Equipment

Furniture for an early childhood classroom should be movable, durable, and scaled to the children's size. Tables and chairs should be of varying heights since children in any age group vary in size. Tables of different shapes can be used for both art work and eating. Trapezoidal tables are nice to have in a class since they can be grouped and arranged to create many different shapes. Stackable chairs and tables can be stored in a corner of the room when not in use.

If young children stay in school for a full day, they will need cots for rest. Lightweight cots that stack for easy storage can be purchased. It is not necessaary to have cots for children in a half-day program. Various cabinets, shelf units, and racks should also be provided for storing supplies, equipment, and books. If supplies are kept on open shelves, the children can help themselves to materials they need. In addition to providing storage, cabinets and shelves can be arranged to screen different centers from one another. Other furniture and equipment, such as housekeeping furniture or a water/sand table, will be needed in the activity centers.

When you are selecting equipment for the classroom, the following criteria should be used:

Safety. This is the first and most important consideration in selecting materials. The Public Action Coalition on Toys (1983) suggests that the following questions be asked about the children's toys and equipment:

> Are there any sharp edges or points, exposed nails, sharp wires or straight pins?
> Is it large enough so that it can't be swallowed?
> Does it have detachable or (poorly glued) small parts that can be removed and lodge in the windpipe, ears, or nose?
> Is it made of unbreakable material?
> Is it labeled "nontoxic," since infants put everything into the mouth?
> Does it have parts that can pinch fingers or toes or catch hair?
> Are the cords for crib toys shorter than 12 inches to avoid strangulation?

Is the projectile toy (rocket, dart, model airplane) capable of inflicting dangerous eye injuries?

Does the toy require electricity?

Will the toy be safe when used in its surroundings?

Are there any hidden hazards?

Is the toy easily cleaned? (pp. 6-8)

Cost. All programs have limited supply budgets. Thus, the cost of an item often determines whether it will be purchased. While money spent for an object is critical to many programs, price should not be considered alone. Often more expensive items will last longer and cost less in the long run. Teachers should select materials and equipment that will be interesting to children and help further their educational goals.

Appropriateness for the Children. Materials should be matched to the interests, ages, and learning abilities of a particular group of children. You need to look at the individual children and judge what will work for them to achieve the program's goals.

Quality and Durability. Equipment that is considered adequate for home use is often inappropriate for school. It may not be durable enough for heavy use or it may require too much supervision. The design and construction of each piece of equipment should be considered in relation to its use by a group of children.

Flexibility of Use. Equipment should be selected that can be used in a variety of ways and situations. Dramatic play equipment that has few details can often be used most flexibly. A child's imagination can turn a simple box into a boat or an airplane. Of course, equipment designed for specific purposes should not be overlooked.

A number of guides are available for the selection of equipment for early childhood education. Useful lists include:

ASSOCIATION FOR CHILDHOOD EDUCATION INTERNATIONAL, *Selecting Educational Equipment for School and Home.* Washington, DC: The Association for Childhood Education International, 1976.

EVANS, A. M., "How to Equip and Supply Your Prekindergarten Classrooms." In J. L. Frost (Ed.), *Early Childhood Education Rediscovered.* New York: Holt, Rinehart & Winston, 1968, pp. 567-76.

FOSTER, J., AND N. HEADLEY, *Education in the Kindergarten* (3rd ed.). New York: American Book Co., 1969, chapter 7.

HEFFERNAN, H., AND V. TODD, *The Kindergarten Teacher.* Boston: D.C. Heath, 1960, pp. 59-65.

PROJECT HEADSTART, *Equipment and Supplies: Guidelines for Administrators and Teachers in Child Development Centers.* Washington, DC: Office of Economic Opportunity, n.d.

Free and Inexpensive Materials

Early childhood teachers will save *anything*, and anything that they save can be used as some part of a learning activity. Few teachers have enough money to purchase all the materials they feel they need. Most teachers of young children collect materials from various sources—parents, shopkeepers, and just about anyone else who has something usable to contribute. While no complete list of those things that can be obtained for free can be written, here are some ideas:

- Parents can save buttons, string, cloth, milk cartons, yarn, old shirts, old toys, bottle caps, dress-up clothes, and magazines. Often a note sent home with the children will bring more than you will need.
- Shopkeepers can provide meat trays, props for dramatic play, cardboard boxes, old coupons, window advertisements, posters, wood scraps, carpet scraps, and wallpaper samples. You or your parent group need to ask for these things. Be sure that what is collected is *safe* and *useful*.

Other sources for materials include the Red Cross, post office, fire station, National Dairy Council, agricultural agencies, senior citizen centers, other teachers (who may be willing to trade materials), and local, state, and federal agencies.

Although there is no limit to the materials you can collect, don't collect more than you can comfortably store. Messing up a classroom with a lot of free "stuff" that you can't store can be counterproductive.

DESIGNING OUTDOOR PLAY AREAS

Local climate and weather conditions, as much as anything else, will determine what kinds of activities can be offered to children outdoors and in turn, will influence how the outdoor play area should be designed. Additional considerations include the problems of vandalism and the other uses that might be made of the area when school is not in session. The outdoor area should be considered an extension of the classroom, providing opportunity for exciting learning experiences.

Joe Frost and Barry Klein (1979) recommend that children's playgrounds be carefully planned, even before schools are planned, in order to preserve the natural terrain. Permanent facilities such as fences, storage sheds, waterlines, water fountains, hard-surfaced areas, and shade structures, should be installed at the beginning. The range and arrangement of equipment in the playground should take into account such factors as: (1) the need for complex multifunction structures; (2) the availability of varied kinds of equipment to allow many different forms of play; and (3) the arrangement of equipment to allow play to take place across different structures. Zones can be created for different kinds of play and should be arranged to allow for movement across zones. Space should

Many elements should be considered in designing outdoor space.

also be provided in the outdoor area for creative arts and activities using natural materials. In addition, safety, maintenance, and supervision must be considered when one is planning the outdoor space and its use.

Mildred Dickerson (1977), in describing the process of developing an outdoor learning center, refers to a number of concerns that need to be addressed. She suggests that the complete site be planned initially, even if it is going to be built in stages. The planners must consider regulations, insurance requirements, budget and resource limitations, and the labor needed to build and maintain a site. She also suggests basic criteria to be considered in developing an outdoor learning center, including:

1. Children who will be using the area—their age, size, and abilities.
2. Space and location—closeness to toilets and to the classroom; whether it can be adequately supervised; the elimination of "blind spots" where children can hide.
3. Security—a fence is essential. It should be at least four feet high with no toe holes for climbing. It should have a single gate to allow children to come and go, and a double gate for maintenance.
4. Surfaces—the area should have good drainage and variations in terrain. There should be hard surface areas for some activities, as well as grassy areas, sand areas, and earth areas. A paved path for wheel toys is helpful.
5. Sun and shade—there should be a balance of both.
6. Storage—handy storage areas will keep things from having to be moved long distances.
7. It should support a variety of play opportunities.
8. It should allow for different equipment arrangements—to facilitate equipment use, and to accomplish the goals of the center.
9. Water—a convenient source of water for drinking as well as for water play should be provided.

Selecting Outdoor Materials and Equipment

Outdoor equipment should provide for more than the exercise of large muscles. It should promote creativity and imagination, allowing children to act out ideas and themes in dramatic play.

The equipment provided in an outdoor play area is as important to the child's learning as the equipment provided indoors. Dramatic play props, wheel toys, balls, water play and sand play equipment, construction materials, and gardening materials are all necessary to the outdoor experience. A well-planned, well-organized, and well-equipped outdoor learning environment is an important part of the young child's program.

Besides program concerns, teachers should be concerned about potential safety hazards that may exist in outdoor equipment. Peter Werner (1983) reported that, according to the Consumer Product Safety Commission's 1975 study, playground equipment such as that in a school's outdoor area ranked sixth on the list of 100 most hazardous consumer products. Since that time, however, steps have been taken to improve the quality of equipment.

The Consumer Product Safety Commission published *A Handbook for Public Playground Safety* (1981) that offers the following suggestions for designing a safe outdoor play area:

1. Sixty to 80 percent of playground injuries are caused by children falling off playground equipment onto a hard surface. Using more resilient material under equipment such as bark, sand, or wood chips can reduce injuries.
2. No component or groups of components of a piece of equipment should form an angle that could entrap any part of the child's body.
3. Accessible parts of equipment should be designed so that they cannot catch a child's clothing.
4. Playground equipment should present no sharp edges, protruding points, sharp corners, or other items that could cut, puncture, pinch, or crush a child or catch the clothing.

Teachers should check their outdoor play settings to see if safety problems do exist and make whatever repairs or modifications are needed to protect children.

SCHEDULING ACTIVITIES

Scheduling is the teachers' arrangement of time for children's activities. Half-day, full-day, and extended-day programs require different schedules, but all schedules should be based on an understanding of young children: their patterns of movement, how fast or slow they respond, how much excitement or rest they need. In addition, when activities take place in a regular order each day over a long period of time, a sense of security develops based on a knowledge of what can be expected.

Schedules that are established should be followed. Children like the sense of order this provides. While young children may not be able to tell time, they do know when their day has been rearranged. There are special occasions, such as field trips, visitors, and holiday celebrations, when schedules should be modified.

In developing a schedule for a group of young children, you need to consider a number of factors. A time for the entire group to get together at the beginning of the day is helpful. It allows the teacher to inform the children of what might be happening that day as well as to get a sense of the children. It also helps to establish a feeling of groupness. A similar period at the end of the day can be used to summarize what happened and to set the stage for the next day.

There needs to be adequate time built into the schedule for self-care activities, such as dressing and undressing (on entering school, before and after outdoor play, and before going home), eating (breakfast, if needed, snacks, and lunch), and resting. Times for toileting should be provided, though the children should not be placed on a rigid schedule. High-energy activities should be scheduled as well as quieter activities to give children the opportunity periodically to rest, relax, and calm down and to make sure that children don't get lethargic.

When you are planning schedules, you need to consider the calendar as much as the clock. Time should be allotted during the year for special activities or themes. Most programs include units based on holidays, seasons, animals, or other interests that should have a place in the schedule.

Time must also be allocated for transition from one activity to another. Teachers must plan for adequate cleanup time and make sure they warn children when the end of an activity is coming. Telling children a few minutes ahead that an activity needs to be ended is a good way to help them anticipate cleanup.

A number of factors contribute to difficulties around transition time: boredom, the insistence on conformity, the absence of a future orientation in some children, the absence of clearly defined tasks, and a possible fear of failure (Hirsch, n.d.). Planning for transition can ease potential difficulties. Sometimes specific children have problems during transitions, and a teacher can provide special support for them. Making a game of cleanup can help to make it less overwhelming. Giving children specific directions and setting expectations so that they are able to do what's expected of them also help. Having available some short games, stories, poems, and finger plays can help fill periods of waiting for some children while others are completing their task. Most important, the teacher's sense of calm and order will help the children overcome whatever problems arise.

Extra time must also be allocated for moving the children from one room to another. If children go to a special place for lunch, a teacher has to plan for time to cleanup, to move children to the lunch room, eat, clean up, return to the classroom, use the toilet, and prepare for the next activity.

Although activities should follow the same order each day, teachers should not worry about varying the pace of activities from day to day. Some days children may have a very productive outdoor period, and providing additional time is a reasonable thing to do. On other days disinterest or fussiness may lead to cutting a period short. The teacher must be sensitive to children and be flexible enough to change to meet their needs.

The following schedule is suggested for a morning half-day nursery school and kindergarten:

8:15–8:45 A.M. *Teacher planning and preparation.*

8:45–9:00 A.M. *Arrival.* The children may enter the classroom at various intervals during a prescribed arrival time. Spaced entry allows the teacher to greet each child individually and allows the children an opportunity to make a gradual transition from home to school. During the arrival period they browse through books or work with manipulative materials. They might also be able to view displays the teacher has placed on the bulletin board or science table.

9:00–9:20 A.M. *Group time.* The teacher sits with the entire group to plan the day and take care of necessary routines such as attendance. Group time also allows for discussions on a variety of topics. A sharing or show-and-tell period might be appropriate if the children do not take the initiative in discussions. Once skills in group discussions are developed, the formal show-and-tell could be dispensed with.

9:20–10:10 A.M. *Activity period.* During this period the children are given a choice of activities and may change activities at any time during the period. Many of the children may work individually or in small groups. The teacher may work with a single child or a small group or may supervise the entire room. Included in the activities offered are an arts and crafts activity, dramatic play, and other activities planned by the teacher. Some children may work with manipulative materials. Others might work at a sand table or a water basin or might be involved in a planned science experience. All the activity is under the guidance of the teacher.

10:10–10:30 A.M. *Cleanup, snack, and rest.* After an activity period children need to clean their room and put away the materials they have been using. Time should be allowed for young children to go to the bathroom and wash up. Milk or fruit juice, crackers, raw vegetables, or fruit may be provided as a snack. This period can provide productive learning opportunities. Informal discussions can be stimulated, new food can be tasted, responsibilities and skills can be learned, and children can become aware of the characteristics and functions of the things used. A quiet period, such as listening to a story or record, might be substituted for a formal rest period.

10:30–11:00 A.M. *Music and story time.* A period of time is usually set aside for activities involving the entire class. Group singing or rhythmic activities allow the children to explore music as well as the use of their own body for creative expression. Teachers can read from picture books or tell stories.

11:00–11:20 A.M. *Outdoor activity time.* Children can be encouraged to climb, run, jump, and use wheel toys and large pieces of equipment. Sand and water play can also be included. The amount of time spent outdoors will probably vary with the climate and the opportunities children have to use the outdoors productively at home.

11:20–11:40 A.M. *Preparation for dismissal and dismissal.* The children need time to get ready and collect their things before departing for home. If parents are expected to pick their children up, this time provides an excellent opportunity for mini-conferences and informal chats about the children.

11:40–12:00 *Teacher cleanup period.* At the end of the morning, teachers need time to reorder themselves and their rooms and take care of records before preparing for the next group.

In a program lasting fewer hours, periods can be compressed somewhat. In an extended or all-day program, other periods might have to be added. There might be an extended informal activity period at the beginning of the day to accommodate children who must be dropped off earlier. Breakfast might be served then, if needed. In addition, time for lunch, rest, snack, and individual activities might be added in the afternoon for an all-day program.

A day care program might use the schedule presented here for the morning. However, the day might start earlier for most children, who may arrive at 8:00 A.M. or as early as 6:00 A.M. Along with serving food, where appropriate, teachers might plan for informal activities for the early part of the morning, or they might shift the times of the various activities if most children arrive early. The rest of the day might look as follows:

11:30–12:00. *Lunch.*

12:00–1:30 P.M. *Rest on cots* (many children will nap). The teacher should arrange quiet activities for those who do not. Looking at books or playing with soft toys might help to relax the children. Sometimes playing quiet records on the phonograph helps.

1:30–2:30 P.M. *Outdoor time,* similar to that in the morning.

2:30–3:00 P.M. *Cleanup and snack.*

3:00–3:30 P.M. *Music and/or story time.*

3:30–4:30 P.M. *Activity time.* More emphasis will be given to table activities and less physically demanding activities than in the morning.

4:30–5:00 P.M. (or later). *Informal activities* until the children are picked up.

The afternoon in an all-day kindergarten might be as follows:

11:30–12:00. *Lunch.*

12:00–12:45 P.M. *Quiet time.* Activities that do not require high levels of activity might be offered here. Table activities, including those related to preacademics, might be offered.

12:45–1:45 P.M. *Project time.* Children might work on long-term projects that have been developed over time. Mural paintings, cardboard box constructions related to a social studies unit, or plantings related to a science unit are examples.

1:45–2:30 P.M. *Outdoor activity time.*

2:30–3:00 P.M. *Cleanup, story time, preparation for dismissal.*

3:00 P.M. *Dismissal.*

A full-day program must provide for children's lunch and nap, as well as additional play activities.

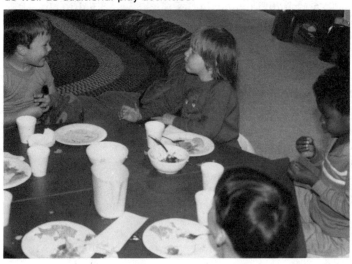

Each day will vary from this schedule, of course, as teachers modify their programs to meet the specific needs of their class or to carry on special projects. The schedule should be characterized by both regularity and flexibility.

SUMMARY

The physical environment includes the early childhood classroom, everything in it, and the outdoor area. These represent the context for children's learning. A room that is poorly equipped will present children with relatively few options for educational experiences. One that is well equipped with developmentally appropriate materials can be a stimulating and engaging learning site. The difference between the two is in the planning, organizing, and provisioning that is done by the teacher. Teachers need to consider the physical environments in which they work and arrange that environment to serve the goals established for their programs.

REFERENCES

BLAKE, H. E. (1977). *Creating a learning-centered classroom.* New York: Hart.

CONSUMER PRODUCTS SAFETY COMMISSION (1981). *A handbook for public playground safety.* Washington, DC: Consumer Products Safety Commission.

DICKERSON, M. G. (1977). *Developing the outdoor learning center.* Little Rock, AR: Southern Association for Children Under Six.

FROST, J. L., AND B. L. KLEIN (1979). *Children's play and playgrounds.* Boston: Allyn & Bacon.

HIRSCH, E. S. (n.d.). *Transition periods: Stumbling blocks of education.* New York: Early Childhood Education Council of New York City.

PUBLIC ACTION COALITION ON TOYS (1983). Guidelines for choosing toys. *Day Care and Early Education,* **11**(1), 6-8.

ROUP, R., J. TRAVERS, F. GLANTZ, AND C. COELEN (1979). *Children at the Center: Final report of the National Day Care Study,* Vol. 1. Cambridge, MA: Abt Associates.

WERNER, P. (1983). Children's needs and safety standards. *Dimensions,* **11**(2), 11-14.

SUGGESTED ACTIVITIES

1. Plan a tentative one-day schedule for a group of three-year-olds. Do the same for a group of five-year-olds. Describe how the schedules are the same and how they differ.

HW

2. Interview a teacher of young children about the importance of planning for transitions. List the suggestions for having smooth transition times.

3. Develop a folder of sources of free and inexpensive materials (continue to add to that folder). Draft a one-page letter requesting materials from these sources.

4. Critique the room arrangement that appears in Chapter 6. How could the arrangement be improved?

5. Design one activity center on any topic for children below the age of six in any curriculum area. Show it to a teacher for suggestions of ways to improve it.

7

PLANNING
AND ORGANIZING
THE SOCIAL
ENVIRONMENT

OBJECTIVES

After completing this chapter on planning and organizing the social environment, the student will be able to:

1. Design an appropriate physical setting to support children's interactions with other children and significant adults.
2. Identify several ways of organizing young children.
3. Plan different types of grouping patterns to facilitate individual and group activities.
4. Describe and compare a number of models to improve young children's classroom behavior.
5. Develop a system of classroom management to help children develop self-control and responsibility.
6. Explain the strategies to teach young children positive social interactions.
7. Discuss appropriate ways of working with adults in the classroom, including paraprofessionals, volunteers, and resource people.

Once teachers establish educational goals for their class, they often focus on creating a proper physical setting. The next step is to plan and organize the social environment, one that will support children's interactions with other children and with significant adults. They must also help young children develop self-control, as well as ways of dealing with the needs and feelings of others. This chapter will deal with the social elements of the classroom, for both adults and children.

ORGANIZING CHILDREN

When young children enter school for the first time, they give up the natural rhythm of their daily activities. They must now attend school at a specific time, sit in an assigned place for a determined period of time, take care of bodily functions at a prescribed time, and eat and play together at specified times. Children are expected to do all these things and others at the same time as their peers. They must adapt their behaviors to what the school considers appropriate and conform to group norms, regardless of how they function at home.

Teaching children in groups instead of one at a time requires the teacher to become aware of the need for individuals to adapt to the group. Yet, within this expectation, teachers must be sensitive to individual differences within the group. In achieving the complex task of organizing children, teachers use various types of organization, grouping children and adults in a workable classroom management system. Children must also be helped to learn the positive social interaction skills they will need.

Grouping

Children in any classroom are different from one another. However, since some will have similar interests and needs and will not differ in profound ways, teachers can often individualize through grouping. In addition, some children may work better in a group situation than alone; they can learn from each other's reactions and model one another's behavior. Some children may also feel less pressured in a group setting.

Four or five young children working together often constitutes a manageable group. Younger children like to sit close to the teacher. They feel that the nearness allows them to get a verbal or physical response easily, which may not be possible when they are lost in a large group. If the teacher has some help (such as an aide, mother helper, college student, or volunteer), the class should be divided into smaller groups to make it more manageable. As children learn to work in groups, group size can be increased. Even if the teacher keeps the entire class together, an assistant can help, joining in and participating with the group, and promoting the children's interests. Three-, four-, and five-year-old children are sometimes all brought together to introduce a unit, tell a story, or talk about an object or event.

Young children may be grouped for story time provided the teacher (1) plans for a smooth transition which allows the children to anticipate what will happen, (2) prepares the setting so that children can listen quietly, (3) has the story and any materials ready in advance, and (4) plans follow-up activities.

Group time should be used to develop receptive and expressive language, encourage thinking processes, and provide positive social experiences for young children. Group experiences should integrate logical and language activities by means of a variety of experiences such as poems, stories, action plays, songs, rhythms, creative movement, and discussion. Not all of these will be used on any one day. Long-range planning guarantees that children have a variety of experiences over time, whereas short-range planning ensures flexibility in teaching.

A word of caution: When teachers develop well-organized instructional plans and prepare all the resources necessary, they often feel the need to stick to them under any circumstances. There should be enough flexibility in planning to take into account any unanticipated events and to make use of opportunities that arise, even if it means dropping a set of planned activities. A frog that jumps into the room on a rainy day during story or sharing time, for example, will instantly distract the children. Rather than fight the distraction, teachers can change the topic and permit the children to become actively involved in the unexpected event. The teacher might seek out storybooks about frogs or use frogs as a theme for a movement activity. The teacher can achieve the same goal and, at the same time, build on an exciting occurrence, especially if the children have been physically confined for a long period of time.

Although formal instruction is seldom found in early childhood classes, children are grouped for a variety of activities. Many kinds of grouping patterns can be used to individualize instruction, including open grouping, paired grouping (Wilson & Ribovich, 1973), and multi-age grouping (Spodek, 1985). Learning centers, discussed in the previous chapter, can facilitate individual and group activities.

Open Grouping   In open grouping children choose a group based on their interests. Children might, for example, choose to join a group in which a story is being read, or they may go to the block center to build with others. This type of grouping requires that activities be known to the children ahead of time to allow them to anticipate activities, plan their selection, and choose to participate in one of several group activities.

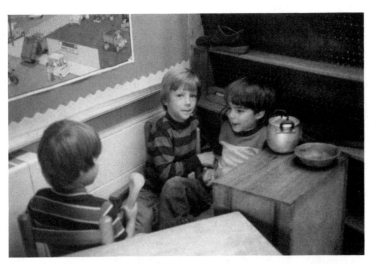

Children often group themselves according to their interests.

Paired Grouping. In paired grouping, a child works for a while with one other child, the two helping each other learn. It assumes that all children can teach and be taught and that all children have strengths and needs that will complement each other. A child's strengths can be demonstrated and internalized by his or her teaching another child, while at the same time each child's needs are met by receiving help from another.

Multi-age Grouping. Multi-age grouping, which is also called *family grouping*, develops an enriched community of young children and provides an opportunity to mix the ages within a group (such as having three- to five-year-olds in the same class). This group of children of different ages functions much as a family does, with children helping, protecting, guiding, and teaching each other. There is also less concern about age level expectations in such groups so that pressure on individuals may be reduced.

Children vary in styles, interests, and needs. Classroom strategies that gear activities and expectations to the average child should be avoided. They create pressures and place restrictions on activities. These strategies punish children for their unique qualities. Individual differences need to be valued and enhanced in the classroom. Grouping practices that work well accommodate the class to differences among children.

Using Children to Extend Teaching

In any classroom, the children themselves should assume some responsibility for classroom tasks. Children can restore toys and materials to their proper places when they are finished using them. They can serve snacks, clean up spills from tables and floors, and maintain a clean, neat, and orderly environment. They can monitor their own behavior and make sure that others do not break the classroom rules. Teachers can use this assistance to provide themselves with more time to teach and interact with the children. This is a good way for children to learn to assume responsibilities.

CLASSROOM MANAGEMENT

Classroom management focuses on maintaining order in the classroom. Many teachers make proper management their primary teaching goal, although different teachers may achieve that goal in different ways. Some teachers punish, lecture, guide, or persuade children to behave appropriately, with all the classroom controls coming from them. Other teachers help children develop self-control and responsibility. Some teachers strive for absolute quiet and limited movement. Other teachers value the movement and noise that come from purposeful activity. Generally teachers want children to behave as they are expected, to not defy the teacher, to be on task, to assume responsibility for classroom materials, and to have good interpersonal skills.

Discipline is an important part of any classroom management system. Discipline is not the same as punishment. It represents an appropriate way of organizing and managing the classroom for children and adults. Simple rules for appropriate behavior should be established, and these rules should be taught through a variety of experiences. The teaching of appropriate behaviors should be planned and worked at just as language arts and other curriculum areas are planned and worked at.

Teachers need to develop a workable management system to meet the range of individual differences in the classroom. A classroom management system should help young children develop self-control in appropriate ways. Children should become more independent, learn to help themselves, and learn to cope with their environment. At the same time, children should be helped to manage their own impulses and drives.

For young children, learning to be independent includes acquiring self-caring skills such as dressing, toileting, feeding, and other essential tasks with the least amount of help. It also includes learning to keep busy, to develop positive relationships with other children, and to make independent decisions to the extent possible. Children should be helped not to be destructive, intrusive, exhibitionist, overly proud, overly assertive, or inappropriately competitive. Developing constructive patterns of self-care and work requires children to direct their impulses. In addition, children need to understand clearly the difference between acceptable and unacceptable behavior. Teachers are responsible for making sure that areas of appropriate, acceptable behavior are spelled out for the children and that children develop self-control.

Some educators and psychologists believe that children's behavior can be improved through specific approaches to discipline. C. M. Charles (1981) describes several models for the classroom environment that promote optimal learning. These include the behavior modification model, the Kounin model, and the Dreikurs model.

Behavior Modification

Psychologists consider behavior modification, or applied behavior analysis theory, to be a systematic way of changing children's behavior. Teachers study the behavior problem, then systematically apply reinforcement and punishment which moves children toward the desired behaviors. Once children acquire the desired behavior, the teacher can eliminate the strategy.

A behavior modification strategy usually consists of four procedures: *pinpoint, record, consequate,* and *evaluate* (Masden & Masden, 1974). Teachers *pinpoint* the specific problem behavior. They observe and *record* how often the behavior occurs under different conditions. They develop a strategy to focus on this behavior. At the *consequate* stage, teachers reinforce the acceptable behavior. Reinforcement can consist of positive statements, a pat on the back, or material rewards (such as tokens, candy, toys, or time to play or to participate in valued activities). Tokens are usually exchanged for some other type of reward. If the child shows negative behavior, it is ignored (if possible) while an alternative behavior that is acceptable is reinforced. After teachers have implemented the strategy to modify children's behavior, they *evaluate* their efforts to determine its success. If the strategy has succeeded, it is eliminated since it is no longer needed. If the strategy has been unsuccessful, then a new one may be devised to be implemented and tested.

Kounin's Model of Classroom Management

The teacher's capacity to manage groups becomes the focus of Kounin's (1970) classroom management model . Teachers need simultaneously to cope with the whole class, subgroups, pairs of students, and individuals. In managing the classroom, Kounin's model avoids punishment and harsh teacher responses. He suggests that teachers should:

1. Be aware of what is going on everywhere in the classroom at all times and let the students know this.
2. Cope simultaneously with more than one problem.
3. Correct the appropriate target behavior immediately to avoid the increase of the misbehavior.
4. Learn to employ the ripple effect efficiently.

5. Use and keep a smooth and consistent momentum.
6. Sustain group focus by alerting and accountability.
7. Offer nonsatiating teaching strategies by using progress, challenge, and variety.

Kounin has identified the *ripple effect* in working with children. What a teacher does to one child, for instance a remark made to suppress behavior, modifies the behavior of all the children who witness the act. Kounin studied kindergartens to determine how teachers deal with misbehaviors, and he found three attributes of *desists,* or ways of stopping misbehavior, used by teachers:

1. *Clarity.* The desist provided information that identified the deviate behavior along with the acceptable behavior and provided the reasons for the desist.
2. *Firmness.* This attitude projects "I mean it" and continues until the misbehavior disappears.
3. *Roughness.* The desist is composed of anger, threats, physical handling, and punishment.

According to Kounin, the degree of clarity of the desist increased conformity of behavior in the children who witnessed the scene. Firmness in the desist increased conformity only in those children who misbehaved. Roughness failed to improve any behavior and made children upset, anxious, confused, and restless. These observations suggest that it is important to be clear and firm in handling problems; they also suggest that roughness should be avoided.

Kounin uses the concept of *withitness* to describe the teacher behavior that communicates that they know what is going on everywhere in the classroom at all times. This sense of what is going on often allows teachers to anticipate and avoid problems by intervening before situations get out of hand.

Timing affects the withitness strategy. Teachers who display withitness correct misbehaviors as soon as they occur. They take action before a misbehavior spreads. Kounin found that withitness induces more work involvement and less misbehavior, particularly in teacher-directed lessons. Correcting the child at once is more important to classroom management than the firmness or clarity of a desist.

Overdwelling refers to teachers' spending time providing directions and explanations that are not necessary. There are some teachers who overdwell on students' behavior, lecturing beyond what is required to eliminate the misbehavior and communicating that they are displeased. They may even lecture long and hard about misbehaviors that have not occurred. Students have a tendency to tune out this type of nagging, letting their mind wander while teachers talk on.

In effective classroom management, *variation* in teaching plays a crucial role in keeping children from becoming bored. Teachers need to change the dynamics of instruction and avoid repetition. Repetition reduces student involvement in and enjoyment of an activity. Teachers must vary the content of classroom activities to achieve better classroom management and more effective instruction.

Dreikurs' Model of Discipline

Rudolph Dreikurs developed a model of discipline based upon psychodynamic principles. It is concerned more with the causes of misbehavior than with the actual behaviors themselves. Dreikurs (1968) suggests that children misbehave for one of four reasons: (1) they wish to gain attention, (2) they wish to display power, (3) they wish to gain revenge, or (4) they wish to display a problem to gain them special attention. Rather than punish children for their transgressions, Dreikurs suggests that teachers and parents use what he calls *logical consequences*. These consequences express the reality of the social order, are directly related to the misbehavior, communicate no moral judgment to the child, and are related only to the immediate problem. That is, the child is still valued but the behavior is not (Dreikurs & Grey, 1968).

In applying logical consequences, it is important that the teacher become aware of the child's reasons for the misbehavior. Rather than allow the child to achieve a desired goal through misbehavior, it must be demonstrated to the child that the behavior is both inappropriate for the situation and ineffective in achieving that result. The logical consequence should be inconsistent with the child's desired goal and the child should be informed of the reason the particular consequence was selected. For example, if a child plays around with his or her clothing instead of getting ready for outdoor play in order to have the teacher do the dressing, a logical consequence might be that the child remains indoors. A logical consequence for messing up the paint at an easel might be having the child clean up while others are engaged in different activities. While logical consequences can work in many situations, they should be avoided where dangerous physical conditions might be created.

Redirection

Teachers of young children often deal with a misbehavior by moving the child from the problem activity and redirecting that child to another activity. If a child is in conflict with another child over blocks needed for a building, the teacher might suggest that the child might enjoy woodworking, firmly guiding the child to the workbench. To be effective, the teacher must know which activities a child finds appealing and be able to offer attractive alternatives.

Teachers need to accept
children's feelings and behaviors.

While redirection works for the short term and is used successfully and often by teachers, it does not help children learn to deal with and resolve conflict. There may be times when a teacher would find it more appropriate to help children negotiate a conflict, developing verbal skills at communicating and social skills at working together. These skills would allow children to be more socially independent in the classroom.

Guiding Children's Behavior

A major goal of education is to help children become self-directed and self-disciplined. Children become independent of authority by thinking and analyzing situations in order to make appropriate decisions. Teachers can guide children, influencing their behavior through social interactions and warm personal relationships. Teachers also help develop appropriate behaviors by arranging the physical environment and providing specific equipment and materials that guide children indirectly.

A well-planned environment helps maintain orderly traffic patterns while allowing for a variety of simultaneous activities. Providing children with sufficient materials (such as paper, scissors, and paste) so that they do not have to wait turns or compete for scarce resources will also lead to fewer arguments. Teachers can also remove equipment that stimulates competition and elicits conflict.

Teachers can guide children's behaviors directly through speaking, demonstrating, helping, leading, approving, disapproving, restraining, and punishing. Dealing with children positively is usually most effective; negative strategies should be used only in extreme situations. Punishment stifles learning, develops negative attitudes toward school and teachers, and provides no directions that children can use for behavior change.

Teachers also may guide young children through physical actions, helping, demonstrating, leading, restraining, or removing the children. Physical guidance can be effective with young children when it is accompanied by verbal guidance.

When teachers speak to children, they should be sure they have the children's attention. They should also be careful to use language that children can understand. Teachers may squat or sit at the children's eye level, looking at them directly, then use simple words, appropriate facial expressions, and gestures to extend communication. When possible, teachers should speak to one child at a time or to small groups, rather than to the whole class. They should give clear and simple directions, telling children exactly what to do. Using the word "don't" in a command may confuse young children. For instance, the statement "Walk" tells children what to do, while the statement, "Don't run!" does not include information about what is acceptable. Teachers should also explain why some behaviors are unacceptable, building on children's reasoning. Teachers can help children learn to follow directions by making them simple and providing enough time to complete tasks. Before moving to another activity, teachers should caution children that it will soon be time to change activities. The children will be able to anticipate change and can finish their project and get ready for the next activity.

All teachers serve as models of appropriate behavior. Children will do what their teachers do. Consistency, patience, and firmness are essential in working with children. The rules children are expected to follow need to be communicated clearly and enforced consistently. They should be specific, concrete, simple, and inclusive. They should be explained and discussed regularly. Teachers should avoid unrealistic expectations of children, which can create frustrations and other problems.

Managing Problem Behavior

Even when teachers have taken all precautions to manage the children's behavior, situations do get out of hand. Teachers can stop and request the children's help. They can be honest, sometimes saying: "We have a problem to solve. This is not working. The problem is that..." Children can suggest solutions to the problem, establish and enforce realistic rules, and assist in organizing the situation.

One of the most important strategies teachers can use to deal with behavior problems is to provide children with a good educational program. Teachers need to carefully examine the children's entire day, including their daily routines like scheduling, toileting, cleanup, dressing, and snack. Every component of the program contributes to each child's behavior and to the dynamics of the group. Problems may easily emerge during transitions as children move from one activity to the next.

TABLE 7-1 Guidelines for Managing Behavior

1. BEHAVIORS EXPECTED OF CHILDREN SHOULD BE KNOWN TO THEM. Children should be told what is expected of them. Children's improper behavior may be a result of ignorance. Instructions will have to be repeated many times in many contexts before they are understood.

2. CHILDREN NEED TO BE TOLD WHY RULES ARE IN EFFECT. Even if they cannot fully *understand* them, children need to be given the reasons for rules. Most rules for school behavior are reasonable. Children can begin to see the purpose of lining up at a slide or limiting the amount of time one child can ride on a bicycle. They can understand why they should behave differently in a crowded lunch room than in their own room and why rules are promulgated for behaving certain ways in class, others in the hall, and still others on a school bus.

3. CHILDREN SHOULD HAVE OPPORTUNITIES TO OBSERVE AND PRACTICE PROPER BEHAVIOR. Children need demonstrations; they learn through modeling. They must also have opportunities to *practice* proper behavior, with feedback from the teacher.

4. THE BEHAVIOR EXPECTED OF CHILDREN OUGHT TO BE POSSIBLE FOR THEM. Children are not miniature adults and should not be expected to behave like adults. Teachers should develop goals of reasonable childlike behavior.

5. CHILDREN CANNOT ALWAYS BE EXPECTED TO BEHAVE PROPERLY AT ALL TIMES. Nobody is perfect, including adults. We do not expect adults always to be on their best behavior. The same is true for children. They should not be expected to conform to standards of model behavior at all times any more than adults should.

6. TEACHERS SHOULD BEHAVE WITH CONSISTENCY. The teacher's behavior communicates a message to the children about what is acceptable and appropriate and what is not. If teachers vacillate or accept certain kinds of behaviors one time and reject or punish the same behavior another time, they confuse children and blur their goals. Though teachers cannot always behave consistently, this is a goal for which they should aim.

Spodek, *Teaching in the Early Years,* 3rd ed. (Englewood Cliffs, NJ: Prentice-Hall, 1985), p. 241.

Scheduling should provide a balance between active and quiet activities. Children may get restless if teachers schedule a long sequence of activities in which children have to be inactive. They will become restless and will seek their own relief by fidgeting, moving, and possibly disturbing others. Having several consecutive active periods, such as free play, creative movement, and outdoor play, can also cause problems. Children may become too tired to be attentive.

Inappropriate tasks can also produce management problems. Having all the children line up to go to the bathroom at the same time, for example, should be avoided. Young children do not have the self-control to wait. Children who cannot perform these tasks can be individually guided or held by the hand. Children should be permitted to drink water or go to the bathroom at times that suit their needs. A few children at a time can wash up while the rest of the class is busy working.

Keeping young children in a straight line when they move about a building or through the streets demands a great deal of the teacher's energy and can cause frustration. Children can be guided to walk on sidewalks instead of lawns and they can learn to walk the halls without running or bumping into someone. Lines are not needed to achieve these purposes, although there are times when teachers use lines to maintain safety.

Activities in which children assume responsibility and develop autonomy should be planned to help children develop self-control. Learning opportunities that are appropriate for individual children need to be provided to help them use learning resources, both in and out of school, to become a responsible group member, working with others without having their wishes submerged but considering the feelings of others.

Teaching Positive Social Interactions

Children often have had no contacts with adults except for those in their home, until they enter preschool. These children need help in adjusting to a new situation and responding to new adult authority figures, including the classroom teacher and other staff members. They need to learn to function effectively in society. The socialization process requires children to interact with others in appropriate ways. Young children need to become sensitive and considerate of others' feelings. They need to develop social competence and learn to work and play with other children.

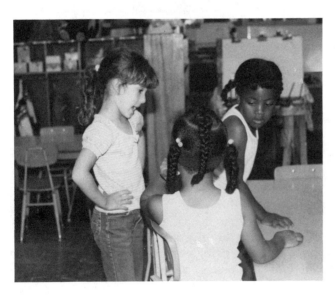

Children need to learn to deal independently with social problems.

The younger child or older children with little experience in playing with others may not be ready to cooperate and engage in play with other children. Children who spend many hours watching television and little time playing with others often lack social skills. Their play requires the teacher's support.

Teachers need to accept a child's patterns of play as it exists, gradually inviting children into small-group activities without forcing any child to function in a way he or she is incapable of. When children join the group for a music or story time activity, a child who refuses to participate should be excused and provided with an acceptable substitute. Children's cooperative play behaviors require the children to consider others, to cooperate with others, to conform, and to become assertive without being aggressive. Some children prefer to play alongside a friend, other children prefer to play together, while still others prefer to play alone with materials, investigating their properties and creating themes.

Play Intervention

Teachers can prolong and extend children's interaction to enrich their social experience, intervening when necessary, but otherwise staying out of play activities. They must be careful to avoid becoming the center of attention or the source of most of the play ideas, thus discouraging the children's play initiatives. On the other hand, teachers can go to the other extreme and fail to promote children's play, allowing situations that lack richness to fall apart too soon. Intervening appropriately in children's play is important in developing children's social skills.

Children's play does not always take a positive turn. Sometimes play bogs down, becoming overly repetitive and not seeming to go anywhere. Sometimes play can lead to conflict among children. It can even lead to destructive behavior. When such things occur, teachers must intervene in order to make the children's play more educationally productive.

Ann Spidell (1985) studied a number of preschools and analyzed how teachers intervened in children's play. She identified a number of strategies that teachers used. One form of intervention was labeled *instruction*. In this intervention teachers told children a fact or concept they felt would move the play along. Teachers also used *praise* to intervene in children's play, showing approval to a child whose behavior they wanted to support or to have other children model. Teachers also used *maintenance* strategies, dealing with issues relating to crowded space, not enough materials or equipment, disputes about rules, or similar housekeeping details.

Among the other strategies that teachers used were *conversation*, engaging children in a dialogue about their interests or activities; *demon-

Teachers may enter into children's play for a short time in order to extend that play.

stration, showing children how to do something or how to carry on an activity; and *redirection*, suggesting alternative activities. *Participation* was also used as a play intervention, with teachers joining into play for brief periods of time.

Not all of these interventions were used to the same extent by all teachers. Each teacher seemed to use some interventions more often than others. Nor were all the strategies equally effective in moving the children's play along. In most cases, teachers used a combination of intervention strategies in helping play remain dynamic and productive.

One of the most powerful strategies teachers use for play intervention is never observed in the classroom. It is not seen because it occurs before the children being their play. This strategy consists of setting the stage for play before the children arrive in school. The teacher intervenes best in children's play by organizing a play center, providing enough space and materials, and establishing proper ways of behaving in the classroom. As the stage is set, the teacher makes suggestions for play activities and provides resources that allow the activities to unfold. Feeding information about the play theme to children by reading books to them, holding discussions, inviting resource persons, or taking a field trip allows children to extend their play and elaborate on what the teacher has originally provided.

Teachers need to keep in mind that play intervention may only require a suggestion or a supportive comment. Teachers can also add accessories to encourage children to participate in a play activity.

Children who prefer to play by themselves should not be forced to engage in cooperative play. Teachers can foster cooperative actions by asking these children to help clean up after snack time or put away library books or housekeeping equipment. These kinds of activities can also be supported by the children who have been playing in these areas. Cleanup activities also provide the teacher with an opportunity to model appropriate behavior for children and encourage them to engage in cooperative activities. The children will soon initiate cooperative play behavior upon the teacher's suggestion or on their own initiative.

ORGANIZING ADULTS

Staffing patterns vary among early childhood centers. The number of persons who are employed in any early childhood center depends on the size of the center, the kind of agency sponsoring the program, and the level of funding provided. The type of staff employed, their relationship, and the program's administrative system depend on the setting.

Adults play a number of different roles in these programs. Directors and supervisors perform administrative duties, though they may also be responsible for some teaching. Head teachers, teacher-directors, and classroom teachers are primarily responsible for planning and implementing the classroom program. Teacher aides and assistants, along with volunteers and community resource people, may do some teaching and engage in other supportive activities under the guidance of a classroom teacher. Every staff member who is in contact with the children has some influence on them. The cook, custodian, and bus driver, for example, have no responsibility for instruction but still influence the children's education in significant ways. They can facilitate program development or retard activities. Although teachers are not responsible for the children's experiences with these school personnel, they must be aware of their experiences and use them to support positive learning opportunities.

Adults working in the classroom must know the school's philosophy, its routines, teaching strategies, classroom management, and appropriate ways to guide children. Teachers need to define clearly each volunteer's specific roles. Adults may be expected to perform duties in school in ways that differ from those they have performed before. Teachers also need to tell others the reasons for the procedures used and provide practice sessions.

A good management system is essential when a number of people (such as specialists, parent volunteers, college students, or teacher aides) participate in the educational process. The teachers must work cooperatively with the adults and communicate to them all decisions that have been made. Teachers should possess the academic and practical knowledge required to plan creatively, schedule appropriate activities for young children, and develop a good management system, including working with paraprofessionals, volunteers, and community resources. The teachers are responsible for ensuring that each child succeeds in some learning experience each day.

Working with Paraprofessionals

Paraprofessionals, such as teacher aides and assistants, generally share classroom responsibilities with the teacher and provide important assistance. Those who work in the classroom can help with routine jobs to support children's learning experiences and can be used to individualize interactions. Aids and assistants can also help teachers with exceptional children who may need special attention. However, it is the teachers who are responsible and who assess the children's individual needs and plan their educational activities.

The teacher aide or assistant can extend the teachers' influence, managing the classroom environment, working with a small group of children, and monitoring the children's behavior and activities. The teacher assistant's supportive role is crucial in the effective functioning of the classroom and may reduce disruptions. The aide or assistant should be included in the planning of the daily and weekly schedules. Open lines of communication must be maintained so all can work effectively as a team. Planning sessions are important for maintaining communication and providing an opportunity to discuss any problems that have emerged.

Working with Volunteers

Some early childhood programs, including parent cooperatives, do not employ adults to assist the teacher in the classroom. Parents may participate in the classroom but the teacher is the one responsible for supervising. Teachers might use volunteers such as parents, community persons, and students to help in the classroom.

Volunteers can be valuable resource persons in a center. Teachers can invite them to the classroom on a regular basis to join with the regular teaching staff, as in cooperative schools, or they can bring them in for short visits. Teachers must coordinate all of the experiences children have with volunteers in school to maximize their use. This means that the

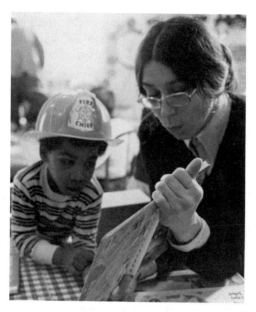

Reading stories to a child is a worthwhile task for a volunteer.

teacher must plan and organize for the use of volunteers, orient them to the school, and even train them.

In training and organizing these volunteers, teachers can meet with them to explain their responsibilities and show how to carry them out. Volunteers can also be asked for their reactions to daily and weekly plans. At the beginning, teachers should explain the basic ground rules for functioning in the classroom and should try to make the volunteers feel at ease. Sharing a list of possible tasks, such as reading a story to the children, cooking with them, discussing a picture, or providing additional adult supervision on a field trip, can give them a sense of the duties they might perform. The volunteers should be able to select from these activities so they can feel comfortable in working with the groups. Some volunteers may have to be given very specific directions in order to function adequately. Teachers should sense what is necessary and respond to each volunteer as needed.

Teachers need to make the volunteers feel truly welcome and comfortable and show them that their assistance is appreciated. Volunteers deserve to be thanked for their help and encouraged to return. They can become a continuing source of help in the class.

Working with Community Resources

Though most of the early childhood program is offered inside the classroom, teachers also can make use of resources outside. Taking young children into the community on field trips can provide a great deal of interest, enjoyment, and information but these field trips must be properly planned. The children should know the purpose and focus of the trip and be able to anticipate what will happen. Although there is much incidental learning on a field trip, its planning cannot be left to chance.

Field trips need not be elaborate excursions. Simple trips can be meaningful to young children: A walk to the corner to watch the traffic lights and cars, or a visit to a local bakery to see bread baked, can provide an enriching experience. Even though some children may have the same experience outside of school, the teacher's planning and preparation can help them focus differently and learn new concepts within a familiar situation.

In addition to taking field trips, teachers can invite resource persons to visit their classroom. Persons in the community who have specific skills or knowledge can help extend the children's knowledge and motivate their interest. Community resource persons can include firefighters, mail carriers, garbage collectors, police officers, highway patrol officers, retired persons, musicians, baton twirlers, dancers, clowns, football players, artists, hobbyists, storytellers, nurses, mothers and babies, custodians, weavers, anthropologists, and anyone else who has some firsthand knowledge that would be of interest to the children.

Before the resource person visits the classroom, the teacher should be sure that both the children and the resource person know the purpose of the visit, what will take place, and the basic ground rules for participation. Children can serve as hosts to the visitor in their classroom.

SUMMARY

Teachers must create a social environment in their classes to help children function well with both adults and other children. Teachers can group children in a variety of ways for different activities and support children in helping one another. There are a variety of classroom management techniques that can be used to maintain order. Good techniques help children manage their own needs and develop autonomy. Through careful teacher interventions children can be helped to develop positive social interactions and can have their play activities extended.

Paraprofessionals, parents, community volunteers, and student teachers can provide assistance to the teacher in the classroom, but teachers must be prepared to spend the time to maximize their effectiveness. Teachers need to plan for each person's involvement, introducing them to the philosophy of the program and the roles of adults in the classroom. Teachers also need to orient volunteers to specific activities in the classroom: reading to young children, supervising outdoor play, assisting at meals, or teaching a concept are all helpful. Having the extra pair of "helping hands" in the classroom, though, will require a teacher to shift some attention from the children to the other adults.

REFERENCES

CHARLES, C. M. (1981). *Building classroom discipline: From models to practice.* New York: Longman, Inc.

DREIKURS, R. (1968). *Psychology in the schools* (2nd ed.). New York: Harper & Row.

DREIKURS, R., AND L. GREY (1968). *Logical consequences: A handbook of discipline.* New York: Meredith Press.

KOUNIN, J. S. (1970). *Discipline and group management in classrooms.* New York: Holt, Rinehart & Winston.

MASDEN, C. H., JR., AND C. K. MASDEN (1974). *Teaching/discipline: A positive approach to educational development* (2nd ed.). Boston: Allyn & Bacon.

SPIDELL, R. A. (1985). *Preschool teachers' interventions in children's play.* Unpublished Doctoral dissertation, University of Illinois at Urbana-Champaign.

SPODEK, B. (1985). *Teaching in the early years* (3rd ed.). Englewood Cliffs, NJ: Prentice-Hall.

WILSON, R. M., AND J. K. RIBOVICH. Ability grouping? Stop and reconsider. *Reading World,* **13,** 84-91.

SUGGESTED ACTIVITIES

1. Visit an early childhood center. Record instances where the teacher attempts to modify a specific child's behavior. Describe the teacher's strategy and the child's changed behavior after intervention.

2. Describe the personal and professional qualities that a teacher needs in order to successfully organize adults for classroom instruction.

3. Interview a teacher of a group of toddlers about problems of teaching them to share. Interview a kindergarten teacher on the same topic. Compare their responses.

4. Interview a preschool teacher to find out how the children in the classroom are managed. Prepare a short report about the teacher's major procedures or principles.

5. Observe a session in an early childhood classroom and note the following:
   a. Number of children working in groups
   b. Ratio of boys and girls in each group
   c. Ratio of children and adults in each group
   Ask the teacher what factors were considered in grouping these children.

6. Interview a nursery teacher, a day care teacher, and a kindergarten teacher to find out how and why they developed their daily schedules.

8

WORKING WITH PARENTS

OBJECTIVES

After completing this chapter on working with parents, the student should be able to:

1. Define blended family, nuclear family, extended family, single-parent family, and foster parent family.
2. Explain different kinds of parent programming, including parent involvement, parent education, and parent advisory groups.
3. Describe ways to involve parents who cannot come to the center, those who can come to the center but who do not want to work with children, and those who want to work directly with children.
4. Discuss the teachers' obligations to parent volunteers.
5. Specify guidelines for parent education.
6. Develop formal and informal ways of communicating with parents.
7. Explain why parent education is a necessary part of any early childhood program.

While the child is the first priority in early childhood education, parents are the second priority. Parents and teachers are partners in helping children to learn. Parents are their children's first teachers, and they continue to have the primary responsibility for their children's development even after the beginning of school. While teachers have an important role in guiding a child, an early education program that does not respect the importance of the parent cannot be successful. A review of the Urban Education Project (Norwood, 1984) noted that one common quality of the most successful schools in the country was the active involvement of parents and citizens in planning curriculum and instruction.

This chapter focuses on working with parents: parents as learners, parents as volunteers, parents as decision makers, and parents as members of the teacher–parent team, providing the best possible support for the young child's optimal growth and development.

The importance of parents being involved in early childhood education can be seen by the results of a number of studies that have been completed over the past twenty years. These results have led to the requirement of parent involvement in Head Start programs.

Rebecca S. Heinz (1979) suggests that three things occur when schools and parents cooperate: (1) parents' and children's self-concept increases, (2) children's motivation accelerates, and (3) children's achievement advances. Heinz also reported that the mothers in Ira Gordon's Florida Parent Education Program who perceived improvement in their children's growth experienced growth in their own self-esteem as women. At the completion of the program, many of the parents moved to better homes, found better jobs, and returned to school. Heinz also suggests that parent involvement in the preschool years is crucial to the formation of achievement motivation in children.

Ira Gordon, Pat Olmstead, Roberta Rubin and Joan True (1979) reported that the Follow-Through Parent Education Program Model had an impact on two areas: (1) changes in the home–school partnership and in parental teaching behavior, and (2) changes in the school, community, and career development of parents, paraprofessionals, and professionals. These Follow-Through parents exhibited more desirable teaching behaviors with their children than did non-Follow-Through parents. They functioned as decision makers, adult learners, and audiences.

This chapter will describe various kinds of families. It will also discuss different ways of working with parents in school, including forms of parent involvement, the use of parent advisory groups, and different kinds of parent education. In addition, it will examine both formal and informal ways of communicating with parents.

FAMILIES

At one time teachers who worked with parents could assume that all families consisted of a mother, a father, and a few children. Today, there are many different kinds of families. While someone takes the parenting role(s) in each, each type of family has its own particular needs and expectations from early childhood programs. Family types include but are not limited to the following:

Finale exam

> *Nuclear families* consist of mother, father, and children.
>
> *Extended families* include more distant relatives (possibly grandparents) living with the nuclear family.
>
> *Single-parent families* have just the mother *or* the father, but not both, living with children.
>
> *Foster parent families* consist of parents who care for children other than their own for temporary periods of time.
>
> *Blended families* are formed when two single parents, each with children, marry and form a new family group.

Blended families (or stepfamilies) present the teacher with a special situation. Patsy Skeen, Bryan Robinson, and Carol Flake-Hobson (1984) report that there are approximately 25 million stepparents in this country and that most blended families are formed by divorce and remarriage. Since most adults have not had prior experience in living with a stepfamily, it is difficult for them to acquire stepparenting skills. Teachers may have children who are members of a blended family and are experiencing difficulty in learning their place. They may also have to communicate with parents who are at a loss as to how to best respond to children in the new family situation.

Yet, when you consider the number of changes that can occur in a nuclear family—moving to a new home, the birth of a baby, mother or father going back to work, or family illness—it is apparent that teachers need to be aware of changes in the families of all the children. Foster families are also continually changing. Since foster children come into a new family for only a short period of time, the family unit is always evolving. This constant shifting affects not only the new children, but the children who are permanent members of the family.

In fact, no single type of family can guarantee that children will not need special assistance from a teacher at some time. Skeen, Robinson, and Flake-Hobson (1984) offer the following suggestions for working with children from blended families; most of them are appropriate for children from all types of families:

1. Observe carefully, looking for clues that can help you understand what a child is feeling.
2. Make a plan on how to help the child. Talk with parents and counselor, observe the child, and read related literature before forming a plan.
3. Provide opportunities for the child to work through feelings via dramatic play, art, or media.
4. Help the child to understand the new family.
5. Maintain a stable classroom environment.

6. Work with the parents, and be supportive of their efforts to help the child.
7. As needed, refer families to competent counselors who specialize in family matters.

While each family type has different needs, an understanding teacher can be an asset to all families.

WORKING WITH PARENTS

Working with parents in early childhood education includes both parent involvement and parent education. *Parent involvement* refers to parents participating in their children's education as classroom volunteers as well as serving on advisory committees or policy boards. *Parent education* refers to providing parents with the skills and knowledge necessary to be more successful parents. The two components complement each other, though they have different purposes and require different teaching approaches.

Parent Involvement *final exam*

Parent involvement programs benefit parents in a number of ways. As parents participate in these programs, they have an opportunity to learn about the teacher's way of guiding children's growth and development. They also gain a sense of competence and a feeling of being needed by the program. In addition, they have an opportunity to develop relationships with other parents in the school (Feeney, Christensen, & Moravcik, 1983).

John McKinney (1980) reported on parent participation in early childhood programs in Philadelphia. In the ten programs described, parents contributed a total of 188,966 hours of volunteer work. Four times as much volunteer time was done than time spent in workshops. Parent participation during the school day may be more difficult to arrange today. With an increase in the percentage of working mothers and of single-parent families, and with a rise in the birth rate, many parents do not have the time to serve as volunteers.

Parent involvement in the schools can take many forms. Regardless of the form, however, planning for involvement takes time and thought. The level of involvement that the teacher will be able to handle should be considered. Shari Nedler and Oralee McAfee (1979) suggest that beginning teachers might start involving parents slowly, setting limited, short-range goals. They can plan to expand the levels of parent involvement as they grow into the teaching role. Rebecca Heinz (1979) suggests that teachers who involve parents in a classroom need to be able to listen to these parents in an active and accepting way and should be skilled in the art of confrontation without explosion.

Doreen Croft (1979) provides some guidelines for increasing the success of parent–teacher interactions in classrooms. Teachers should:

1. Recognize, understand, and accept the concerns and expectations each person brings to the classroom.
2. Carefully plan training sessions.
3. Provide clear rules.
4. Have goals that are agreed upon by both parents and teachers.
5. Offer careful instructions about the options that are available to parents during the decision-making process.
6. Show genuine commitment, patience, perseverance, and a good sense of humor.
7. Develop an atmosphere of mutual cooperation and interdependence.
8. Provide time to talk.

When making arrangements for parent involvement, you need to be able to see things from a parent's point of view and consider the parent's needs. You may need to arrange for child care for other children in the family. You may also need to:

- Provide for alternate times for workshops in order to meet the varied schedules of parents.
- Plan for more than one type of involvement.
- Consider the needs of the single parent.
- Avoid creating father–son or mother–daughter activities that may limit some parents' and children's participation.

Parent involvement can range from doing things at home for school to assisting the teacher in the classroom. Parents who help in the classroom can either work directly with children or be involved in tasks that assist the teacher. All parents are different, with individual needs and interests. Providing a range of activities helps to ensure that parent participants will be doing something they enjoy and that is useful as well. It is helpful to communicate the kinds of tasks that parents can do so they can anticipate what they will be doing. Teachers should also look beyond using only parents as classroom volunteers and include other persons from the family and from the community.

Parents who can come to school but who are not comfortable working directly with children may:

- Record attendance.
- Assemble samples of children's work for booklets or displays.
- Arrange details for field trips.
- Help file pictures or collections of poems, songs, or finger plays.
- Gather information for some of the reports teachers must do, such as the number of children eating meals at school, or types and numbers of health services.

Parents can make an important contribution by participating in classroom activities.

- Prepare materials for class activities such as art, games, and water play.
- Locate resources and materials in the community for the teachers and children to use at school.

Not all parents can come to school during class time. There are other ways to involve parents. Parents who cannot come to school can:

- Launder or mend dress-up clothes from the dramatic play area.
- Collect scrap materials for craft projects.
- Paint or fix school toys that need repair.
- Serve as telephone tree coordinators to facilitate communication regarding meetings or other topics.
- Make instructional materials.
- Arrange field trips.

Parents who are interested in working with children in school could be asked to:

- Assist a small group of children (under the teacher's guidance) with a language game or a short math or science activity.
- Read (or tell) a story or poem.
- Help with art and music activities.
- Be available to talk with and listen to the children as they work.
- Supervise children's activities, such as cooking, caring for pets, or fingerpainting.
- Assist during transition periods by helping with cleanup or preparing for the next activity.

- Help a child with table activities such as counting, seriating, or classifying.
- Take one or two children on short trips in the neighborhood.
- Help with arrival and dismissal times.
- Be available in emergencies (for example, taking a child to the toilet in a hurry, or soothing a child who skins a knee).
- Let the teacher know if any child seems to need special attention.

Teachers who invite parents into the classroom have an obligation to help them learn more about children. One way to do this is to provide opportunities for parents to observe in the classroom before they begin working with children. K. Eileen Allen and Betty Hart (1984) suggest providing parents with a clipboard with a simple observation form as a way to focus observations. Teachers would then arrange time for parents to discuss their observations. Teachers must always respond to parent questions about children, program, or participants' work. Talking with volunteers not only broadens their knowledge about children but also indicates that you value their work.

An orientation meeting can also be provided before parents begin participating with children. During the meeting parents can learn about the program, they can be provided with a schedule of activities, they can go over rules for behavior and the sanctions that are used in class, and they can learn their specific responsibilities (Spodek, 1985). It is far easier to orient parents to the program before they begin to work with children than it is to do so while they are working. It is also important to allow time for parents to talk together informally so that they can become acquainted with one another.

Parent Advisory Groups

Another level of involvement includes parents on advisory or policy committees. At this level parents have input into the educational decision-making process. Advisory committees give advice to teachers, supervisors. and administrators regarding the educational program.

Parent *policy councils* allow parents to make decisions about programs, in contrast to parent *advisory groups,* which provide advice. These councils are generally found in parent cooperative nursery schools and in federally funded preprimary programs such as Head Start (Nedler & McAfee, 1979). The parents in a parent cooperative own the school and so they must be involved in making decisions. Many federal programs, including Head Start, have regulations which require that parents be involved in program decisions.

Regardless of the level of involvement, when parents participate, both parents and children benefit. Parents and teachers come closer together as teachers learn more about the children's families and parents come to value the school more highly.

Parent Education

Parent education programs are not limited to teaching parents to teach their children. Rather, they range broadly from programs that help parents develop positive self-concepts to programs designed for unwed teenage mothers. No one parent education program can meet the needs of all parents. Each teacher or school should develop programs that reflect the specific needs and interests of their parents.

Christine Cataldo (1980) has identified four basic clusters of early childhood parent training programs. The first is parent training when the child or family is thought to be at-risk. A second provides the parent with social and informational support but teaches and supports parents in a less direct manner. A third cluster consists of programs for children with the parent receiving adjunct services. Finally, there are parent-oriented activities through which a relationship is formed between parents and professionals and which serve a significant role in the child-rearing endeavor.

One form of parent education has been to involve parents in the classroom as volunteers and then to discuss the parents' observations with them. This gives the parents an opportunity to learn more about children while working with them. This strategy was used in Head Start as a way to reach the program's objectives. It allows low-income parents to gain skill and confidence while encouraging them to become involved in the classrooms (Travis & Perrault, 1980).

Parent education meetings can put parents in touch with specialists in the field.

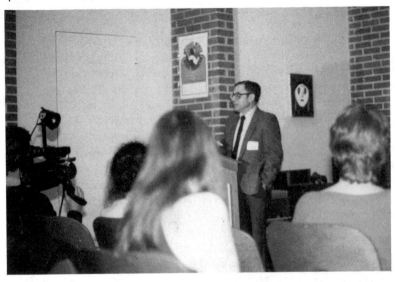

Kevin J. Swick (1983) suggests five guidelines for developing parent education programs:

1. Always begin with the premise that parents are learners.
2. Parenting behaviors are developed early in the parenting process. The most effective programs have focused on first-time parents.
3. While parent education should begin with the early stages of parenthood, it should be continuous and based on a developmental approach.
4. Effective programs involve the parent in planning the content and process of the program.
5. The psychological facets of parenting should become the primary basis upon which all programs are developed.

Swick's guidelines are intended to help the parent become an integral part of the learning process rather than a passive recipient of knowledge.

Alice Honig (1979), referring to a "Parents Bill of Rights," suggests that parents have the right to:

1. Knowledge about child development.
2. Observation skills for more effective parenting.
3. Alternative strategies for problem solving and discipline.
4. Knowledge about how to use a home for learning experiences with children.
5. Language tools and story reading skills.
6. Awareness of being the most important early teachers of their own children.

These parent rights also suggest some guidelines for parent education programs. Parents' right to acquire both skill and knowledge means parents need to have opportunities to learn about children and how to work with children. Parent education programs should provide information about the child's physical development, social development, emotional development, and cognitive development. They should also help parents develop the skills necessary to work with their own children. Parent educators should show parents what to do, give them an opportunity to practice what they should do, and provide feedback on how well they are performing (Spodek, Saracho, & Lee, 1984). Guided practice is more likely to bring about change in a parent's behavior than is a lecture.

One way of providing parents with a knowledge base is through the use of family-based programs. These programs, which are set in the child's home, provide professional support to teach the parents how to be effective educators. Alice Honig (1982) refers to family-based programs that can increase the level of consciousness of parents, help them obtain information they need to be effective parents, and make them aware of their importance in their children's lives. Again, in a family-based program parents have the opportunity to refine their skills by doing.

Group meetings allow parents to develop a sense of fellowship.

Another form of parent education that has been particularly successful is parent group meetings. Group meetings give parents an opportunity to gain knowledge and to obtain a sense of fellowship that comes from being with others who have similar concerns or needs. Groups can focus on either children's or parents' needs. Some groups have helped parents to gain self-esteem; others have focused on training parents for new job skills.

The large number of children born to teenagers in this country has necessitated the development of parent education programs designed for young adults. In 1979, according to Alice Honig (1982), 29 percent of births to white teenagers and 83 percent of births to black teenagers occurred outside of marriage. Further, one out of five babies in the United States is born to a teenage girl. Programs for these mothers should focus on nutrition and health care as well as on parenting and child development knowledge. They also have to encourage and help the mother to complete high school.

COMMUNICATING WITH PARENTS

Parents have a right to know about their children's progress. Teachers have a corresponding obligation to respond to parents' requests for information. However, the communication process should not be just one way, from the teacher to the parent. Effective communication requires that both the teacher and the parent send and receive information about the child.

Communication techniques range from informal to formal, from those that take little time to those that take a great deal of time. They are all important and they all increase parents' and teachers' insight into the nature of the child and his or her learning.

Parents are not as concerned about global generalization as they are about the specific things their own child is doing. Generally, they want to know about:

1. Their child's activities in school.
2. How their child responds to other children.
3. How other children respond to their child.
4. How their child gets along on the playground.
5. What their child likes and dislikes about school.
6. Whether or not the teacher is truly concerned about their child. (Heinz, 1979)

Informal Communication Techniques

Informal techniques are those simple procedures that convey information about what happened during the day or about special situations that have arisen. One informal technique is to greet parents and speak to them briefly when they drop off children in the morning or pick them up in the afternoon. Teachers can find out if Joey had a bad morning or if something happened at home that may affect his behavior. The afternoon provides an opportunity to tell the parents about an interesting event that happened in school or a special milestone that Debbie accomplished that day. These brief encounters can provide important pieces of information. Because these encounters are public, the topics should be ones that are not confidential and that can be discussed in front of the child (Allen & Hart, 1984).

Another type of informal communication is the personal note. By taking the time to write to parents about an important event, you indicate to them that you care about them and their child. Sending notes home with children of this age has an inherent danger: Children may lose the notes before they arrive home. It is a good idea to pin such notes to the children's clothing or tape them to their lunch boxes as they leave for home.

Telephoning parents is another way to communicate with parents. Sometimes calls can be made during the school day, but often they need to be made in the evening. If the topic is such that the child should not be involved, it might be wise to prearrange a time to call or to call after a child is asleep.

Formal Communication Techniques

Formal techniques include all endeavors that have a set agenda and specific theme. Parent conferences, home visits, parent meetings, and newsletters all provide formal ways to communicate information to parents.

Parent Conferences. For many teachers, parent conferences are the least favored way of communicating with parents. It takes time to confer with each parent and even more time to plan for each conference. In addition, teachers may feel threatened by having to report a child's progress to parents in a face-to-face situation.

There are some guidelines for conferences that, if followed, can help make the conference a positive, productive meeting. The first guideline is to use everyday speech that can be understood by parents. Educational terms may not be understood and may intimidate some parents. In addition, if you are meeting with parents who are not fluent in English, it might be helpful to arrange for an interpreter.

Keep in mind that the parent is coming to you for a conference and needs to be made as comfortable as possible in an unfamiliar environment in which you work daily. Be prepared for the conference.

TABLE 8-1 Guidelines for Parent–Teacher Conferences

BEFORE THE CONFERENCE

---

1. Identify the purposes for the conference (e.g., reporting, information sharing, problem solving).
2. Prepare an agenda.
3. Review the child's record.
4. Prepare specific materials to show parents (e.g., observation notes, test results, work samples).
5. Set a time for the conference that is convenient for all.
6. Invite both parents, if possible.
7. Find a comfortable, relaxing, quiet place for the conference.

DURING THE CONFERENCE

---

8. Be friendly—establish a positive atmosphere.
9. Inform parents about the class program, schedule, and routines.
10. Make positive comments about the child; talk about strengths as well as problems.
11. Be specific about the problems you present.
12. Use language that parents can easily understand.
13. Provide opportunities for parents to speak as well as listen; be a good listener.
14. Work cooperatively with parents on specific solutions and activities for the child; identify responsibilities.
15. Summarize the meeting; make sure you and the parents are clear about the next steps.

AFTER THE CONFERENCE

---

16. Make a brief record of the content of the meeting.
17. Plan for follow-up.

From: B. Spodek, O. N. Saracho, and R. C. Lee. From *Mainstreaming Young Children*, p.166 © 1984, Wadsworth, Inc. Reprinted by permission of the publisher.

Have notes and files on each child as well as children's work samples ready before the parent arrives. Rely on your professional training and ethical standards. Be gentle with parents in commenting on children. Parents identify closely with their children and criticism often implies criticism of the parents as well. Negative comments should be stated in a positive way and qualified, if necessary. Concrete examples are more useful than generalizations in helping parents understand their children. Most important, a complete picture of the child, presenting strengths along with weaknesses, should be offered. Guidelines for parent conferences are presented in Table 8-1.

Home Visits. Home visits follow many of the guidelines for a parent conference. You should arrive at the home on time and you should not overstay your welcome. Limit the discussion to prearranged topics and *listen* to what the parent says. Listening is an important part of any successful communication. It needs to be practiced regularly. In addition, observe the home carefully so that you have a good sense of the setting in which the child is growing up.

Parent Meetings. Teachers are often called upon to plan or direct parent meetings. These meetings might be used to orient parents to the schools, providing information about the school's philosophy, school policies, or school rules and procedures. Such a meeting is helpful at the beginning of the school year. Other meetings might be called to tell parents about the program, to show them their children's work, or to answer questions about what the children are doing. Parent meetings are a good vehicle for parent education as well. Experts might be asked to talk about a particular topic, or a film or videotape might be shown, or a discussion might be held.

Teachers need to be aware of the purposes of the meeting and see that the activities are related to that purpose. Resources need to be collected before the meeting and the physical setting arranged to be as comfortable and as helpful as possible. Meetings should be scheduled so that most parents can attend, or the schedule could be varied so that all parents have a chance to attend some meetings. Sometimes it is necessary to provide some form of baby-sitting for parents who don't have a place to leave their children.

In addition to the formal meeting, it is helpful to schedule an informal time when parents can get to know one another and where teachers can chat with them briefly. It is also important that the meeting not take too long. Table 8-2 presents guidelines for parent meetings.

TABLE 8-2 Guidelines for Parent Meetings

BEFORE THE MEETING

---

1. Involve parents in planning the meeting.
2. Establish a convenient time for the meeting.
3. Find a comfortable, convenient place to meet.
4. Announce the topic and format of the meeting well in advance; inform parents of what they should bring.
5. Send out notices of the meeting with return slips.
6. Follow up on parents who do not return slips.
7. Arrange for transportation and baby-sitters if necessary.
8. Check with parents about refreshments.

DURING THE MEETING

---

9. Start and end the meeting on time.
10. Establish ground rules early (e.g., smoking, breaks, confidentiality).
11. Be flexible in following the agenda.
12. Vary program activities (e.g., discussion, role playing, lecture, film, games).
13. Provide opportunities for everyone to be involved in the discussion.
14. Allow some time for informal interaction at the end of the meeting.

AFTER THE MEETING

---

15. Make a brief record of what happened.
16. Plan for follow-up activities.

From: B. Spodek, O. N. Saracho, and R. C. Lee. From *Mainstreaming Young Children*, p.169 © 1984, Wadsworth, Inc. Reprinted by permission of the publisher.

Newsletters. A periodic newsletter is a good way to inform parents of current school events and to provide them with ideas for working with their own children. Thelma Harms and Deborah Cryer (1978) offer the following purposes for a newsletter:

1. To keep parents informed about current classroom activities.
2. To give parents some insight into the educational purposes underlying instructional activities.
3. To enhance children's and parent's abilities to communicate with each other.
4. To reinforce and extend school learning into the home and family, especially in the area of language development.

To be most effective, newletters should be sent home on a regular basis and they should be short enough to be read by busy parents (Hanley, 1980). A two- to three-page newsletter might work well. Table 8-3 offers some suggestions for what to include in a newsletter.

TABLE 8-3 Ideas for a Parent Newsletter

1. Describe special events that are happening or will happen in your center.
2. Bring parents up to date about ongoing activities (e.g., how the garden is growing or how the baby guinea pig is doing).
3. Provide parents with activities that they can do at home with their children. Describe very specific activities so parents know exactly what to do.
4. Provide parents with a "talk-about" section discussing children's school activities that can be extended at home. The children enjoy discussing their "work" with parents; a "talk-about" section stimulates communication.
5. Highlight one staff person in each newsletter. Detail his or her background, training, special interests, and experience.
6. Describe special projects that individual children have completed. Be sure to feature each child at some time during the year.
7. Request materials or assistance that you might need.
8. List community services and activities of interest to parents.
9. Provide short descriptions of articles or books that parents may find helpful.

WORKING SUCCESSFULLY WITH PARENTS

Working with parents is an important element in educating young children. In order to do this successfully, teachers must understand and value the beliefs and cultural backgrounds of each family. They must be willing to accept the parents as the final authority in matters relating to their own child, except in cases of abuse and neglect. Teachers must be willing to modify their own program to meet the expectations of parents while educating parents in relation to what they see as important. Forcing parents to adhere to the value orientation of the teacher often leads to mistrust of teachers' motives and an impression that the teacher feels superior and is insensitive.

Teachers must understand that no two families are alike; each will treat their children differently. There is no single set of behaviors and experiences that leads to optimal child development. Nor is there one body of knowledge that would enable a person to be an effective parent. Any approach to working with parents must take into account the individual differences that occur in any family group. Joseph H. Stevens, Jr., (1980) feels that parent programs should be considered developmental and should be designed to be appropriate for all parents. This is important, since parents function at their own levels of development. Teachers must be able to identify the needs and interests of the parents and plan programs flexibly to include their changing interests and concerns.

Teachers need to be aware of the forces that are affecting family life today. Included in these are:

•Economic forces	the need for two salaries in many families
•Technological forces	new household utensils and tools changing the nature of housekeeping
•Political forces	provision of special services for families; concern for child abuse and neglect
•Social forces	many smaller families, nonnuclear families, high mobility
•Psychological forces	changing identity of women (Swick, 1984)

Similarly, Doreen Croft (1979) suggests that the significant social changes that have affected the lives of parents include:

1. The increasing number of divorces, leaving only one parent in the family.
2. Occupational mobility.
3. The breakdown of friendly, stable neighborhoods.
4. School districts that require children to leave their neighborhoods in order to attend school.
5. The development of separate patterns of social life for different age groups.
6. The delegation of child care to institutions.

In working with parents, teachers must keep two ideas in mind. The first is that the role of the teacher is not to do something to parents but rather to provide an opportunity for parents to influence as well as to be influenced (Spodek, 1985). Second, the parent–teacher relationship need not be confrontational in nature. Too often inexperienced parents and teachers tend to think the worst of each other. Receiving a note from the teacher requesting a conference frightens many parents. They automatically assume the child is having a problem. Conversely, many teachers who receive a note or call from a parent requesting a meeting assume that they will be accused of having done something wrong to the child. The more parents and teachers know about each other and the more they work together, the more comfortable and trusting the relationship will become.

SUMMARY

Working with parents is critical to working well with children. In planning a parent program, teachers need to be sensitive to the kinds of families represented in their classroom. Different families will have different needs as well as different ways of responding to the school.

In working with families, teachers need to determine what levels of parent involvement are appropriate for the school and community. Parents might participate in the classroom, serve on various committees, or serve the program in other ways. Teachers must also determine what kind of parent education program is most reasonable.

Teachers must also develop both formal and informal ways of communicating with families. Parent conferences are most useful in communicating with individual parents, but meetings, home visits, newsletters, and informal chats are also helpful. A teacher's insight into the needs of children and families, and the range of options the teacher has available, will determine the success of any parent program.

REFERENCES

ALLEN, K. E., AND B. HART (1984). *The early years: Arrangement for learning.* Englewood Cliffs, NJ: Prentice-Hall.

CATALDO, C. Z. (1980). The parent as learner: Early childhood parent programs. *Educational Psychologist,* **15**(3), 172-186.

CROFT, D. J. (1979). *Parents and teachers: A resource book for home, school and community relations.* Belmont, CA: Wadsworth.

FEENEY, S., D. CHRISTENSEN, AND E. MORAVCIK (1983). *Who am I in the lives of children: An introduction to teaching young children* (2nd ed.). Columbus, OH: Merrill.

GORDON, I. J., P. P. OLMSTEAD, R. I. RUBIN, AND J. H. TRUE (1979). How has Follow Through promoted parent involvement: *Young Children,* **34**(5), 49-53.

HANLEY, P. E. (1980). Working parents: Ideas for classroom participation. *Dimensions,* **8**(2), 45-57.

HARMS, T. O., AND D. CRYER (1978). Parent newsletter: A new format. *Young Children.* **33**(5), 28-32.

HEINZ, R. S. (1979). *Practical methods of parent involvement.* ERIC Document Reproduction Service No. ED 188776.

HONIG, A. S. (1979). *Parent involvement in early childhood education* (2nd ed.) Washington, DC: National Association for the Education of Young Children.

————(1982). Parent involvement in early childhood education. In B. Spodek (Ed.), *Handbook of research in early childhood education,* pp. 426-455. New York: Free Press.

McKINNEY, J. (1980). Evaluation of parent involvement in early childhood programs 1979-1980. ERIC Document Reproduction Service No. ED 204 388.

NEDLER, S. E., AND O. D. McAFEE (1979). *Working with parents: Guidelines for early childhood and elementary teachers.* Belmont, CA: Wadsworth.

NORWOOD, G. R. (1984). Schools need parent power in the 80's. *Dimensions,* **12**(4), 4-5.

SKEEN, P., B. E. ROBINSON, AND C. FLAKE-HOBSON (1984). Blended families: Overcoming the Cinderella myth. *Young Children*, **39**(2), 64-74.

SPODEK, B. (1985). *Teaching in the early years* (3rd ed.). Englewood Cliffs, NJ: Prentice-Hall.

SPODEK, B., O. N. SARACHO, AND R. C. LEE (1984). *Mainstreaming young children.* Belmont, CA: Wadsworth.

STEVENS, J. H., JR., (1980). Our romance with parenting. *Dimensions*, **8**(2), 78-81.

SWICK, K. J. (1983). Parent education: Focus on parent needs and responsibilities. *Dimensions*, **11**(3), 9-12.

———(1984). *Inviting parents into the young child's world.* Champaign, IL: Stipes Publishing Co.

TRAVIS, N. E., AND J. PERRAULT (1980). *Day care as a resource to families.* ERIC Document Reproduction Service No. ED 190198.

SUGGESTED ACTIVITIES

1. Collect parent newsletters from a number of centers. Compare them as to layout, content, and clarity. Discuss the characteristics that seem to make the most attractive newsletter.

2. Attend a parent orientation session at a child care center. List the topics covered that relate to parent involvement and to parent education. List some of the things that made the meeting effective. Describe how it could have been improved.

3. Visit a home-based program along with a parent educator. Describe the techniques the educator uses to train the parent.

4. Ask a number of parents what schools could do to help them become more involved. Compare and contrast mothers' responses with fathers' responses.

9

EVALUATION IN EARLY CHILDHOOD PROGRAMS

OBJECTIVES

After completing this chapter on evaluation in early childhood programs, the student will be able to:

1. Identify and describe the different ways to gather information for evaluating children.
2. Describe different ways of observing young children that can be used in an early childhood classroom.
3. Design an evaluation plan that reflects important elements of an early childhood program.
4. List the characteristics of a classroom environment that supports educational activities.
5. Describe screening procedures for identifying exceptional children.
6. Record and interpret the results of an evaluation.
7. Identify several ways of reporting to parents about their child's progress.

Evaluation is helpful in making classroom decisions as well as in developing educational policies. Many agencies and organizations use it to improve their performance. It is equally useful to teachers as an aid in improving the education of the children in their classes.

At one time educational evaluation was considered the same as testing. Test scores were used to assess individual children in school, and their performance on a test was used to evaluate the school program. Children's test scores, however, provide only a limited amount of information about a child's performance. Achievement tests do not provide information about children's interests or about how they learn. They are only one narrow method of evaluating learning and have limited use for early childhood classrooms. In addition, we need to know much more than just the children's levels of achievement to evaluate a program.

This chapter will describe ways of gathering and analyzing information about children, including different kinds of tests and observations. It will discuss the evaluation of classrooms and programs. Forms of screening handicapped children and recording and communicating the results of evaluation will also be presented.

WAYS OF GATHERING INFORMATION

An evaluation that provides insight on an entire program (e.g., its rationale, development, operations, achievements, and problems) requires different ways of gathering information. Such an evaluation assesses the school context, the children's learning environment, the teaching method used, and the program's outcomes. It should use a combination of methods including different types of observations along with standardized and informal tests. Each of these will be discussed separately.

Observations

An observation is a way of gathering information about a situation by looking at and listening to what is happening, then recording it accurately. The observer receives impressions and records ongoing events, just as a camera might. Teachers can use observation to understand what is happening to children in a classroom. A number of observation methods have been developed over the years for these purposes. Olivia Saracho (1983b) describes the different kinds of observation strategies that can be used in an early childhood class, including anecdotal records, rating scales, semantic differential scales, and checklists.

Anecdotal Records. An anecdotal record is a brief account of a situation. By means of words, it draws a picture and provides a factual description of an incident, behavior, or event. Several guidelines should be followed in recording anecdotes:

1. *Descriptions should be specific.* Specific descriptions of what actually happened and the children's reactions, actions, and comments need to be carefully recorded. Care should be taken not to use words that are easily misinterpreted (such as "yelled" or "screamed"). In recording factual descriptions of events, observers must select words or phrases to be used consistently throughout the description. (For example, every time someone talks, the word "said" is recorded.)

2. *The collection of anecdotes should be purposeful.* Although ancedotal records identify unanticipated behaviors, observations should describe specific situations and focus on a selected behavior.

3. *Recordings should be systematic.* A system must be designed to record descriptions of events in order to identify patterns in young children's behavior. For example, a child may be observed during outside play so the teacher can record his or her progress in motor development.

4. *Background information should be provided.* The date, time, child's name, and setting in which the event occurred should be recorded.

Figure 9-1 presents an example of an anecdotal record.

Figure 9-1 Anecdotal record.

Child Ralph Samson	Age 5 yrs. 1 mo.	Sex male

Date November 21, 1987   Time 9:15 – 9:30 (a.m.) / p.m.   Setting Story Hour

Observer Janie Smith   Observation No. 6

Record exactly what you observe under observations and record any interpretations under interpretations.

Observations	Interpretations
The teacher read the book *Snails, Where Are You?* Ralph said, "In the book." The teacher said, "Look, very carefully and raise your hand." Ralph did not raise his hand and said, "At the beach." The other children said, "On the cat's tail!" The teacher finished the story, put the book away and told the children to go back to their chairs. Ralph sat on the carpet and would not move until the teacher talked to him and both went together to his chair.	Ralph seems to like to participate in group discussions. He likes to answer questions even if they are not correct. He seems to have trouble following directions and paying attention. He will follow directions, but he requires the attention and assistance of the teacher.

Rating Scales. Rating scales are used for making an estimate of a child's specific behavior or trait. To develop a rating scale, you first identify traits that need to be evaluated. Statements, units, or categories relating to the trait are written as statements on the scale. A teacher or observer can mark along a continuum the extent to which they agree or disagree with a description of that trait or behavior as represented in a child.

Placing equally distanced units, points, numbers, or descriptive statements along a continuum can help an evaluator make the judgment. An odd set of intervals (for example, three or five) are often used in order to provide a neutral midpoint. On a five-point scale, the highest score will be a five while the lowest score will be a one, or vice versa (see Figure 9-2).

Teachers can design a rating scale with as many items as they feel are necessary and appropriate. Each statement needs to be clearly defined and represented by a set of rating units. The teacher observes the behaviors and places a mark on an appropriate point on each rating scale line. Rating scales can easily be used to develop a profile of each child's strengths and needs.

Semantic Differential Scales. A semantic differential scale is similar in many ways to a rating scale. The person using it makes an estimate of a behavior or trait, but makes the estimate by judging where on a scale between two opposite adjectives the individual fits. For example, some pairs of opposite adjectives that could be used to describe a person are "happy–sad," "strong–weak," "reflective–impulsive," "interesting–boring," and "active–passive." Each set would allow the teacher to make a judgment on that particular characteristic.

Each adjective pair is placed at opposite ends of a line. As many as seven equally separate points between the adjectives can then be marked along that line. The observer checks that point on the line that most closely describes the characteristic being assessed in relation to these adjectives. The closer to the end of the continuum the mark is made the more strongly the observer considers that particular adjective as describing the behavior or trait (see Figure 9-3).

Checklists. A checklist is a list of items, behaviors, or traits; the teacher is to determine whether these traits exist in a child or not. Behaviors or traits that are essential in learning are used for a checklist to assess young children in a school setting. The observer checks off the presence of the items by placing a check mark or marking a "yes" or "no" next to each item. This is an easy method of assessing behaviors or traits (see Figure 9-4).

STRUCTURED OBSERVATION TECHNIQUES

Examples of rating scales

1. The child engages in cooperative play.

1	2	3	4	5
never	seldom	sometimes	often	always

2. The child likes to look at pictures.

1	2	3
disagree	unsure	agree

Figure 9-2

Examples of semantic differential scales

active	— — — — — — —	passive
happy	— — — — — — —	unhappy
misbehaves	— — — — — — —	behaves

Figure 9-3

Examples of checklists

Check off the presence of each behavior.

_____1. Child can categorize objects.

_____2. Child looks at books.

Circle a "yes" to indicate the presence of each behavior and circle a "no" to indicate the absence of each behavior.

yes   no   1. Child manipulates objects.

yes   no   2. Child plays in dramatic play area.

Figure 9-4

Summary. Each observation method above represents a way to systematically assess children's behaviors or traits. They each provide a different kind of information that is helpful in identifying the strengths and needs of a program or an individual child. A more detailed description of observational techniques can be found in the following books:

ALMY, MILLIE, AND CELIA GENISHI, *Ways of Studying Children* (rev. ed.). New York: Teachers College Press, 1979.

BOEHM, ANN E., AND RICHARD A WEINBERG, *The Classroom Observer: A Guide for Developing Observation Skills.* New York: Teachers College Press, 1977.

COHEN, DOROTHY H., AND VIRGINIA STERN, *Observing and Recording the Behavior of Young Children* (2nd ed.). New York: Teachers College Press, 1978.

Standardized Tests

Standardized tests include a fixed set of items that are carefully developed to evaluate a specifically defined area of achievement. Precise instructions are used in administering and scoring the tests. In addition, standard criteria are established at a national level for such tests, based on the average scores of large numbers of individuals who are similar to those who will be taking the test. These standard criteria or norms allow teachers to compare an individual's test score with those of a representative group who have taken the same test. Thus, they are able to make judgments about that child's performance in relation to all other children's performance. Standardized tests provide a national frame of reference in judging an individual's achievement. The content and procedures that are estabished for such a test are also standardized. Since an identical test is administered in the same way to all individuals everywhere, comparisons are considered to be valid.

Each standardized test assesses certain elements of school content and academic skills, has different objectives, and uses different testing materials. Even tests with similar titles may be very different from one another. Because of these differences, standardized tests need to be carefully selected by the teacher in relation to the purpose for which the information will be used (Gronlund, 1981).

The standardized tests that are used in early childhood education usually assess the children's readiness for learning tasks. They measure basic concepts and skills that are important in order for children to achieve those learnings that will be expected of them. For example, the *Boehm Test of Basic Concepts* (Psychological Corp., New York, NY) indicates the children's knowledge of verbal concepts (e.g., biggest, nearest, several) which are essential to understand oral communication and gain from school experiences. Children listen to test items read aloud to them and then mark an X on pictures that indicate the proper response. Similar tests include the *Cooperative Preschool Inventory* (Addison-Wesley Testing Service, Reading, MA), *Stanford Early School Achievement Test* (Psychological Corp., New York, NY), and *Tests of Basic Experience* (CTB/McGraw-Hill, New York,

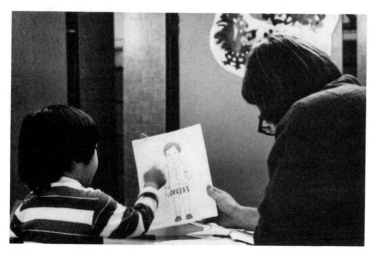

Individual tests are often used to assess young children's
learning and development.

NY), which measure basic concepts and other kinds of preschool learning
(for example, knowledge of the child's environment). Although these other
tests have a broader scope than the *Boehm Test,* their purpose is essentially
the same: to evaluate the children's knowledge of important concepts and
skills as well as to identify learning deficiencies.

Reading readiness tests are widely used in preschool, kindergarten, and first grade to determine the children's ability to benefit from
reading instruction and to be a basis for grouping for such instruction.
Examples of reading readiness tests include the *Metropolitan Readiness Tests*
(Psychological Corp., New York, N.Y.) and *Murphy-Durrell Reading Readiness Analysis* (Psychological Corp., New York, NY). These tests attempt to
identify whether children have the knowledge and skills needed for
beginning reading instruction, but test scores are only one indication of
children's readiness to read. They do not provide information about
children's mental ability, physical development, experiential background,
social and emotional adjustment, or the desire to read. All of these
elements are also important for beginning readers (Gronlund, 1981).

Although there are advantages to using standardized tests, they
also have some disadvantages, as noted. For a proper assessment, other
kinds of information need to be gathered.

Informal Tests

Another way of gathering information is through informal testing. Informal test scores cannot be compared nationally. The tests are based on what
the children are actually being taught in a particular class, and the
information can be used directly by a teacher in planning and modifying
the instructional program. (See Figure 9-5.) Once a teacher determines the

Figure 9-5 The following are examples of items which can be included in an informal reading test for five- or six-year-old children.

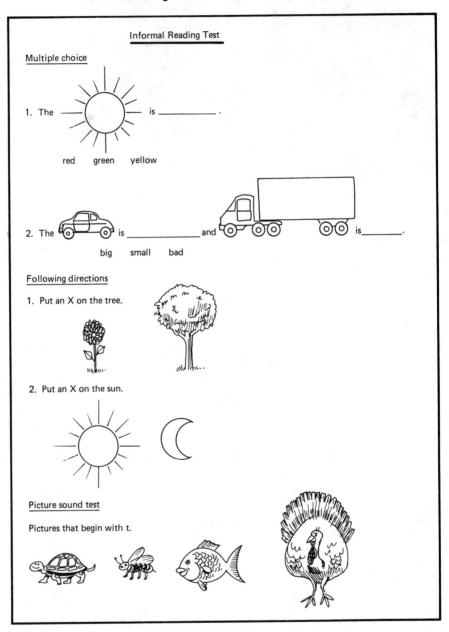

purpose for testing children, items related to what they are learning can be developed or selected. For example, informal placement tests can help determine the children's readiness for planned instruction. Informal formative tests given during teaching can be used to gather information about how well children are learning from the activities presented; the results will help to improve and guide the selection of future activities. Informal prescriptive tests can be used to identify what instruction needs to be provided and to plan activities designed to teach to the goals. These tests can also help improve children's performance and identify any learning problems. Informal summative tests are given at the end of a unit of instruction in order to evaluate the degree to which children have achieved the expected learning outcomes (Gronlund, 1981).

Since informal tests are related to the specific goals of a particular class, teachers can use them to determine if they are succeeding in helping the children achieve the educational goals. In developing these tests, teachers must carefully select items that are developmentally appropriate, since no norms are available to provide guidance. Irrelevancies that might influence the children's responses must be eliminated.

PROGRAM EVALUATION

There is no single early childhood program that meets all the needs of all children or their parents. However, all programs must meet the general needs of the children they serve for good education and care, providing opportunities for children to develop physically, socially, intellectually, and emotionally and helping them to overcome or cope as much as possible with any handicaps they may have.

Each early childhood program uses its own specific ways to achieve its particular goals. These goals need to be evaluated along with the educational program that is designed to achieve them.

Bernard Spodek (1975) has suggested that each program be evaluated on the basis of its *worth, practicality,* and *effectiveness*. The program's worth depends on its underlying values. These may be made explicit, or they may have to be extracted by one's identifying the program's priorities. Information on the program's practicality can be gathered by one's examining the way a program works and identifying the resources it uses. An assessment of student outcomes can provide one type of information on the program's effectiveness.

A careful evaluation plan can guide teachers in understanding the important elements of an early childhood educational program and how these elements operate within their specific context. It should include an analysis of all components of the program. One way to get at such an understanding is through *responsive evaluation* (Stake, 1976), which focuses on actual program experiences rather than on what the program intends to do. Responsive evaluation looks at "what people do naturally." Information about the program is gathered through observations, interviews, and reactions. The perceptions and values of individuals are observed; records are examined. The report of such an evaluation may be presented formally or informally, orally or in writing, and in a variety of forms. It might consist of brief narratives, portrayals, product displays, or graphs, depending on the needs of the audience (Saracho, 1983a).

An early childhood program evaluation may also focus on the success of different types of curriculum, such as one based on applied behavior analysis. Some teachers have difficulty evaluating their early childhood curriculum, lacking the background or competence to do it by themselves. They can work with an evaluator who has the particular expertise necessary. Since teachers are the ones who implement the program and thus have the practical knowledge of their classroom and their children, their judgments provide important and practical information that should be included in any evaluative process (Saracho, 1983a; Spodek, 1985).

Huber Walsh (1980) believes that all teachers can formulate effective strategies for assessing children's learning if (1) the learning objectives are stated clearly and accurately, and (2) the teachers have a rudimentary knowledge of evaluation techniques.

Teachers who work with children under six years of age should limit the use of pencil-and-paper testing. Instead they should use more informal evaluation techniques such as observations, structured interviews, and analysis of children's products. These techniques can be used to evaluate the total early childhood program or just a specific area such as language arts, mathematics, or dramatic play.

In evaluating a literacy program for a group of three-year-old children, teachers can check to see if the children are attentive while listening to stories, if they can describe things in pictures, and if they can remember the sequence of events. Teachers can also note if the children ask to see the pictures relating to a story or repeatedly ask for a particular book or one on a particular topic. Olivia Saracho (1984) suggests that the way young children feel about reading may be as important as their reading skills in getting ready to learn to read. She developed a checklist teachers can use to determine how children feel about reading.

The evaluation of young children's learning experiences should include both *feedforward* and *feedback* dimensions. Feedforward is a preliminary assessment, an evaluation of the children's knowledge about the topic, setting, and objectives before a topic is introduced. Feedback is a final evaluation, referring to the children's responses after a learning activity. It provides information on how well the children have learned and what else they need to learn about a specific topic. These processes are similar to what is called *formative evaluation* and *summative evaluation*.

Formative evaluation consists of frequent judgments that are made while an activity is taking place, whereas summative evaluation refers to the overall worth of an activity and is usually made at the completion of the activity to be evaluated. These judgments are designed to improve the ongoing activity (Scriven, 1967).

EVALUATING CLASSROOM SETTINGS

The classroom environment is composed of objects and people organized into some relationship with one another. This environment is deliberately designed to support activities that the teacher values and that are expected to lead to learning outcomes. If teachers know about the characteristics of a classroom environment, they can act on this information and change the environment to improve a program's effectiveness.

Children react to all aspects of a classroom environment—the physical environment, the interpersonal environment, the activities, and the time schedule. The physical environment communicates many messages, including those about the kind of child-teacher and child-child relationships that are valued in the classroom. For example, when chairs are placed in a circle, they communicate the expectation of child-child learning interactions. The interpersonal environment should be warm and accepting. The environment should also include challenging and complex activities. In addition, long periods of unbroken time should be provided to enable children to become deeply involved in the activities.

Each setting must be individually assessed in relation to the unique combination of children, facilities, and staff. Thelma Harms (1979) has developed an evaluation checklist that consists of questions organized into four categories: physical environment, interpersonal environment, activities to stimulate development, and schedule. Rating the environment in relation to these questions allows teachers to become more aware of the setting. The following are examples of each:

The Physical Environment

1. Can quiet and noisy activities go on without disturbing one another? Is there an appropriate place for each?
2. Is a variety of materials available on open shelves for the children to use when they are interested? Are materials on shelves well spaced for clarity?

The Interpersonal Environment

1. Is there a feeling of mutual respect between adults and children; children and children?
2. Do children feel safe with one another?

Activities to Stimulate Development

1. Are there many opportunities for dramatic play indoors and outdoors: large housekeeping corner, small dollhouse, work-related props, dress-up clothes for boys as well as girls?
2. Is there a variety of basic visual art media: painting, drawing, clay, salt-flour dough, wood-glue sculpture, fingerpaint, collage?

Schedule

1. Is the time sequence of the school day clear to both teachers and children?
2. Has the schedule been designed to suit the physical plant and particular group of children in the school?

Harms' checklist has proven helpful to many teachers. Other, more direct systems of observing the environment can also help determine an early childhood program's quality and its effects on children. Ilse Mattick and Frances J. Perkins (1973) provide a set of observation guidelines which contain three major categories: (1) physical setting, including spatial structure (use of space), materials, and temporal structure (timing); (2) interactional setting (relationships), including teacher–child, child–child, staff, and teacher–parent interactions; and (3) program, including curriculum content, teaching strategies, and socioemotional climate. The following are examples of items from their guidelines:

Physical Setting. The guidelines take into consideration ways in which the physical environment provides for each child's developmental progress in physical, social, cognitive, and affective areas.

Spatial Structure (use of space)

Are facilities adequate, both inside and outdoors, in terms of numbers and ages of the children and the number of hours they spend at the center?

Materials

What specific materials are there in activity areas that indicate intended use of the area?

Temporal Structure (timing)

Is the sequence of different segments of the day's program clear and comprehensible to the observer (without having to ask)?

Interactional Setting. The guidelines take into consideration relationships regarding a variety of learning that can occur only in an environment of trust, pleasurable involvement, and support for autonomy.

Teacher–Child

Note the teacher's facial expression as she talks and reads to children or engages them in learning projects. (Animated, impassive, "bored to tears," angry?)

Child–Child

What kinds of overtures do the children make to each other? How are these responded to? Can give-and-take encounters be observed frequently? Is there conversation between children?

Staff

Do individual staff members give evidence of being responsible for particular children?

Teacher–Parent

How many parents are involved in the instructional or caretaking aspects of the program?

Program.   The guidelines take into consideration ways in which the program helps children to increase their understanding of self, other people, and the world around them and to be able to act upon this understanding.

Curriculum Content

Describe (a) a water play sequence, (b) a cooking project, (c) a discussion guided by the teacher, and (d) a music period. (What learning is going on? Which educational goals are being met?)

Teaching Strategies

Does the teacher guide different children toward different activities for specific reasons (e.g., hammering for a restless child, table games for a timid, inhibited child on a certain day)?

Socioemotional Climate

How are good working and learning conditions ensured? (e.g., Do children have minimal interference with the activities, get the supplies they need in order to follow through on a project, etc.?)

Teachers must be concerned with the quality of the physical setting in early childhood education because of its effects on their interactions with young children. Both the degree of creativity and the opportunity for discovery provided in the classroom environment are directly related to the number and types of elements in it. For example, research has shown that young children's preferences for toys and the kinds of social interaction they display depend on the kinds of materials provided to the children and on the opportunities available to carry out activities without disruptions or distractions. Elizabeth Phyfe-Perkins (1980) offers the following criteria for judging educational toys:

1. *Holding power, attention span, and social value of materials.* Children interact with a variety of materials in different ways. They prefer to use some materials more often and to be involved with some activities for longer periods of time. These social interactions among children differ with the materials.

2. *The variety and complexity of materials related to an overall index of space quality.* Each play material differs in its play potential. Play equipment can be analyzed, according to Elizabeth Prescott (1978), by level of complexity, the variety, and the quantity for each child. Simple materials can be used only one way and do not have subparts. Complex units (such as a play house with furniture or a water table with equipment) have subparts or require the juxtaposition of the different kinds of material, permitting children to improvise and manipulate. Super complex units require three or more types of materials (such as water and measuring equipment added to the sandbox, boxes and boards for use with the jungle gym). A more complex unit provides children with more choices as they play. Complexity sustains attention and promotes dramatic play and social interaction. According to Elizabeth Prescott (1978), complexity, variety, and amount to do for each child, influence such young children's behaviors as attention span, group participation, dramatic play, nondisruptive free choice of activities, and goal-directed behaviors.

3. *The amount, type, and display of materials as they influence children's behavior.* Deciding which behaviors must be fostered depends on educational philosophy and values. The type of materials provided for young children is important to increase their attention, to facilitate their social interaction, and to elicit their cognitive play modes. Raw materials (clay, sand, blocks) are popular; sand and clay encourage solitary and parallel play as well as functional cognitive levels of play. A number of different materials can provide a purposeful activity, and a sufficient number of play spaces must be available for each child in order to promote the flow of children from one activity to another during play. An appropriate amount of materials encourages positive behavior in children who are required to follow a rigid schedule of activities.

One who evaluates an early childhood program needs to assess the classroom environment from the children's point of view. Children respond to the total setting: the way people treat them, the materials that are available on the shelf, the space available in the play areas. Everything in the classroom, including the spatial arrangement and the materials available, communicates to children what is valued. The teacher's way of speaking, as well as the teacher's gestures and even the pace of walking, are part of the overall setting. The children's interactions with adults and other children are also important elements of the preschool setting. Since the preschool setting provides strong messages to young children, it must be evaluated and modified as necessary to provide a high-quality learning environment.

SCREENING EXCEPTIONAL CHILDREN

Sometimes teachers identify particular problems in a child beyond those usually found in a regular class of children. If the teacher's assessment suggests a serious handicap, the teacher should request the assistance of a specialist to make additional assessments. For example, a speech and communication disorders specialist could be called in to assess communication skills, examining the child's ability both to articulate sounds and to use normal communication procedures. The teacher and the specialist can then discuss specific problems and, together with a team including parents and others, can develop an individual educational plan for the child. Specialists may suggest activities for the teacher to use in class. They may also provide special activities for the child outside of class.

The teachers' observations can help to develop a problem list to serve as a focus of the assessment. This list may contain a series of questions, and the responses from the specialist would help them make plans for working with the child. For example, if a teacher's classroom

A variety of screening devices are used to identify handicaps in children.

observation indicates that a child's leg movements seem impaired, the teacher may want to ask the physical therapist the following questions:

1. What is the extent of the child's impairments?
2. How will the child's leg movements affect his or her other skills (such as walking)?
3. What type of skills will the child be able to perform?
4. What types of activities should be planned for this child?
5. Who should be involved in working with this child?
6. What precautions need to be taken to safeguard the child?

Once information is gathered, a program needs to be developed by a team, including, in the above instance, the teacher and the physical therapist. The therapist might work with the child regularly for a period of time. The teacher could supplement this treatment with additional activities within the regular class. Educational activities might be combined with leg exercises, for example, through movement exploration, games, and creative dramatics. The progress of the treatment would be continually assessed.

Teachers need to assess the instructional program they are offering to be sure they are meeting the needs of both their handicapped and nonhandicapped children. Evaluation can help teachers judge the effects of any modifications they make in the instructional program and can help to improve educational services for all children, including exceptional students.

RECORDING AND COMMUNICATING THE RESULTS OF THE EVALUATION

Information collected about each child in class should be regularly and systematically recorded. Carefully maintained records help teachers plan the child's instructional program and assist in individualizing instruction by identifying further learning possibilities, assessing individual growth, determining the child's personal characteristics, and planning for materials and resources needed to enrich the instructional program.

Teachers need to keep their students' records up to date, including those that document diagnostic-prescriptive processes, checklists related to particular performance areas, and work plans developed for the child, which might contain goals, objectives, materials, procedures, and evaluations. For the exceptional child, the resource team should check and discuss these records at regular intervals.

It is the teacher's responsibility to evaluate carefully the instructional program designed for every child. The most expert consultant can make a mistake about a remediating procedure. The teacher's assessment can also monitor the effects of a special procedure or an entire program designed to eliminate or reduce a child's problem. The teacher should consider the information that is on file and organize it to present to others in a comprehensive report about the child.

Reporting to Parents

Reporting on the evaluation of children is an important element in an early childhood program. The five methods that are most often used are informal reports, individual conferences, report letters, check sheets, and report cards (Decker & Decker, 1984). Report cards are seldom used in early childhood classes. The first two of these are also described in the discussion of parent programs in Chapter 8.

Informal Reports. Informal reports are usually provided in early childhood programs. They include casual conversations with parents in which the staff member discusses something about the child, such as the child's learning to skip, language development, vocabulary building, or self-care skills such as buttoning a sweater.

Individual Conferences. Individual conferences are usually scheduled with the children's parents, providing face-to-face contact. Teachers need to plan intensively for a successful conference. A letter should be sent explaining the purpose of the conference and inviting parents to make appointments during specified times. A schedule of appointments should be made and each appointment confirmed. A place for the conference should be identified and a waiting area provided for parents who arrive early. A baby-sitter may be needed for parents with younger children.

A guide sheet is helpful in planning a conference on children's progress. It can include an outline of what will be covered at the conference. While teachers should focus on the most important items, they should also present a picture of the whole child. Teachers must examine records on the child, and carefully transfer to the guide sheet all of the information that needs to be shared with the parents. A copy of the guide sheet can be given to parents.

Supplementary material should also be made available during a conference. Samples of children's work can be collected that represent all or most developmental areas, and these can be shown to parents to offer a fuller picture of their children's progress. The last step of the conference is to summarize it. After the conference the teacher should write a report of the conference to keep in the child's file.

Report Letters.   Writing individual letters can be burdensome. Therefore, report letters are usually designed as a form that can be used for each child. Several headings may be used, such as psychomotor learning, personal-social adjustment, cognitive development, language growth, work habits, problem solving, aesthetics, and self-reliance. Whatever headings are used, teachers should be sure that all parents understand their meaning. Teachers can record brief comments about a child's progress under each heading. In using report letters, teachers are able to concentrate on a child's specific strengths and needs without recording letter grades or satisfactory/unsatisfactory ratings. Individual report letters take a lot of time to complete, and teachers need to be careful not to stereotype their comments after writing the first few letters.

Check Sheets.   Check sheets contain checklists of expected achievements. Teachers check off the child's development of a particular skill or concept. While check sheets can be one of the methods of reporting, they should not be the only means of reporting. They are generally most helpful when shown to parents during an individual conference or when enclosed in a report card or letter.

SUMMARY

Evaluation helps teachers make judgments about the programs they are offering and about their children's learning and development. A number of different techniques can help teachers gather and record information about children and about their classroom. Once this information is recorded it can be compared over time to assess the children's progress and the program's appropriateness. The results of evaluations can be communicated to parents and to others.

Although the pressures on children to achieve are not as strong at the preschool level as at the elementary school level, it is essential that parents work with teachers to evaluate their children's progress. Teachers must consider the progress of each individual child as they keep in mind that there are differences in parents from group to group. Reports should be presented based on the needs and interests of the parents and the extent of their participation in preschool activities. For a group of parents not familiar with the evaluation process, the report may include a brief, encouraging note at the end of the year to increase parental pride, parental appreciation of the child, and parental participation in preschool group activities.

REFERENCES

DECKER, C.A., AND J. R. DECKER (1984). *Planning and administering early childhood programs* (3rd ed.). Columbus, OH: Merrill.

GRONLUND, N. E. (1981). *Measurement and evaluation of teaching.* New York: Macmillan.

HARMS, T. (1979). Evaluating settings for learning. In D. W. Hewes (Ed.), *Administration: Making programs work for children and families,* p. 187-190. Washington, DC: National Association for the Education of Young Children.

MATTICK, I., AND F. J. PERKINS (1973). *Guidelines for observation and assessment: An approach to evaluating the learning environment of a day care center.* Washington, DC: The Day Care and Child Development Council of America.

PHYFE-PERKINS, E. (1980). Children's behavior in preschool settings—A review of research concerning the influence of the physical environment. In L. G. Katz (Ed.), *Current topics in early childhood education,* Vol. 3, pp. 91-125. Norwood, NJ: Ablex.

PRESCOTT, E. (1978). Is day care as good as home? *Young Children, 33*(2) 13-19.

SARACHO, O. N. (1983A). New dimensions in evaluating the worth of a program. *Education,* **103**(1), 74-78.

——— (1983b). Using observation techniques to plan inservice education. *Child Care Information Exchange,* 14-16.

——— (1984). Using observation to assess young children's reading attitudes. *Reading Horizons,* **25**(1), 68-71.

SCRIVEN, M. (1967). The methodology of evaluation. In R. Stake (Ed.), *AERA Monograph Series on Curriculum Evaluation,* No. 1, pp. 37-83. Chicago: Rand McNally.

SPODEK, B. (1975). *Evaluating teacher education.* Paper presented at the annual National Association for the Education of Young Children Conference, Dallas.

——— (1985). *Teaching in the early years* (3rd ed.). Englewood Cliffs, NJ: Prentice-Hall.

STAKE, R. E. (1976). *Evaluating educational programmes: The need and the response: A collection of resource materials.* Paris: Organisation for Economic Cooperation and Development.

WALSH, H. M. (1980). *Introducing the young child to the social world.* New York: Macmillan.

SUGGESTED ACTIVITIES

1. Observe and compare two play areas for young children. List the characteristics you would evaluate.

2. Observe a preschool or kindergarten class and identify specific examples of appropriate and inappropriate uses of evaluation

methods. Describe the evaluative situation and the role of the early childhood teacher in each situation.

3. Interview a school psychologist concerning the value and the confidentiality of records. Discuss professional ethics and the dangers involved when a child's file is used inappropriately.

4. Develop a checklist to assess the physical environment of a classroom.

5. Develop and use an informal test on reading or language for a group of young children.

6. Observe an all-day preschool program and write an anecdotal record of one child in the early morning and another of the same child in the late afternoon. Compare the child's behavior at both times.

7. Construct a semantic differential scale to assess the extent to which you have achieved the objectives of this chapter.

10

PLAY
IN EARLY
CHILDHOOD
EDUCATION

OBJECTIVES

After completing this chapter on play in early childhood education, the student will be able to:

1. Define play.
2. Describe classical and dynamic theories of play.
3. List several criteria to identify play.
4. Describe the classical theories of play.
5. Compare stages in play development.
6. Describe and compare ways to support outdoor play.
7. Describe and compare ways to support indoor play.
8. Develop outdoor play activities.
9. Develop indoor play activities.

From the time when special programs were first developed for young children, there has been a belief that play is the way that these children learn. Not all early childhood programs include play as a learning activity, however. While traditional Montessori programs provide environments to support a wide range of manipulative activities, Montessori activities are considered work rather than play. In addition, fantasy activities, dramatic play, and activities that nurture creative expression are not a part of Montessori programs. There are also programs for young children consisting of direct instruction that do not view play as a form of learning. These programs focus primarily on academic achievement and exclude play activities except as a form of relaxation from the work the children do. Even when the activities are in the form of games, they do not meet the criteria for play that we will present in this chapter. Barring these exceptions, however, most early childhood programs contain a significant amount of play activities. Teachers consider these to be an important part of the education of young children.

This chapter will discuss definitions and theories of play. It will also describe ways of developing play activities and supporting play indoors and out-of-doors.

DEFINING PLAY

Play as a phenomenon has intrigued educators, psychologists, philosophers, and others for many decades. They have tried to define it, explain it, understand it, and see it in relation to other activities in which humans engage. Play has been a particularly difficult concept to understand because it appears in so many different forms. In addition, play is not only an activity of young children but of adults and nonhuman animals. In this chapter we will deal with play only in relation to the activities of young children.

We see play so regularly in our lives that we have no problem identifying it, although there are times when we are not sure when someone is serious or "merely playing." It is not an easy matter, however, to spell out exactly what makes an activity play and what makes it nonplay, that is, work or serious activity.

Often we define play in terms of what it is not. Helen B. Schwartzman (1978), for example, states:

> Play is not work; play is not real; play is not serious; play is not productive; and so forth....[Yet] work can be playful while sometimes play can be experienced as work; and likewise, players create worlds that are often more real, serious and productive than so-called real life. (pp. 4-5)

You will note that even a serious scholar can sometimes have trouble in formally separating work from play.

One possible explanation for this confusion is the fact that play and work are not concepts that can be identified in an all-or-none manner. Often activities will be "more work" or "more play." Eva Neumann (1971) has identified criteria that can help us in judging the nature of an activity as more work or more play. Neumann's criteria for play include *inner control, inner reality,* and *intrinsic motivation.* To the extent that children control their own activities rather than being subjected to the control of outsiders, the activity may be considered play. To the extent that the child allows fantasy to operate rather than being limited by the outer reality of the situation, the activity may be play. And to the extent that the child is motivated to engage in the activity for its own sake rather than for some external reward, the activity may be play.

In a similar vein, Kenneth Rubin, Greta Fein, and Brian Vandenberg (1983), after reviewing definitions of play, suggest that most definitions identify play by the state of mind of those who are playing. A person's motives for being involved in an activity provide a clue to whether they are playing or not. We need to consider also the individual's concern for goals, concern with the material involved in the activity, and concern for rules and for other elements. They suggest, then, that play can be identified by the following criteria:

1. Play is personally motivated by the satisfaction embedded in the activity and not governed either by basic needs and drives or by social demands.
2. Players are concerned with activities more than with goals. Goals are self-imposed and the behavior of the players is spontaneous.
3. Play occurs with familiar objects, or following the exploration of unfamiliar objects. Children supply their own meanings to play activities and control the activity themselves.
4. Play activities can be nonliteral.
5. Play is free from rules imposed from the outside, and the rules that do exist can be modified by the players.
6. Play requires the active engagement of the players.

Understanding Play

There have been a number of theories developed to explain play. J. Barnard Gilmore (1971) identified some of these theories including the following classical theories of play:

1. The *relaxation theory* suggests that play serves to restore the energy we use up during work. Thus, after a period of sustained work we need a period of play in which we can relax. During that time we generate and store enough energy so that we may resume work once more.
2. The *surplus energy theory* suggests that, as organisms, we generate energy continually. Most of that energy is used up by working. When we

have energy left over beyond what we need for work, we rid ourselves of it by playing.

3. The *recapitulation theory* suggests that individuals go through stages in their personal development that are similar to the stages we have gone through in the development of the human race. Play is an instinctive way of getting rid of primitive skills and drives that have been carried over through the epochs of civilization through heredity. By allowing a person to move through these primitive stages, play allows the child to become prepared for the activities of modern life.

4. The *preexercise theory* suggests that play is an instinctive way of preparing children for the activities of adult life. Young children's play activities parallel the activities they will engage in as adults. In this way, play allows the child to practice skills that will be important in adult life.

The first two of these theories seem to have a ring of truth to them. We ourselves often become tired at the end of a week of work. The weekend gives us a chance to relax and store up enough energy to allow us to face the serious tasks of a Monday morning. Similarly, if we watch a class of children after a long spell of bad weather, we seem to feel their pent-up energy. The energy that was not used in vigorous outdoor activities seems to build up. We will probably find the teacher looking for ways to help the children rid themselves of their excess energy.

Early theories of child development built upon the recapitulation theory. It was attractive to think of the young child maintaining continuity with the entire human race. Play provided the link between the young child, the new generation, and the oldest generations of mankind. Children's play did seem primitive when compared with how adults functioned.

Play also seems to have a preexercise function. If you walk through a toy store, or the toy department of a larger store, you see toys that are simplified miniature replicas of what adults use in their lives. There are rows and rows of dolls and miniature homemaking equipment. There are mechanics' tool sets, doctor kits, toy typewriters, and many other playthings that reflect adult reality. These toys allow the children to engage in activities that parallel those of adults. In many ways the world of child's play does serve as preparation for the world of adult work.

Despite the fact that there is a certain attraction to each of these theories, none of them is adequate in helping to explain children's play. Other theories have evolved within the last several decades to help us understand what happens in children's play and what occurs as the result of this play. These include the following:

The *psychodynamic theory* of play has its roots in the psychoanalysis of Sigmund Freud. According to Freud, play allows children to express and get rid of fears and anxieties by bringing them to a level of consciousness and having them expressed in play. Children use the fantasy of play to deal with those parts of reality that they cannot deal with directly. Problem situations are scaled down in play. At the smaller, simpler play level children may be able to handle problems that cannot be handled on a larger scale, or situations can be changed in play so that they can be mastered. Because of the way play is used by children to express conflicts and problems, psychoanalysts are able to use play as a form of therapy. The language of play serves the same function that verbal language serves for adults in psychoanalysis.

Constructivist theory is rooted in the work of Jean Piaget. Piaget viewed the development of knowledge in children as being created by two complementary processes. One process, called *assimilation,* allows the individual to take in information that is gained as a result of experiences. As that information is fit into the individual's already developed sense of understanding, it is considered to be assimilated or absorbed. Sometimes new information cannot be fit into an existing framework of understanding; it may be in conflict with what a person seems to know or it may contradict past understandings. As a result, people are required to change their way of viewing and understanding the world: They must become involved in *accommodation,* changing their sense of what they know in relation to the new information. They create a new balance or *equilibrium.* Play is a way of taking in information from the outside world and working that information through so that it fits with a person's already developed scheme of understanding.

Other theories also exist that help explain various aspects of children's play. According to Vygotsky (1967), play is helpful in the development of language and thought. Mental structures are formed through the use of signs and tools, and play helps in this formation. Play also frees the child from the constraints of the real world that surrounds the child. In this way play gives children greater control over a situation than they would have in reality. Children play with meanings as well as with objects as a result of being freed from reality. They are thus allowed to engage in higher-order thought processes through play.

Jerome Singer (1973) views imaginative play as children's efforts to use their physical and mental abilities in an effort to organize their experiences. Play, according to Singer, is used by children to explore the world, to develop competence in dealing with the world, and to develop creativity.

Michael Ellis (1973) seeks to understand play as a form of information processing. He suggests that human beings normally are mentally active. They continually work at making sense out of the information they gather. If the individual has too much or too little information to process, there is an uncomfortable feeling, and a proper balance needs to be created. Thus, we stop paying attention to some things in our environment that seem overwhelming. We also daydream when we get bored, that is, when too little information is coming our way. The young child uses play as a way of creating that balance. The child can create information internally through fantasy play.

Robert White's theory of competence motivation has also been used to explain some things about children's play. Children require no rewards for playing; they play for play's sake. White (1959) suggests that children gain personal satisfaction from feeling competent. Being able to do something well or having an impact on the surrounding world carries its own rewards. Play serves as a way that children can act on their own in an effective manner. Thus, play activities are themselves rewarding.

While no one of these theories alone explains all about children's play, when taken together they can be used to help us understand that play serves many functions. Play is an activity that children engage in naturally; they do not need to be prodded to play. Play is useful to children in helping them understand and express the world, both at a thinking level and at a feeling level. Play gives children a sense of mastery or control over some aspects of their world. Play involves the use of symbols, actions, or objects that stand for something other than themselves. Because play is not tied to reality, it allows flights of fancy in children which are as important in the developing of their understandings as in the development of their creativity.

Stages in Play Development

Another complicating factor in studying the play behavior of children is that it changes as children grow. Changes in the social and intellectual dimensions of play have been noted by a number of child development specialists. As early as 1932 Mildred Parten identified the changes in the social play of children as they move through the early childhood period. Parten (1932) observed children at the age of three as either *unoccupied* (not playing), as *solitary* players (playing alone), or as *onlooker* (looking on at the play of other children). By age four children were involved in *parallel* play (playing side-by-side with other children), and by age five they were observed in *associative* or *cooperative* play (play in which they engage other children).

Parten saw parallel play as a bridge between solitary play and cooperative play or group play. There have been a number of more recent studies that suggest that children often move directly from solitary play to social play, with parallel play serving as a bridge to allow children to adjust to social situations in play. Other studies suggest that solitary play may not be entirely age related and that both older and younger children engage in solitary play, although it is used in a more constructive or educational manner by older children (Johnson & Ershler, 1982).

Jean Piaget (1962) outlined early stages in play development as *practice* play, *symbolic* play, and *games* with rules that correspond to *sensorimotor*, *preoperational*, and *concrete* operations stages of intellectual development. The sensorimotor stage of play builds on the infant's and toddler's existing patterns of social behavior. Symbolic play is best represented in the dramatic play we see in preschool children. Children in kindergarten and beyond shift from overwhelming involvement in dramatic play and spend more and more time playing games.

Sarah Smilansky (1968) adapted Piaget's play stages for studying preschoolers. She defined *functional* play as the routine or stereotyped use of play materials or as simple motoric activity. *Constructive* play was defined as sequential and purposive play that resulted in a finished product. *Dramatic* play was seen as thematic role play that involved transforming situations or objects.

Teachers can combine the work of Parten with that of Smilansky to get a sense of the level at which children are playing in their classes. Kenneth Rubin and his colleagues (1976) have done this in researching the impact of interventions on the play behavior of children. Teachers can observe their children's play, noting the level at which they play in various activity centers. They can then intervene by modifying the setting, by adding new materials, by raising questions of the children who are playing, or by stepping in momentarily to move play in a particular direction and then stepping out again. Knowing the criteria for play, the teacher can be sensitive that the activity remains play even when there are adult interventions. It should not be distorted to the point that the children become so reality oriented or sensitive to authority that the activity loses its playfulness.

DEVELOPING PLAY ACTIVITIES

Reviewing the theories and definitions of play has helped to pinpoint the fact that play is an important activity for young children. Play serves as a way for children to express ideas and feelings as well as to explore understandings about the world. Play also helps to build social relations among children. Thus, it is valuable in supporting the well-rounded development of young children. The important point for the teacher is to be aware of children's play and especially the kinds of play we want to support. By nurturing selected play activities, we can increase the educational power of children's play in school.

Almost all nursery school and kindergarten programs devote a considerable portion of the school day to play. The teacher needs to plan for this play, providing the necessary supporting environment, making sure that enough materials and equipment are available, feeding into the positive social relations that develop among children at play, and helping the children to extend their play.

Play takes place both indoors in the classroom and out-of-doors in the play yard. Most outdoor play differs in important ways from indoor play, and therefore different supports and controls need to be provided.

Outdoor Play

Outdoor play is usually noisier and more vigorous than indoor play. There is more space out-of-doors, so it is a better place for children to run, jump, and use wheel toys like tricycles and wagons. Also, because there are no walls or ceilings, loud noises are less disturbing. There may be grassy, dirt, or sandy surfaces outdoors which make falling less dangerous for children than the wood or concrete floor indoors.

Even though all this is true, outdoor areas should not be limited to large-muscle activities. Many of the activities of the classroom, including music, art, storytelling, and dramatic play can take place outdoors as well. Of course, some of these activities will be limited by climate and weather.

Most schools, including preschools, are in session from about the beginning of September until some time in June, although summer sessions are often held. In some regions of the country this period includes severe winter weather. Not only may it be too cold to do many of the things we do indoors, but the clothing children wear outdoors in winter limits their mobility and the activities in which they can engage. At other times of the year extreme heat or rain may also limit the outdoor activities that can take place reasonably and comfortably.

There are almost always times, however, when useful play activities can take place outdoors. The play should be designed to support a range of activities. There should be areas for vigorous activity, where climbing equipment can be placed and a proper ground surface arranged to support safety. There needs to be some paved surfaces for wheel toys. There should be a sandpit or dirt area for digging. Many large-muscle activities can be extended to include elements of dramatic play if teachers provide props and suggestions for play themes.

There should also be areas that support quieter activities. Arts and crafts or less vigorous dramatic play can take place outdoors. Construction with large hollow blocks is also a basic outdoor activity. Much of the year water play can be provided as well. These ideas may suggest the need for a zoned outdoor play area, with different places developed for different activities, much like activity centers in the classroom. A further discussion of the physical setup of outdoor play areas is presented in Chapter 6.

More important, however, outdoor play time is not a recess for children. We do not send young children outside so that they can rid themselves of excess energy. Rather, this is a setting for valuable play activities. If value is to be gained, then teachers must do more than monitoring for safe, nonaggressive behavior. True, teachers must be on guard to see that children are not hurt or that children do not fight, but they need also to observe the children's outdoor play so that they can extend it just as they do indoors.

Indoor Play

Indoor play is usually a little quieter and more constrained than outdoor play. The room should be arranged so that different kinds of play can occur in different areas at the same time without interfering with one another. To this end, the classroom is arranged into activity centers. Each center has space allocated and materials available for one type of activity or play, such as dramatic play, block building, or manipulative and fine motor play. In addition, if gross motor play is provided indoors, there is usually a room set aside with a lot of space, some large pieces of equipment, and some gym mats.

Each activity center is designed to serve a particular purpose. The materials and equipment are readily accessible to the children, and the boundaries of the center are carefully delineated, although children should be able to carry their play beyond those boundaries when necessary.

Some ways we guide play apply to all activity centers; others apply only to specific centers. After we present here some general strategies for guiding play, we will look at each type of play separately.

Initiating Play Activities

Sometimes it is enough simply to make play materials available to children to start a play activity. If the materials are attractive, if they offer reasonable play opportunities, and if there is some novelty to the materials and the setting, that may be enough. It is helpful, however, to have a short meeting with the children to present a new piece of equipment or a new toy. You can talk about the uses that can be made of the materials and the limitations on its use. If the new equipment seems to be particularly attractive, it may be helpful to develop another, equally attractive activity, to limit conflict or arguments over taking turns.

Often you can stimulate new interest in a play activity by bringing a degree of novelty to it. Rearranging the block area, setting up some signs in the dramatic play area, or introducing a few new materials will make something that has become "old hat" an attractive new activity once again.

In starting a new play activity, it often helps to stimulate the children's imagination. A walk through the neighborhood, reading a book related to a particular play topic, or showing a film or filmstrip will each serve to get children's play started.

Moving Children's Play Along

Every preschool teacher is presented with a dilemma in guiding play. On the one hand, we want children's play to be as productive as possible; we need to involve ourselves in it to some extent to achieve this goal. On the other hand, we want children to be independent in their activities. We do not want to structure the play for the children. If we impose ourselves too much, the activity is limited and stops being play. Teachers need regularly to check on the consequences of what they say and do. If a teacher goes too far, it is easy to pull back without causing too much distress, if that teacher is sensitive to what is happening in the play.

Teachers can guide children's play by adding or taking away material from the play situation. At the beginning of supermarket play, for example, there are a number of things that can be provided: A doll carriage or other wheeled toy can be a supermarket cart, boxes and empty food containers can represent the store's merchandise, and tables can serve as shelves. Signs can be written, indicating what kinds of food are on what table, and even the price can be noted. The teacher might ask the children what they need, or might suggest materials, or might simply put some things out so the children themselves can choose what to use. As the play progresses, a toy cash register and some play money might be added.

Sometimes the teacher will guide play by suggesting roles that children can play. "Who is doing the shopping?" or "Who is the supermarket clerk?" may be enough to suggest new roles and move play along. A teacher might also join the play for a while. The teacher could become a shopper for a period of time, purchasing, asking about the price of things, and asking who should be paid as a way of suggesting roles.

If the children seem blocked in their play, the teacher might take them on a field trip or bring in a book to provide more information. For example, the teacher could take just a few children or the whole class on a trip to the supermarket. A few purchases might be made to show the children the entire shopping process. They will pay more attention in this situation than when they visit the store with their parents. The children also could observe the way the store is arranged, how food is stored, and so on. If plans are made in advance, you might be able to take the children to the storage area, the butchering area, the bakery, or other places not normally seen in the supermarket.

Teachers must be careful not to disrupt the flow of activities when intervening in play. They must also be careful not to provide too much for the children—too much material, too much information, or too much structure. If there is too much, children either ignore what the teacher introduces or may lose interest in the activity. Teachers can intervene in other play areas, through the way we have suggested they intervene in dramatic play.

Large structures allow a range of outdoor play activities.

SUPPORTING OUTDOOR PLAY

Much of the outdoor play of young children consists of large motor activity: climbing, running, jumping, swinging, and crawling. Other outdoor activities involve wheel toys, building structures, playing with sand and water, engaging in dramatic play, and playing games. Each of these will be discussed separately.

Large Motor Activity

Relatively little intervention is required when children engage in large motor activities. Equipment needs to be provided that is both challenging and safe, and that avoids creating frustration. Whatever equipment is available must be carefully checked to ensure that it is in good condition. It should also be matched to the developmental level of the children. For very young children a set of low steps provides plenty of challenge for climbing. You will see little children going up and down such steps repeatedly. When children are older and more capable, wooden or metal ladders can be introduced, along with ramps, rope ladders, platforms above ground level, cargo nets, and climbing ropes. Often these pieces of equipment are integrated into large play structures that provide a range of options so that children can establish their own challenges. Some children's centers are even fortunate enough to have trees in their play yards that are suitable for children to climb.

The ground surface under any climbing equipment should allow children to fall or jump without being injured. Sometimes dirt or grassy

A large see-saw extends both physical and social play.

surfaces are adequate. At other times sand, tanbark, corn cobs, or other appropriate material needs to be provided. If the play area is subject to heavy traffic, the grass will not survive.

In addition to climbing apparatus, there ought to be things for children to crawl under, jump over or down from, swing on, and slide on. Although separate pieces of equipment can serve these purposes, larger pieces of stationary equipment are sometimes placed permanently in the play area for children's use. These can be augmented with other props to extend the children's play. Barrels and large cardboard cartons are fun for children to crawl through. Smooth boards can be used to provide added slides, and hanging pieces of cloth can provide privacy.

Wheel Toys

Some space which is paved with concrete, asphalt, or a similar material should be provided so that children can use wheel toys. These can include tricycles, wagons, Irish Mails, Big Wheels, miniature trucks, or similar vehicles. Children will use wheel toys in a variety of ways. They will ride on them alone or with others; they will carry things or pull things with them. Traffic patterns and rules need to be established. Since there are often more children than wheel toys and these toys may be quite popular, the teacher may want to work with the children to develop rules for taking turns.

Building Structures

Not many years ago the *Adventure Playground* movement which had been popular in Europe caught the imagination of American educators and recreation workers. Adventure playgrounds provide children with the opportunity to create their own play structures. Children are given tools and raw materials and, with help and supervision from adults, they create their own play equipment. Supervisors check that the structures are safe before children use them. The beauty of the structures rested in the fact that they were built by children for their own use rather than for their visual beauty.

Few children of kingergarten age or younger are capable of constructing their own adventure playgrounds. However, young children are capable of combining pieces of equipment to create their own play structures when the proper equipment is available. In many large city playgrounds and school yards the play equipment is solid and permanent, anchored into place to be safe and vandal-resistant and to require little maintenance. Too often these structures leave little flexibility to children. However, smaller pieces of equipment can be given to young children outdoors to allow them to create their own play structures. Sawhorses, ladders, cleated boards, large hollow blocks, large wooden packing crates, and other such pieces of equipment can be combined and recombined to provide a variety of play structures. Often these can be used in combination with more permanent structures in the play yard. The fact that children can continually modify and elaborate the structures they build means that these structures are continually being renewed, providing novelty and a sense of adventure and challenge that permanent structures cannot offer. Since they are created by the children themselves, such structures are even more attractive.

For children to build adequate play structures, there must be enough equipment to allow them to extend from what is provided. There also needs to be some storage facilities available outdoors so that when the play is over, the structures can be taken down and the pieces stored. This way new ones can be created at a later time.

Sand and Water

Sand and water can be used both indoors and outdoors. When used indoors, they are usually in a large basin or tub set on a table, or in a special lined sand or water table. When they are used outdoors, more freedom can be allowed and, since there is more space, more sand or water can be provided.

Outdoors a large sandbox or sand pit can be used. It can be

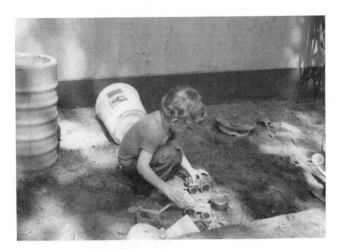

A sand pit will allow children to use many props in their sand play.

recessed or placed low to the ground so that children can kneel over the edge or even be allowed to play inside it. It is important that a sandbox be designed to drain easily and that it can be covered and kept clean.

Children can play with sand with no tools, just feeling, molding, and modeling damp sand. Nevertheless, tools are useful for children to use. Pails and shovels, large wooden spoons, strainers, funnels, plastic jars, and empty cans all make excellent tools to use with sand. Toy trucks or construction vehicles might also be provided. If the weather is good, a water hose, a sprinkling can, or a plastic bottle filled with water will allow the children to dampen or wet the sand.

Sometimes the ground itself serves children's play well.

Indoors or out, water play can be provided with water made available in galvanized or plastic tubs. There should also be various containers to pour the water into. Hoses, funnels, plastic boats, and other objects that float or can be filled with water can be used to extend the child's play.

As in other areas, rules need to be established for children who use sand and water. Wetting other children or throwing sand may need to be clearly indicated as taboo. Proper protection, such as plastic aprons, may be needed to protect children's clothing, or shoes and socks may need to be removed when children step into a sandbox. Also, children can help with cleanup here, as in all areas.

Dramatic Play

Although most of the dramatic play of children takes place indoors, children will engage in such play in the yard if we allow them to and if we provide supports. Many of the elements of dramatic play, discussed later in this chapter in relation to indoor play, also apply to outdoor dramatic play. Climbing apparatus can be turned into homes, castles, airplanes, or any number of other settings that will allow the children to extend their activities through their imagination. Interventions here will be much like those indoors. The teacher needs to observe the children's play, keeping it going by making sure there are enough props, feeding ideas when necessary, and maybe even moving into the play for short periods of time.

Games

Teachers can help to develop outdoor games with children. Games differ from other forms of play in that there are rules that provide structure. Many children's games are too elaborate for the preschooler. It is difficult for young children to follow the rules or even remember the intent of the game. Many simple games, however, can be played with the teacher providing the leadership. Simple singalong games like "Ring Around the Rosie," "Paw Paw Patch," and "Loobie Loo" can be played by preschoolers. Other games might also be played as children develop skills in game playing and an understanding of how games work. Ruth F. Bogdanoff and Elaine T. Dolch (1979) provide a set of developmental guidelines that can help in selecting games that match the developmental level of any particular group (see Table 10-1).

There is usually more room outdoors to allow a large number of children to play a game together. In addition, there is usually plenty of space for other activities, so that all children do not have to be required to participate.

TABLE 10-1 Developmental Guidelines For Choosing Games

LEVEL	CHILD'S THOUGHT DEVELOPMENT	GAME REQUIREMENTS	SUGGESTED GAMES
I	*Preoperational*	Pattern or sequence game Two-step sequence	Ring Around the Rosie Roll the Ball (small group)
	Very limited verbal understanding	No verbal instruction necessary to teach game	Hokey Pokey (modified) Humpty Dumpty and other nursery rhymes
	Strong egocentrism	Continuous participation by all No waiting necessary Two to four children	This is the way the _____ walks (tune of Mulberry Bush)
	Little group awareness, child involved primarily with adults	Game depends on adult action No role alternation required	
II	*Preoperational*	Basic pattern game Not more than three steps in sequence	Punchinello (circle style) Did You Ever See a Lassie?
	Verbal understanding not dependable	No verbal instruction required	Hide the clock Little Sally Walker
	Egocentrism still strong	Continuous participation Five to eight children	Paw Paw Patch
	Awareness of other children's presence but most interest in adult's expectation of child's behavior	Role alternation with help of the leader only	Variation of Mulberry Bush (with child's choice of action)
III	*Preoperational*	Basic pattern game Four to five steps in sequence Limited choice of action within framework of game	Looby Loo Doggie, Doggie, Where's Your Bone? Musical Chairs (modified) Are You My Kitten?
	Coordination of language with action nearly complete	Some verbal instruction supported by demonstration	Duck, Duck, Goose (modified)
	Egocentrism less strong in game situation	Wait short periods for turn with group action interspersed	
	Good awareness of all players but limited understanding of their roles in game	Six to ten players One-to-one interaction possible	Mulberry Bush

TABLE 10-1, continued

Primary interest in own role	Role alternation between players may now be part of game	

IV	*Late preoperational*		
	More objective understanding of role in action of game	Players required to make some choices of action	A Tisket-a-Tasket
			Squirrel in the Trees
	Good verbal understanding	May use verbal clues as well as action	Charlie over the Water
			Find My Child
	Egocentrism diminishing	Turn taking can be part of game	London Bridge
			Knock, Knock
	Enjoy coordination with group	Understand and enjoy role alternation and some role reversal	
	Will subject own interests to group effort	Eight to twelve children	

V	*Concrete operational*		Word games (G-H-O-S-T)
	Reversible thought and lessened egocentrism	Decisions of strategy determine outcome of game	Tag (modified)
	Understand rules as objective framework for action		Hide and Seek
			Kick the Can
			Competitive races and relays
	New interest in competition within coordinated effort	Competition may be used Team action may substitute for personal involvement	Follow the Leader
			Darts
	Use language easily for thought	Verbal element can be definitive part of game	Horseshoes
			Pease Porridge Hot
			Simon Says

R.F., Bogdanoff, and E.T. Dolch, "Old Games for Young Children: A Link to Our Heritage. In L. Adams and B. Garlick (Eds.), *Ideas that Work with Children,* vol 2. (Washington, DC: National Association for the Education of Young Children, 1979), pp. 169-177.

SUPPORTING INDOOR PLAY

Indoor play is usually organized into activity centers. The most important centers for play are the Block Center, the Housekeeping Center, and the Table Activities Center. Other centers are also provided for other activities.

Block Building

Wooden blocks provide an excellent material for children's construction. There are two types of wooden blocks that preschool children use: large hollow blocks and the smaller solid wooden unit blocks. Cardboard blocks are also available and are less expensive to purchase, but they are much less durable and, because of their lightness, they are not as productive in children's use.

Hollow blocks are usually based on a unit of about one foot square by one-half foot deep. The blocks also come in half units and double units as well as triangular ramps and boards. Some sets of hollow blocks are made of hardwood with two open sides to allow children to slip their hands inside to carry them easily. Other sets are made of plywood, closed on all sides, though often with hand-holes on two sides. Because of their size and their sturdiness, children can build structures that are relatively stable and strong enough to climb on or crawl into. Children build them to their own specifications to serve their own purposes. While providing a good medium for construction, hollow blocks also serve as props for dramatic play, substituting for many structured play props. Blocks can represent buildings, vehicles, or funiture. When the children are through with a particular prop, it can be taken apart and reassembled in a different way to represent another prop.

Unit blocks are much smaller than hollow blocks. The structures created with them are used by children in a very different way. Unit blocks are solid pieces of wood, the best ones made of hardwood. They are based on a unit with multiples and variations of that unit. The basic unit is a brick-shaped block measuring 5½ by 2¾ by 1⅜ inches. Double units and quadruple units are two and four times the length of the unit, and a half unit is one-half its length. Ramps, triangles, pillars, boards, switches, and curved units are all made in proportion to the unit. Figure 10-1 provides examples of unit blocks typically found in a classroom set.

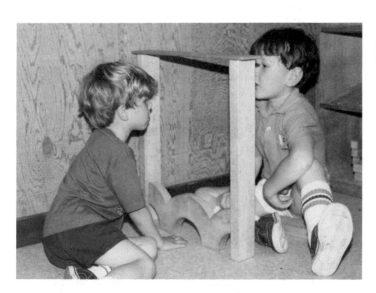

Even the simplest buildings allow for social as well as physical learning.

FIGURE 10-1   Types of Unit Blocks

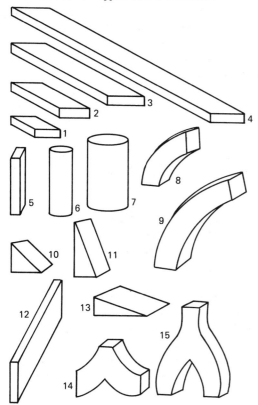

1. Half unit
2. Unit
3. Double unit
4. Quadruple unit
5. Pillar
6. Small cylinder
7. Large cylinder
8. Circular curve
9. Elliptical curve
10. Small triangle
11. Large triangle
12. Floor board
13. Ramp
14. Right-angle switch
15. Y switch

Blocks may come in other sizes and shapes as well.

From Elisabeth S. Hirsch (Ed.), *The Block Book*, (Washington, DC: National Association for the Education of Young Children, 1984). pp. 202-203.

The advantage of basing the dimensions of all the blocks on a unit is that the structures that are built with the blocks, even large, elaborate ones, will be in proportion and will be stable and sturdy. If the blocks are made of hardwood, they are less likely to wear significantly with use; the proportions will remain constant throughout the life of the blocks, and these blocks, if used properly, will last a long time.

Unit block structures are constructed on the floor. They are too small for children to use in dramatic play, but in time they will be used fancifully. At first, children will be content to build simple structures and take them down. As children mature, they will use blocks to represent objects and structures in the outside world. Once children use blocks representationally, their play with unit blocks is much like playing with a dollhouse: they will manipulate objects to represent dramatizations rather than perform in them themselves.

Many years ago Harriet Johnson (1933) identified stages in young children's block building. In the first stage children may simply walk around carrying blocks in their hands. In the second stage children will take blocks and pile one upon the other. Children go from this stage to building towers. They will also lay blocks side by side in rows.

In later stages children will start bridging space with their blocks, separating blocks on the floor and then putting one block over two spaced blocks. After this, children will start to build enclosures of various kinds. In later stages children reproduce elements in their structures over and over again as they make patterns; they also begin to build balanced

As children develop, their block structures become more complex and more representational.

structures through their patterning. In the final stages children use blocks to represent larger objects in the real world. School buildings, city streets, airports, and other real things will be represented and children will use them to play through the processes they observe in the world.

In the early stages of block building, small sets of blocks with limited amounts of space are adequate for children. As children move through the stages of block building, their more elaborate structures need more blocks, as well as more space. These more elaborate block structures take a long time to complete. It helps if block buildings can be left up for more than one day. Children can build and rebuild them and the structures will be used in many different ways as well.

Blocks are expensive. They also take up a lot of classroom space. Nevertheless the learnings that can result from block building make the investment worthwhile. Not every block builder will become a great architect, as did Frank Lloyd Wright, but block building does teach a great many things. Physical coordination and eye–hand coordination are just the beginning. Through blocks children learn math concepts as they balance their buildings and find that equivalent lengths of blocks cover the same space. They learn informal measurement of length, area, and volume and begin to understand topological geometry. Also blocks are representational. They can be used to help in developing social studies understandings. They also help develop abstract thinking, for they allow children to use relatively abstract objects to represent reality in an arbitrary way, developing the rules of representation themselves. (See Elizabeth Hirsch, *The Block Book* [1984] for an excellent discussion of learning through blocks.)

The teacher needs to establish a sense of order in the block area. Blocks should be stored on shelves clearly marked so that children can replace them in the same spot from which they took them. There need to be limits on how children use blocks—leaving space around the shelves so others can move by, respecting the buildings of other children, using blocks safely, not throwing them or hitting with them, and not using them inappropriately. There might also be limits on how high children should build with blocks.

When working with very young children, teachers might show them how to stack or make rows. They might also build alongside the children, making bridged structures. However, teachers should not tell children how to build or what to build. Block structures should always be the children's. Suggestions can show alternatives without imposing them on children. As children mature, teachers should provide props to extend their block play. A pulley system can allow airplanes to land and take off at an airport. A battery, buzzer, and door button can extend children's play in their personally created dollhouse. A field trip to see how things are built and organized in the world outside the school can stimulate more block building.

Blocks can be combined with other toys to extend children's play.

Dramatic Play

Dramatic play is probably the most studied, though not necessarily the most understood form of young children's play. In dramatic play children pretend at being persons other than who they really are and use objects to represent things other than what they really are. Dramatic play incorporates a great deal of fantasy. When it is rooted more in reality, when children act out the roles and relationships they see in the social world that surrounds them, it is often called sociodramatic play.

In dramatic play children develop their own evolving play situations, setting the stage and creating their own dialogue. Even when the play is based upon an observed or experienced situation, dramatic play is an important avenue young children use to express and explore their own personal feelings as well as their understandings of the world they have experienced. In playing with others, children are able to work through their feelings and test their understandings against those of others. Thus, this form of play helps children develop an understanding of their world as well as an ability to cope with their environment.

Most preschool classes have dramatic play centers. Often these represent the home life situation of children. It may be called the "doll corner" or the "housekeeping corner." Miniature tables, chairs, stoves, sinks, refrigerators, and beds are provided along with dolls, toy pots and pans, small brooms, and other things that allow children to act out the roles they see at home. They can be a parent and cook, clean, and feed the doll/baby. Or they may be the baby and have another child nurture them. The way children play out these roles, relations, and feelings reflects how they understand them in their own life.

Dress-up clothes and a housekeeping corner are a part of most dramatic play centers.

Teachers can extend children's play beyond the confines of the home. A range of community settings can serve as the basis for children's sociodramatic play. The supermarket, post office, auto repair shop, barber, or hairdresser, to name just a few settings in the neighborhood, can provide stimulation for interesting play in children.

Judith Bender (1971) suggests creating a set of "prop boxes" as a way of organizing material for dramatic play. The teacher can collect and store material related to each play theme in a box. The following suggestions might prove helpful in creating some prop boxes:

Store. Empty food boxes or cans, a cash register, play money, signs, supermarket advertisements, a white apron. (These can be augmented by shelves, tables, and other equipment that can be found in the classroom.)

Barber/hairdresser. Mirror, combs, brushes, hair rollers, hair clips, shampoo containers, empty hairspray cans, a cloth to cover the child's clothes, a toy razor, a shaving brush.

Post office. Used stamps, envelopes, postcards, rubber stamp and stamp pad, play money, empty milk containers to serve as letter boxes, paper, pencils.

Doctor's office. Stethoscope, gauze bandages, toy hypodermic syringe, white coat or shirt.

Auto repair shop. Screwdrivers, wrenches and other tools, air pump, empty oil cans, clean used automobile parts, toy cars and trucks.

Telephone store. Toy telephones, wire, plastic tape, pliers, screwdrivers and other tools, telephone directories.

Teachers can think of other sets of props to organize into prop boxes as they watch and listen to children to find out what interests them. In each case, some attempt toward authenticity of materials is helpful. Safety, however, is the most important consideration when you are selecting material.

One of the prime responsibilities of the teacher is to set the stage, providing equipment and materials that will invite children to play. In addition, teachers need to observe play to augment the material as needed. The teacher may also provide information that will feed into the play and suggest play ideas. On occasion, the teacher may also join in the play. With all the possible interventions, however, it is important that the teacher does not distort the situation. Play should always remain in the children's control.

Table Activities

Most early childhood classes will have a portion of the room set aside for table activities. Along with tables there will be open shelves to store a variety of small materials for children's play. Each set of material can be kept in its own container, possibly a plastic see-through box, basket, or tray. The children can take a set of materials from its shelf to the table. When they are through, they can gather the materials back into their container to replace on the shelf.

Many of these materials are designed to promote small-muscle development and improve eye–hand coordination. Many of them can also be used to help develop perceptual and conceptual skills. The materials in such a center might contain the following, depending on the developmental level of the children and the resources of the school:

Stacking and nesting toys. Even the youngest preschoolers can use toys that contain smaller and larger parts. These can be ordered by size and stacked one upon the other, placed on a dowel, or nested one into the other. Cups, dolls, and rings are among the more common materials used in these toys. Children learn to distinguish one part from another by size and put them together in the proper manner.

Puzzles. A wide range of wooden puzzles are available for young children. Some of the simplest are formboards, in which spaces are cut out in different forms (such as triangles, squares, rectangles, or trapezoids) and children must put the correct form into the matching space.

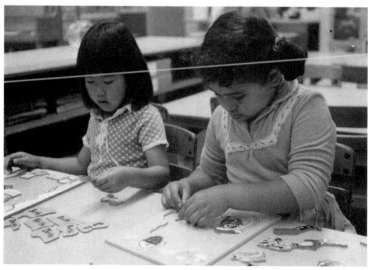

A wide range of puzzles should be provided.

More complex are picture puzzles. These puzzles will vary from a simple one with a single part made up of the pictured object, to complicated puzzles in which the shapes of the pieces have no relationship to the shapes of the objects pictured. There may be as many as two or three different levels of difficulty available in a class. Not too many puzzles are needed at one time, though, since young children enjoy completing the same puzzles over and over again.

Fastening frames. A very useful manipulative device is a fastening frame. This usually has two pieces of cloth stretched over and attached to a wooden frame. Attached to these are one of the many fastening devices that we use in clothing: zipper, hooks and eyes, buttonholes, snaps, or eyelets and shoelaces. The children enjoy fastening and unfastening these devices. Practicing with these frames not only improves motor skills but also helps children learn self-care skills, for the skills learned can be transferred to the fastenings on children's clothing.

Locking devices. There are a number of commercial sets of locking boards available. Sometimes parts of the boards can move to resemble the opening and closing of doors and windows. Often teachers find they can make the same apparatus themselves with materials from a local hardware store. Hinges can be used to fasten the moving parts, and hooks and eyes, sliding door bolts, hasps, cupboard catches, window locks, and even locks that use keys can be mounted for children's use.

Construction sets. There are many excellent sets of materials that children can use to build on a table surface. Table blocks, which are smaller versions of the unit blocks, are the simplest of these. In addition, there are plastic

Sets of construction materials allow children to create many structures.

interlocking blocks, such as *Lego,* as well as *Lincoln Logs, Tinkertoys,* and many others. These are designed commercially and each is given its own brand name. Often these can be combined with small figures of people or animals, with doll furniture, and with small toy vehicles to allow children to add to their constructions as they play out their own dramatizations in miniature.

Games. A number of simple games can also be included in the materials in this center. Some games, like *dominoes,* might be played independently by children. Others, like *Lotto,* might require the attention of an adult working with a group of children. Somewhat more elaborate games such as *Candy Land* or *Chutes and Ladders* might also be included for more mature children.

Academically oriented material. A number of sets of material can be included in this area to provide academic readiness for children. Templates, along with paper and pencil, allow children to trace shapes; this activity prepares them for writing letters. Number cubes or puzzles designed to teach number meanings can also be included, along with wooden or plastic letters that can be combined to make simple words. These materials allow children to explore the meanings of numbers and the uses of letters independently. They let children discover meanings on their own and become more comfortable with academic concepts.

Other manipulative materials. A glance through any early educational catalog will provide illustrations of material far beyond those discussed here. Many of them are worth having in a classroom. Montessori material, for example, has proven useful over the years with young children. These and other materials can also be used in inventive ways. As with other areas of the room, however, there are limits to the way materials should be used. It is helpful to introduce new materials to the children, showing them how they should be used. The routines of caring for and cleaning up the area must also be shown to each group.

SUMMARY

In this chapter we have discussed the nature of play. We have identified both classical and current theories of play. We have also discussed the importance of play for the development of the young child. We have focused on how play can be used in an early childhood class and have identified the role of the teachers in supporting and extending children's play. Finally we have presented the various play areas of the early childhood class, both indoors and outdoors, discussing the significant aspects of each.

Play is a critical element of any early childhood program. It is the responsibility of the teacher to see that the children's play serves an educational function. Equally important, it is the teacher's responsibility to see that the activity remains play. Young children in school must be allowed to maintain their spontaneity and creativity as they use the materials we provide for them.

REFERENCES

BENDER, J. (1971). Have you ever thought of a prop box? *Young Children,* **26**(3), 164-169.

BOGDANOFF, R. F., AND E. T. DOLCH (1979). Old games for young children: A link to our heritage. In L. Adams and B. Garlick (Eds.), *Ideas that work with young children,* Vol. 2, pp. 169-177. Washington, DC: National Association for the Education of Young Children.

ELLIS, M. J. (1973). *Why people play.* Englewood Cliffs, NJ: Prentice-Hall.

GILMORE, J. B. (1971). Play: A special behavior. In C. Herron and B. Sutton-Smith (Eds.), *Child's play.* New York: John Wiley.

HIRSCH, E. S. (ED.) (1984). *The block book* (rev. ed.). Washington, DC: National Assocation for the Education of Young Children.

JOHNSON, H. (1933). *The art of blockbuilding.* New York: Bank Street College (reissued, 1966).

JOHNSON, J. E., AND J. J. ERSHLER (1982). Curricular effects on the play of preschoolers. In D. J. Pepler and C. H. Rubin (Eds.), *The play of children: Current theory and research,* pp. 130-143. Basil, Switzerland: S. Karger.

NEUMANN, E. A. (1971). *The elements of play.* New York: MSS Modular Publications.

PARTEN, M. B. (1932). Social participation among preschool children. *Journal of Abnormal and Social Psychology,* **27,** 243-269.

PIAGET, J. (1962). *Play, dreams and imitation in childhood.* New York: Norton.

RUBIN, K. H., G. G. FEIN, AND B. VANDENBERG (1983). Play. In M. E. Heathering (Ed.), *Carmicheal's manual of child psychology: Social development.* New York: John Wiley.

RUBIN, K. H., T. L. MAIONI, AND M. HORNUNG (1976). Free play behaviors in middle and lower class preschoolers: Parten and Piaget revisited. *Child Development,* **47,** 414-419.

SCHWARTZMAN, H. B. (1978). *Transformations: The anthropology of play.* New York: Plenum.

SINGER, J. L. (1973). *The child's world of make-believe.* New York: Academic Press.

SMILANSKY, S. (1968). *The effects of sociodramatic play on disadvantaged preschool children.* New York: John Wiley.

VYGOTSKY, L. S. (1967). Play and its role in the mental development of the child. *Soviet Psychology, 12,* 62-76.

WHITE, R. F. (1959). Motivation reconsidered: The concept of competence. *Psychological Review, 66,* 297-333.

SUGGESTED ACTIVITIES

1. Observe an early childhood program for young children. Identify the different stages of play development observed. Describe each in concrete terms.

2. Record the shapes of blocks and accessories that young children use in an actual play situation. Describe what the teacher did to support block play.

3. Interview a parent. Ask what his or her child has learned from play.

4. Develop a directory of sources of early childhood play material and equipment.

5. Survey the local community schools for the different types of outdoor play equipment and play surfaces used in their outdoor areas.

11

CREATIVE ACTIVITIES

OBJECTIVES

After completing this chapter on creative activities, the student will be able to:

1. Define creativity.
2. Describe the developmental characteristics of creativity in children ages three to five.
3. Develop activities that support creativity.
4. Prepare a variety of two- and three-dimensional art activities.
5. Design craft activities for young children.
6. Discuss the purpose of music activities for young children.
7. Prepare a variety of early childhood music experiences.
8. Develop a movement program for young children.
9. Design movement activities for children's physical development.

Young children freely express their feelings and thoughts through many different materials. Often the way young children express themselves is more important than what they express. These expressions help them achieve self-satisfaction and acquire self-confidence, helping them develop positive self-concepts. It is more important that young children have personal forms of self-expression than polished products which display well but which might be based upon an imitation (e.g, drawing the same scene as everyone else in class or memorizing a specific poem). Such products are educationally irrelevant and have no relationship to the child who is producing them. A basic goal of education should be to develop in children the capacity to create, using their own abilities, without having to follow a specific pattern or a particular set of directions and without having to depend on external rewards for satisfaction.

In developing these forms of self-expression, children need to be provided with opportunities to use open-ended materials, such as wood, clay, or paints. As they explore these materials, their creative work must be respected and their talent be encouraged. This chapter will discuss issues related to self-expression and creativity. It will also present ideas for offering developmentally appropriate opportunities for children to express themselves in two-dimensional and three-dimensional art work as well as in music and movement.

SELF-EXPRESSION

Young children express themselves in many ways. They use words to communicate ideas and feelings. They also use pictures, sounds, movement, and a variety of other media. Teachers can stimulate self-expression by challenging children to use their imagination. For instance, children can listen to music with their eyes closed. The teacher can ask them to imagine moods or images and to draw or paint what they have imagined. Or teachers can play background music, then invite the children's brushes to dance as they paint. Children's imaginations can also be stimulated by questions such as: "Can you make this ball of clay look like something you eat?" "What parts of your hand can you use to create something from the forest?" "What materials do you need to create a puppet who could be anyone?" or "How many different ways can you draw a castle?" (Lasky & Mukerji, 1980).

In order to stimulate self-expression, teachers can tell stories, present well-illustrated picture books, show films, filmstrips, and other media, and share songs and games about specific topics related to the children's lives. They can ask children to think of how things would look through the eyes of someone else, such as a bird in the sky or a fish under water. Children can be organized to work in groups with one child beginning a project drawing on a large piece of paper, then every other child being asked to continue the work, in turn, until it is finished. It is often helpful for teachers to collect project ideas, writing them on index cards and storing them in a file box which can be shared with children. Often the children themselves will be the source of these ideas. For those children who cannot read, directions can be provided through pictures.

A climate of self-expression should characterize all early childhood programs. Self-expression is healthy for young children and should be fostered and nurtured. Doing so requires providing more than a supportive climate for children. To develop such a program, it is helpful for you to know something about the development of creativity.

Creativity

In the past several decades educators have realized that creativity is as natural to the average person as it is to the genius (Torrance, 1962). Ligon (1957) has identified age-related developmental characteristics for children's imagination. He also suggested methods to use in promoting young children's imagination. These developmental characteristics for birth to six years of age include the following:

Birth to Age Two. Children begin to develop their imagination during the first year of life. As they develop speech, they begin to ask questions about the names of things and try to reproduce the sounds and rhythms they hear. They are very curious and examine everything they touch, taste, and see.

During this period, creative growth can be stimulated with simple materials, large blocks, dolls, and the like. Teachers can encourage verbal play and should accept the names that children use for their creations. Once the children begin to use words with meaning, songs can be sung about objects rather than the child's being asked to "say dog," or "say daddy."

Ages Two to Four. These children learn about the world through their own direct experiences as well as through verbal and imaginative play. They have short attention spans and shift activities at random. They begin to become independent of others as they do things for themselves. They continue to be curious about their environment as they explore the world in their own unique way and ask questions.

Children of this age can be provided with toys that can be used to represent a variety of things. They can be made aware of the wonders of nature in budding flowers, growing seedlings, baby kittens, and the varied colored leaves of fall. These children need freedom to explore, but they also need to be prepared for new experiences so that they can respond to strangeness.

Ages Four to Six. During this third period children begin to develop planning skills. They anticipate play and work and they enjoy planning and working through their plans. They learn different roles through pretend play and experiment with many of these roles.

Many refer to these early childhood years as the age of creativity. An observation of an early childhood school shows a world graced with young children's imagination and inventiveness. Children build with blocks, paint, shape objects out of clay, or work with other materials. Others will sing melodic fragments or familiar tunes or move their bodies to the rhythm of music they hear. Children of this age will play with language as they play with toys.

Teachers need to encourage creative growth by integrating creative activities into the education program. Activities that support creativity include experiences in art, music and movement.

ART ACTIVITIES

Young children express themselves through art in ways that require no words. They enjoy printing, constructing, modeling, painting, stitching, and weaving. They act selectively, interpreting and expressing their experiences as they think and feel about them. In this process, art serves a dynamic and integrative function.

Just as children go through stages in cognitive development, so they go through stages of artistic development. Victor Lowenfeld and W. Lambert Brittain (1982) describe such stages. The stages that are of concern to early childhood teachers are the scribbling stage (ages two to four) and the preschematic stage (ages four to seven).

Children at the *scribbling* stage have a kinesthetic experience through drawing, feeling their drawings through the movement of their arms and hands. They make longitudinal, then circular, motions. As they mature, their actions become more coordinated. Children experiment with material, first making drawings, then comparing what they have drawn to what they see in the real world to give the drawing a name.

In the *preschematic* stage, children discover the relationship between drawing, thinking, and reality. They start out knowing what they wish to represent, even though their picture may change in the process. They are beginning to create representational drawings and they are developing form concepts.

These stages suggest the kinds of activities that are most appropriate for children at various ages. Teachers need to be aware of children's level of art performance and provide activities to move them to somewhat more mature levels. The following are the kinds of material that children can use in two-dimensional and three-dimensional art projects in an early childhood class.

Two-dimensional Art

Two-dimensional art is art that is created with materials on a flat surface. Among the materials young children can use are paints, chalk, crayons, fingerpaints, and collages.

Tempera Paint.   Tempera paint is an opaque water color. This type of paint allows children to work quickly. Tempera paint is easy to control and details can be painted over because the material dries very quickly. Any type of paper, including cardboard, can be used with tempera paints.

Although tempera paints can be purchased premixed, dry tempera or powder paint is often used in schools since it is less expensive. It can be mixed with water to be used with brushes or fingers. Children can paint in solid areas, outline areas of color, or combine interesting mixtures. Dry paint can also be sprinkled on a moistened paper. Children can also dip a wet brush into the dry powder and then brush the paint on an absorbent paper surface.

Young children should probably be offered only a small range of colors so they will have no problems in selecting the colors and there will be little distraction. Small amounts should be given at first, since young children will mix colors until they are unusable. Primary colors (red, yellow, and blue) should be introduced first; other colors can be made by mixing these.

Young children need only a small range of colors for painting at an easel.

As they mature and children's paintings become more representational, the color range should be widened.

Colored Chalk.   Young children enjoy drawing on wet pieces of paper with various colored chalks. Colors should be limited at first. As children mature and acquire more experience with chalk, they learn to blend colors and explore the use of chalk in combination with other media. For example, they may brush over the chalked areas with paint. Chalk pictures can be sprayed with a fixative or hair spray to keep the pictures from rubbing off.

Crayons.   Wax crayons are available for drawing in almost every early childhood class. They are easy for children to use, require little teacher preparation, and need less cleanup than most art materials. Large half-round or hexagonal crayons are easy for young children to grasp and

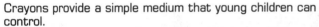

Crayons provide a simple medium that young children can control.

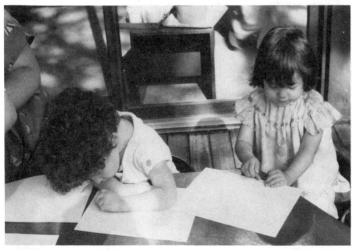

control. Their shape also keeps them from rolling away. A large variety of crayon colors are available, although young children need only a few basic colors. Crayons work best on the rough texture of manila paper, but almost any paper can be used for crayoning.

As children develop greater control over their drawing, teachers might wish to provide marking pens as well. These pens allow children to make pictures with deep vivid color and firm edges. The feel of the marking pen is also different from that of a crayon or a paint bush and offers an interesting alternative to children. Care needs to be taken that the markers selected for young children contain washable and not permanent color.

Fingerpaint. Fingerpaints permit the children to work with color and form more freely than do paint brushes. Glazed paper can be moistened either by dipping it into water or sponging the water on the paper. A tablespoon of fingerpaint can be placed on a dampened paper or spread evenly over the surface. Children can use their fingers, the sides of the hands, their elbows, combs, sticks, or pieces of cardboard to draw an image or design. At the beginning children use one color at a time; as they gain experience and maturity with this kind of painting, colors can be used together. Finger paintings can be dried on a flat surface covered with newsprint. The paintings may have to be pressed flat to avoid curling.

Children do not always need to fingerpaint on paper. Fingerpainting can be done on any smooth washable surface. A print can be made from the surface by pressing a sheet of paper to it if the child wishes to preserve the painting.

You can make fingerpaint by combining tempera paint or powder paint with liquid starch or wheat paste and mixing until smooth. Making fingerpaint in the classroom is fun, but commercially prepared fingerpaint will usually produce a better result.

Collage. A collage is a composition in which a variety of materials are selected and organized to produce interesting patterns, textures, and colors. Colored paper, cloth, feathers, straws, and almost any kind of material that can be pasted on paper can be used in a collage. Materials and textures can be overlaid to add depth. Since the materials are largely flat and are pasted or fastened against a flat background, a collage is still considered two-dimensional art. With collage, young children's primary concern is with form and color.

Colored Sand. Children can paint with ordinary brown or white sand or sawdust that has been colored with tempera paint or food coloring. They draw designs with white glue, which they can squeeze out of a nozzle-topped plastic bottle. Colored sand is then sprinkled over the paper. The sand sets as the glue dries, and the excess sand can be shaken off. This process can be repeated on the same paper with another color of sand.

Murals. Most art projects are independent activities, but children can also be organized into groups to make murals. These can use a variety of materials and a variety of surfaces. Since mural painting uses a larger surface than either painting or drawing, more space will be needed for the project. Children can each be given their own section to work on or they can work on the whole mural together. Children should be helped to plan and work together as a group on a mural.

Other Materials. Children can use other materials to extend the basic use of two-dimensional art materials. Texture can be provided with the addition of materials such as sawdust, sand, flour, salt, liquid soap, and other items with different textures. Each child can take a piece of paper, one color of paint, and a brush and can experiment with mixing these materials in the paint or sprinkling it over the painted paper.

Providing tools other than brushes also adds variety to painting. Rollers, whisk brooms, straws, marbles, dispenser bottles (the squeezable kind), tinfoil pie plates, and cardboard box halves all work well with paint. Children can choose to paint with one or more of these tools.

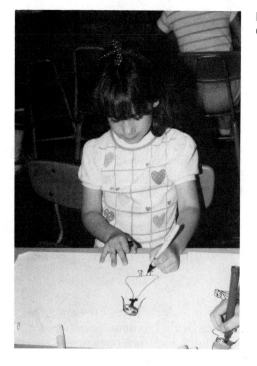

Marking pens allow children to produce vividly colored drawings.

Children can also dip a piece of string into paint and then drag it or drop it on the paper. They can place the string on a paper and fold the paper over, pressing down with one hand while pulling the string with the other. The paper is then opened and allowed to dry. Young children can drip some paint onto a paper and then blow through a straw over the paint to make patterns. If they blow from different points around the paper, the design can be varied.

The teacher can have the children paint with marbles to develop eye–hand coordination while creating pleasing designs. Take a muffin pan, put a different color of paint in each muffin holder, and drop a marble into each. Children can place a sheet of paper at the bottom of a shallow, open-top box. They can then take one of the paint-covered marbles from the muffin pan, drop it in the box, and move the box to allow the marble to roll over the paper. Then a marble of a different color can be substituted and the process repeated.

Three-dimensional Art

Materials that are three-dimensional provide children with the opportunity to produce width, breadth, and depth. Three-dimensional media include blocks, wood, clay, and sand.

Blocks. All early childhood classrooms should have a good set of wooden unit blocks. Unit blocks were discussed in the previous chapter as a play material. They can also be regarded as an art material, since block constructions resemble sculpture. It is helpful to provide accessories that extend the block structures. These can include the following:

Toys are useful accessories. Small cars, rubber or wooden people and animals, pulleys, airplanes, and trucks can all be used.

Colored cubes can be added to blocks, as can parquetry blocks or large dominoes. Assortments of odd-shaped small blocks or sewing thread spools can be put into boxes for use in decorating buildings.

Pebbles, small stones, and little sticks can serve as cargo for trains, boats, and trucks.

Lumber scraps, especially flat pieces for constructing roofs and wide bridges, will enhance block constructions.

Small, familiar signs such as "one way," "school crossing," or "bus stop" can be added to children's construction. Tongue depressors or popsickle sticks stuck in clay or play dough can be used to anchor these signs.

Thin pieces of rubber tubing tacked to a cylinder block can become a simple gas pump.

Excelsior makes good hay for farm animals.

Trees can be drawn on paper, cut out, stapled to a tongue depressor or popsicle stick, and stuck into a piece of clay or play dough to stand.

Pulleys, with ropes and containers, make wonderful elevators.

Dry cell batteries with bell wire and flashlight bulbs are popular accessories.

Magazine pictures of bridges, roads, constructions, or city scenes can be mounted on cardboard and displayed on the walls of the block area.

Children's books can be provided for the class to develop ideas for block construction. For example, if a theme is "city scenes," the books might include the following:

ZION, G., *Dear Garbage Man.* New York: Harper & Row, 1957.
GOODSPEED, J. *Let's Go Watch a Building Going Up.* New York: G. P. Putnam's Sons, 1956.
SCHNEIDER, H., AND N. SCHNEIDER *Let's Look Under the City.* New York: W. R. Scott and Co., 1954.
TRESSELT, A. *Wake Up City.* New York: Lothrop, Lee and Shepard Company, 1957.
ZOLOTOW, C. *The Park Book.* New York: Harper & Brothers, 1944.

Woodworking. Woodworking provides children with visual, motor, and problem-solving experiences. Constructing small objects with scrap wood, tools, glue, nails, and a variety of woodworking accessories helps children learn about tools and develop skills in using them.

A workbench, with a thick wooden top and with wood vises attached, should be provided for the woodwork area. Children learn to work with many types of tools including a hammer, saw, screwdriver, plane, vise, drill, clamp, and rasp. The tools should be of good quality. Hammer heads should be forged, not cast, and all tools should be in good repair, with saws and drills kept sharp to avoid frustration and to maintain safety. Proper care and safety are important considerations in the use of woodworking tools. Tools might be stored on a peg board or on shelves that are marked so that each tool gets placed in its proper position. Having children wear eye protectors while woodworking is a wise precaution.

Wood can easily be combined in different ways with other materials to develop satisfying results and interesting art forms. Since most of the wood used will be scrap material, it is important that teachers select only soft woods that can be worked by the children. Woodworking is especially useful for children who have experience primarily with store-bought toys. Many excellent suggestions regarding woodworking can be found in the NAEYC publication, *Woodworking for Young Children* (Skeen, Garner & Cartwright, 1984).

Clay.   Clay is a plastic art material which allows young children to mold three-dimensional objects. It provides children with an opportunity to create and recreate different shapes and sizes. At first, young children are not particularly concerned with making something with clay. They prefer to manipulate it, sense its feelings, experience its pliability, smell its earth odor, and notice its reaction to patting, pulling, twisting, squeezing, rolling, and shaping.

After they are allowed to spend time manipulating the clay, they can squeeze it into a fat sausage, roll it out into a long coil, or shape it in a variety of ways. They can compare the length and thickness of the coils they make. They can then see how many things they can make with their coils.

When children have had some experience manipulating clay, they can begin making simple pots and bowls. Have them make balls and then use their thumb to make holes in them. By squeezing the hole toward the outside, they can shape a bowl. If they hold the ball of clay in one hand, they can pinch out a pot with the thumb and fingers of their other hand. They can pull up the pots to make them tall, or pull out the pots to make them wide. When they have finished shaping the pots, they can press them gently on the table to make flat bottoms (See Figure 11-1).

Figure 11-1 Making pottery

Clay, like blocks, can be used with accessories. These include paints (to color dry clay objects), rolling pins, tongue depressors, plastic knives and forks for cutting and designing, buttons and yarn, acorns or other vegetables for making prints, and waxed paper or aluminum foil for molding clay objects.

There are several variations of clay which can provide different textures, different feeling, and smell. These include:

Plasticine, an oil-based nonhardening clay. It is stiffer and harder for children to manipulate. It does not dry out, however, and can be used over and over again.

Sawdust and wheat paste mixtures provide a rough texture, but children find they offer a pleasing feeling. This medium cannot be molded too thickly because it will not dry properly. Objects made with this type of clay can be dried more quickly by being placed in a slow oven to evaporate the water.

Papier-mâché is made by tearing newspaper or newsprint into small pieces and adding warm water. Once the paper is completely wet, any excess water is squeezed out and wheat paste is added to make the material into a malleable clay. Once papier-mâché is molded and dried, it will not break. Objects that are molded too thickly may mildew, however. To avoid this, a hole can be made in the bottom of the molded object to allow circulation of air and to hasten drying. While it is drying, the object can be turned from side to side until it becomes hard. Projects using papier-mâché should be simple for young children and should not take so long that children lose interest.

Play dough can be made by mixing two cups of flour with one cup of salt and then adding enough water to make it into a "clay." The children can mold it, or can roll it and cut out forms. Food coloring or tempera paint can also be added. Adding a bit of vegetable oil or glycerine to the recipe will keep the dough from drying too quickly.

Cornstarch clay is made by cooking cornstarch and water until the starch is dissolved. The starch is cooled until it thickens, and then tempera paint can be added for color. When ready, the children can mold it.

Cornstarch clay offers a medium for modeling.

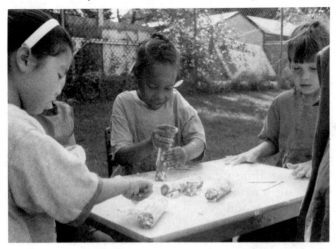

Sand. A sand table kept in class allows for excellent modeling activities. The sand should be sprinkled with water each morning to allow it to become moist enough for the children to mold. Sandboxes can also be used in other ways. Instead of sand in the sandbox, wood shavings, small pebbles, or rice can be substituted. Although these do not lend themselves to modeling, they are fun to have for activities such as measuring and pouring.

Craft Activities

Craft projects have the same characteristics as three-dimensional art projects, though they tend to be more practical. Craft projects can serve different purposes. For example, children can create Christmas ornaments to decorate the tree, or they can create Mother's Day gifts. Although some craft projects require some teacher direction, an emphasis should be placed on the children's personal creativity.

People: Spoons and Clothespins. Help the children to select objects such as corks or short sticks, and add bits of scrap materials to make small people. Only a small amount of scrap material is needed to convert a spoon or clothespin into a little doll. These can be stuck into a wad of play dough or clay so they can stand up straight. Bits of fabric and yarn can be glued on for clothing and hair, and a crayon, felt tip pen, or small pieces of fabric can be used to make the eyes and mouth for the face (see Figure 11-2).

Teachers can help children successfully complete craft projects.

FIGURE 11-2 **People: Spoons and Clothespins**

Walnut Shell Boats. Let children place small balls of clay into unbroken walnut shell halves. A sail the size of a postage stamp can be drawn and cut out of a piece of cloth or soft material, then mounted on a toothpick or dowel and pushed into the clay (see Figure 11-3).

Cupcake Bells. Have the children join three or more cupcake papers with different lengths of strings. The strings can be inserted through the middle of the cups with a tapestry needle. The bells are adjusted so that they fall at different levels (see Figure 11-3). Cupcake papers of assorted colors will be more colorful. Jingle bells can be attached for clappers.

FIGURE 11-3

Walnut Shell Boats

Cupcake Bells

FIGURE 11-4

Easter Basket

**Nut and Candy Dish
for Thanksgiving**

Easter Basket.   Have the children open the top of a half-pint milk or cream container. The container can be cleaned, then painted inside and out with quick-drying paint. The children cut two long ears and a round circle for a nose from construction paper and staple or glue these on the container. Children can add other features, like whiskers made from pipe cleaners or thick strips of paper. A handle made of fancy string can be attached to make this Easter Bunny into a basket (see Figure 11-4).

Thanksgiving Nut and Candy Dish.   Have the children twist two pipe cleaners together and shape them to make a head and long neck. Insert these in the base of an aluminum foil mini-cup, separate them at one end, overlap these ends so that the head remains steady. Shape another aluminum foil mini-cup into a lady's fan to form the turkey's tail and glue or tape it to the outside of the aluminum foil mini-cup, opposite the side where the head and neck were inserted. Adjust it for balance. This can be used as a candy/nut dish, or a table setting (see Figure 11-4).

MUSIC ACTIVITIES

Music is as important a part of young children's experience as it is to adults. Music shows the essence of the human spirit and brings joy to the quality of living. A good music program should be integrated in an early childhood curriculum. Sally Moomaw (1984, p. 7) suggests the following music goals for young children:

- Children should have many opportunities to explore music through their voices, through their body movements, and through making sounds with instruments.
- They should have opportunities to express emotions through music.

- They should gain increased understanding of what makes different kinds of sounds.
- They should have opportunities to expand listening skills.
- They should develop awareness of body image and self-identity.
- They should develop enjoyment of music.
- They should explore their own creativity in music.
- They should have experiences that reflect their developmental needs.
- They should have opportunities for group participation.

Young children become engrossed in music activities. Their eyes sparkle, their body moves, their mind discovers rhythmic language as their mood and feelings surface. Young children enjoy music, singing spontaneously when they work and play, clapping their hands and moving their bodies to the different sounds they hear, and creating their own sounds.

Teachers can provide young children with a wide variety of musical experiences while allowing them to be unique and creative. Music experiences in early childhood education should allow for both individual experimentation and group participation. Just as teachers can have a good art education program without being artists themselves, they can also plan and implement good music experiences with young children even though they are not musicians. Early childhood music experiences should include rhythmic activity, singing, and playing musical instruments.

Rhythmic Activities

Even infants love to experiment with rhythms, playing such rhythmic games as pat-a-cake. Young children sense rhythms and easily match movement with music. Rhythmic activities offer children ways to explore the pulse, relative duration, and flow of sound. They keep time with music when they hear recordings, sing songs, act out nursery rhymes, or chant songs or poems. Exploratory and imitative experiences provide young children with a range of rhythmic movements, both musical and nonmusical.

Children create informal and spontaneous rhythms which teachers can extend by adding a chant, encouraging hand clapping, or playing an instrument. Teachers should not be concerned if the movements do not synchronize with the beat. Repetition helps children to control their rhythmic responses. Young children learn to synchronize movement with the beat as they experience music with instruments, action songs and games, visual devices (e.g., clocks and metronomes), and recordings with predominant rhythmic character.

Children who have better motor coordination can test out rhythmic patterns through clapping and chanting word rhythms of poetry and songs. They can improvise, share ideas, and verbalize their rhythmic knowledge through basic musical terms such as fast–slow, long–short, and even–uneven (MacDonald, 1979). They can further develop their knowledge of low, medium, and high notes by demonstrating these concepts through movement: squatting down for low notes, kneeling or touching their waists for middle notes, or standing on tiptoe and reaching high in the air for high notes. They can also find other ways of illustrating the differences in musical pitch.

Teachers can encourage rhythmic experiences by playing music on a piano, guitar, or record player and having the children walk, run, spin, or slide. Playing different rhythms on an instrument such as a drum or tambourine also helps. Slow beats can be played for walking, fast beats for running, and other beats can call young children to skip, roll over, slide, jump, or stretch. If children move around a circle in the same direction during movement activities, they can avoid colliding as they move. Young children should be given the opportunity to select the music for their movements or asked how the music they hear makes them feel.

Scarves extend children's movement. They can hold scarves above their head and run with them, pretending that they are airplanes, flying, landing, and taking off again. Or they can roll the scarf into their hands, pretending that they are balls, then throw the scarves up high. As the scarves begin to float downward, children can retrieve them and move with them. A scarf can also be a cape. Or if two children hold a scarf up in the air, they can lower it and raise it, pretending they are ocean waves. As children listen to different kinds of music, they can move their arms and the scarf.

Singing with Young Children

As children listen to and learn songs, their listening skills are developed and they gain an emotional release, just as adults do. The use of their own voices provides young children with the concrete experience which is essential to their understanding of what makes a vocal sound. Young children, while singing, test their ideas of soft and loud, high and low, fast and slow.

Young children's first musical experience is often group singing. MacDonald (1979) believes that young children can integrate movement, speech, and singing to develop chants in accord with their melodic configurations, repetitive character, and rhythmic movement. Teachers can employ these chants to describe daily events and as an aid in making transitions from one activity to another as well as to teach the value of singing.

It is not unusual for young children to create spontaneous songs about what they are doing. Young children sing when they work and play, often singing bits and pieces of works that they create to match their rhythmic movements. They may chant, "I'm baking an apple pie," or "See me swing up and down." Teachers can sing the chants and songs children

The autoharp serves as an excellent accompaniment for group singing.

create. They can ask the children to repeat the songs, and the melody and words can be recorded. The children will enjoy seeing their songs written down or hearing them played back on the piano or guitar or replayed on a tape recorder.

Young children usually prefer songs with a good melody, easy words, and actions. Children who do not know the song well will repeat whatever they know over and over again. Their singing may be off pitch or loud and it may have more gusto than skill. Any enthusiastic and repetitive music experience can be an enriching one.

Singing demands that words and vocal pitch be combined. Teachers should present songs that are developmentally appropriate for young children, starting with songs that have a limited melodic range, then gradually introduce songs with greater tonal variety. When young children are ready, teachers can teach them concepts about melody through singing. Appropriate teaching strategies include physical motions according to the direction of a song's melody, and visual cues composed of dashes or musical notes (which do not have to be presented on the musical staff) showing high–low, same, and up–down tones. Visual/tactile music experiences can include song bells, piano keyboard, or step bells. The children's knowledge of pitch can be used as they sing familiar songs and demonstrate the melodic flow.

The variety of cultures and backgrounds of children in our society require that a variety of musical experiences be included. Some appropriate songs can be found in a music textbook. The children themselves are often the best sources in selecting the songs. There are also a variety of songbooks which teachers can use as resources. Bernard Spodek (1985) suggests the following songbooks to use with young children:

DIETZ, B. W, AND T. C. PARKS, *Folk Songs of China, Japan, and Korea.* New York: John Day, 1964.

FOWKE, E., *Sally Go Round the Sun.* Garden City, NY: Doubleday, 1969.

GLAZER, T., *Eye Winker Tom Tinker Chin Chopper: Fifty Musical Fingerplays.* Garden City, NY: Doubleday, 1973.

JENKINS, E., *The Ella Jenkins Song Book for Children.* New York: Oak Publications, 1969.

LANDECK, B., *Songs to Grow On.* New York: William Morrow, 1950.

LANDECK, B., *More Songs to Grow On.* New York: William Morrow, 1954.

LANGSTAFF, N., AND J. LANGSTAFF *Jim Along, Josie.* New York: Harcourt Brace Jovanovich, 1970.

SEEGER, R. C., *American Folk Songs for Children.* Garden City, NY: Doubleday, 1948.

SEEGER, R. C., *Animal Folk Songs for Children.* Garden City, NY: Doubleday, 1950.

SENDAK, M., *Maurice Sendak's Really Rosie: Starring the Nutshell Kids.* New York: Harper & Row, 1975.

WINN, M., *The Fireside Book of Children's Songs.* New York: Simon & Schuster, 1966.

WINN, M., *What Shall We Do and Allee Galloo!* New York: Harper & Row, 1970.

New songs should be introduced in a simple and easy way. Teachers should introduce the songs themselves. The children may not respond the first or second time the songs are presented. It takes a while for young children to understand and remember the words, and it takes even longer to get a clear idea of the melody. Listening capacity and vocal control are acquired more slowly by some children than others, although most children will acquire these skills to some degree if they are exposed to music and no one pressures them. Teachers need to encourage young children to sing, even if they are not singing the right tune. Drill on either words or music should be avoided with preschool children. Teachers should sing a song straight through, helping the children understand its meaning and allowing young children to catch what they can, even if it is only the last note.

Using Musical Instruments

Musical instruments should be provided in early childhood classes for children to play both independently and in a group. While some of these musical instruments can be made by teachers or children, commercial instruments should also be available since most homemade instruments do not have fine tone quality. Drums, tambourines, gourds and maracas, metal triangles, a variety of bells (for example, jingle bells, dainty table bells, cowbells), a xylophone, and cymbals should be included.

Children need to explore the instruments. They can use them with songs, chants, and records, exploring melodic directions (such as up, down, same), tempo (such as fast, slow, getting faster, getting slower), and rhythmic patterns, and producing original tunes and rhythm sounds.

Young children should experiment with both pitched and unpitched instruments. Each type of instrument makes a different sound, and by playing even an unpitched instrument differently (e.g., hard or soft, fast or slow), they can produce a different sound. They also learn that the size of an instrument affects the sound it makes: large drums make a lower tone than little drums, and the long bars on the xylophone make a lower tone than the short bars.

Experiences with instruments develop young children's understandings of sounds and music. Instruments can also help children express their feelings and promote their creativity. In addition, they improve children's eye–hand coordination and fine motor skills.

Sally Moomaw (1984) identifies three different types of instruments to be used with young children: rhythm instruments, melody instruments, and accompanying instruments (See Table 11-1).

> *Rhythm instruments* are those that are struck or scraped to create non-pitched sounds. Rhythm instruments for young children are those usually found in the percussion section of an orchestra. They include tone blocks or wood blocks, rhythm sticks, claves, guiros, triangles, and cymbals.

For the youngest children it is best to experiment with unpitched musical instruments.

TABLE 11-1   Types of Instruments and Examples of Each

RHYTHM INSTRUMENTS	MELODY INSTRUMENTS	ACCOMPANYING INSTRUMENTS
tone blocks or wood blocks	xylophones	autoharps
rhythm sticks	melody bells	guitars
claves	zithers	drums
triangles	glockenspiels	pianos
cymbals		
finger cymbals		
maracas		
castanets		
tambourines		
drums		
jingle bells		
jingle sticks		
cowbells		
sand blocks		

Melody instruments are those that make sounds with certain pitches to create tunes or melodies. These include xylophones, melody bells, and zithers.

Accompanying instruments produce tones or chords, such as do the piano, autoharp, and guitar. Teachers usually play these instruments. While the piano is an excellent accompanying instrument, it requires considerable training for someone to accompany songs.

There are many homemade instruments that can be made by the teacher. Children can make some instruments as well. Kathryn Bayless and Marjorie Ramsey (1978) have provided suggestions for making several instruments, such as coconut shell clappers, rhythm blocks, and hand shakers (see Figure 11-5).

FIGURE 11-5   Homemade Instruments

Rhythm Blocks

Coconut Shell Clappers

Hand Shaker

For *coconut shell clappers,* take a coconut that has the ends rounded to fit in the children's hands. Tap a hole in it and let it dry for several months so that the substance inside shrinks away from the sides. Place the coconut in a vise and saw through the middle, then lift out the substance inside the coconut with a knife. Children can take the shells and clap them together to make a hollow sound similar to horses' hooves.

To make *rhythm blocks,* match two scraps of wood, one inch or less thick, which are similar in shape, size, thickness, and length. Sand the blocks until they are smooth. A design can be painted on them. Attach drawer handles or empty thread spools to be used as holders. Different sets of rhythm blocks of different sizes, shapes, thickness, and length will make different sounds when struck together.

To make a *hand shaker,* carve a handle at one end of a wooden board approximately 1 inch wide, 8 inches long, and ¼ inch thick. It should now look like a paddle. Straighten out four soft drink bottle caps and punch a hole in the middle of each. Place a ½-inch washer between two of these and nail them to the wood on the opposite end of the handle. Nail another set of bottle caps and washer further back.

A *drum* can be made out of a coffee can with a plastic cover. A more authentic drum can be made by removing both sides of the can and stretching rubber or animal hide across the openings at each end. A *gong* can be made by suspending a 50-gallon steel drum from ropes. A garden hose *flute* can be made out of a foot-long piece of garden hose corked at one end, with holes bored down one side. A *washtub bass* can be created out of a galvanized washtub, a broom handle, and a 5-foot piece of heavy string or cord. The tub is placed upside down on the floor. One end of a cord is attached to a screw eye in the end of the broom handle and the other to an eye-bolt set in the center of the tub. The other end of the broom handle is notched and placed on the tub's edge. The cord is tightened and loosened by rocking back with the broom handle. The cord can be plucked like a bass fiddle.

Instruments allow young children to experiment with sounds, join in a rhythm band, observe older children playing instruments, create original tunes, and play spontaneously. Teachers must be careful that they do not pressure young children to participate or to produce rigid patterned musical activities. Teachers of young children should encourage their students to explore and discover musical instruments.

MOVEMENT EDUCATION

Adults enjoy moving in certain ways as well as watching the movement of others. For example, they delight in seeing a person score a point at tennis, make a basket, or win a track race. Precision and grace are qualities that can be found in activities such as dancing, skating, diving, and gymnastics.

Movement education teaches young children physical skills related to moving. Children should learn and acquire the necessary understanding and self-confidence at their own rate. Carol Copple, Irving Sigel, and Ruth Saunders (1979) note three factors relating to the children's early movement development: children respond to music, emotion, or mood. They use these factors to provide an understanding of the representational possibilities of movement. Movement education also emphasizes an appreciation of individual differences, task persistence, self-motivation, self-esteem, and enjoyment.

A movement education program should reflect differences in children's development. Characteristics of children's physical development and their program needs and implications are noted in Table 11-2.

TABLE 11-2 Characteristics, Interests, and Needs Important in Program Planning

PRESCHOOL (NURSERY SCHOOL)

Characteristics	*Program Needs and Implications*
Cognitive Domain	
Is unable to sit still for more than a brief period.	Utilize movement experiences for learning activities.
Constantly explores environment.	Allow for creative effort, exploratory opportunity.
Shows little differentiation of fantasy from reality.	Offer activities that include elements of reality and fantasy so that they can learn to identify both.
Uses numbers without understanding concept of quantity.	Play active games that require simple counting.
Can make a choice between two alternatives.	Provide opportunities for children to make appropriate decisions.
Is capable of following directions if not more than two ideas are given.	Keep directions simple and straightforward, with one or two points of emphasis.
Begins to use words to express feelings.	Emphasize dramatic play.
Affective domain	
Has fear of heights, of falling.	Provide successful experiences in climbing and jumping off boxes (moderate height).
Can have strong fear of failure.	Allow to progress at own rate, but encourage experimentation.
Likes rhythmic activities.	Gross motor activities to rhythm. Simple rhythms. Marching. Action songs.
Is self-conscious.	Avoid sarcasm, ridicule, laughing at children. Seek emotional satisfaction.
May be shy.	Bring out through participation and acceptance. Encourage to "show".
Has great desire to imitate.	Offer opportunities to imitate animals, machines, professional personnel, and parental figures.
Needs constant encouragement.	Place emphasis on effort rather than reward for quality performance only.

TABLE 11-2 continued

Likes to play individually or in small groups of two or three.	Allow time for individual play and aid children in learning to play with others.
Shows great imagination.	Offer play opportunities where imagination is valued. New ways of playing games or creating make-believe characters that move are excellent.

Psychomotor Domain

Is awkward; shows inefficient movement	Keep activity within the maturity level.
Binocular vision is slowly developing.	Provide hand-eye, object-handling experiences.
May walk well, but have difficulty with other locomotor skills.	Provide wide variety of motor challenges. Stress hopping, skipping, galloping. etc.
Climbing skills need development.	Offer experiences of climbing over low, inclined planks, packing boxes, on jungle gyms, stairs.
Balance skills are developing.	Offer activities involving simple balancing.
Begins to develop throwing patterns.	Allow for hand-eye experiences with appropriate balls, beanbags, etc.
Is learning to use the hands.	Offer experiences of handling and guiding objects such as scooters, little cars, building blocks, etc.
May have trouble with eye control.	Provide low-level hand-eye experiences.
Toilet routines may need control.	Get children to accept this responsibility.
Physical growth slows down comparatively.	As physical growth slows, the child's readiness to learn motor skills increases. Allow many opportunities for the child to practice gross and fine motor skills.
Starts to develop agility in movement.	Offer hurdles to jump and mini-obstacle courses as challenges. Offer practice in starting, stopping, dodging, and changing direction. Offer game activities that require few rules and offer activity for all children.
Catching skills begin to mature.	Practice catching skills with objects that move slowly (balloons, beachballs) and will not cause fear.
Many motor learning patterns become ingrained.	Show children the proper way to perform various skills

KINDERGARTEN AND FIRST GRADE

Characteristics	*Program Needs and Implications*
Cognitive Domain	
Has short attention span.	Change activity often. Offer short explanations.
Is interested in what his body can do. Is curious.	Offer movement experiences. Give attention to basic movement.

TABLE 11-2 continued

Wants to know. Asks "why" often about movements.	Explain reasons for various activities and movements.
Expresses individual views and ideas.	Allow children time to do their own thing. Expect problems when children are lined up and asked to perform the same task.
Begins to understand the idea of teamwork.	Allow some opportunity for situations that require group cooperation. Discuss the importance of such.
Sense of humor is expanding.	Insert some humor into the teaching process.
Is highly creative.	Allow opportunity for students to try new and different ways of performing activities. Sharing ideas with friends will encourage them to create.
Affective Domain	Offer same activities for both boys and girls.
Shows no sex differences regarding interests	
Is sensitive and individualistic. The "I" concept is very important. Accepts defeat poorly.	Encourage taking turns; sharing with others; and winning, losing, or being caught gracefully.
Likes small group activity.	Use entire class grouping sparingly. Break into small groups.
Is sensitive to feelings of adults. Likes to please teacher.	Offer needed praise and encouragement.
Can be reckless.	Stress sane approaches.
Enjoys rough-and-tumble activity.	Include rolling, dropping to the floor, etc., in both introductory and program activities. Stress simple stunts and tumbling.
Seeks personal attention.	Recognize children through both verbal and nonverbal means. See that all have a chance to be the center of attention.
Loves to climb and explore play environments.	Provide play materials, games, and apparatus for strengthening large muscles. examples are climbing towers, wagons, tricycles, jump ropes, mini-obstacle courses, and turning bars, to name only a few.
Psychomotor Domain	Offer vigorous games and stunts; games with individual roles—hunting, dramatic activities, story plays; few team games or relays.
Is noisy, constantly active, egocentric, exhibitionist. Is imitative and imaginative. Wants attention.	
Large muscles are more developed; game skills are not developed.	Stress basic movement and fundamental skills of throwing, catching, bouncing balls.
Is naturally rhythmical.	Provide music and rhythm with skills: creative rhythms, folk dances, singing games.

TABLE 11-2 continued

May become suddenly tired, but soon recovers.	Use activities of brief duration. Provide short rest periods or include moderately vigorous activities.
Eye-hand coordination is developing.	Offer opportunity to handle objects such as balls, beanbags, hoops, etc.
Perceptual-motor areas are important.	Offer practice in balance, unilateral, bilateral, and cross-lateral movements.
Pelvic tilt can be pronounced.	Give attention to posture problems. Provide abdominal strengthening activities

Robert P. Pangrazi & Victor P. Dauer, *Movement in Early Childhood and Primary Education* (Minneapolis: Burgess Publishing Co., 1981), pp. 13-15.

Creative Movement

Movement serves both a communicative and aesthetic function. Though the movement components are the same in both, communication is the major function in pantomime, while the aesthetic quality of the movement is more important in dance.

Movement education, based on an understanding of various movement elements developed by Rudolph Laban (1971), is a relatively new approach to learning. The parts of the body vary in their relationship to each other and to objects (near, far; on, around, under). The number and variation of actions (such as stepping, balancing, crawling) are infinite. Movement in space occurs in several directions, at different levels along pathways of certain kinds (such as straight, curved, zigzag), and in a wide range of movement from small to large. Speed and rhythm also affect movement. Their force fluctuates in a continuum from strong to weak and in quality from sudden to sustained, while the flow varies in its degree of freedom. Children experience, experiment, observe, discover, analyze, and formulate ideas as they acquire knowledge and form concepts. Ideas are classified and analyzed to associate information into meaningful concepts. Emphasis is placed on the children's intellectual development and the wide range of skill and maturity which is found among the individuals in any class.

Laban has proposed the use of movement exploration to make children aware of the diverse capacity in the movement of the body rather than dictating to children specific directions in movement. Open-ended problems with wide alternative solutions requiring no right or wrong answers are offered. Follow-up questions encouraging children to explore additional alternatives should also be provided. Laban urges that an understanding of the movement education structure and its process lay the foundation for physical education. He employs the media of games, gymnastics, and dance to promote the child's physical and emotional development through movement concepts such as body awareness, space, quality of movement, and relationships.

Movement Activities for Physical Development

Robert P. Pangrazi and Victor P. Dauer (1981) suggest that movement activities at the early childhood level should include (1) movement experiences and body mechanics, which are locomotor, nonlocomotor, and manipulative; (2) rhythmics; (3) apparatus; (4) stunts and tumbling; (5) simple games; and (6) sports' skills and activities. These activities can provide a balance in games, gymnastics, and dance, although less emphasis should be placed on games.

Games. The main purpose of early childhood games is personal challenge; in games with older children, one challenges an opponent. Competition is an element of all games, but young children enjoy it only when they have mastered the required skills. The skills developed in the early years that are fundamental to games include visual perception (e.g., spatial body awareness, spatial relations, form constancy, figure/ground), auditory discrimination (e.g., sound localization, rhythm discrimination, figure/ground selection), tactile-touch, kinesthetics, sensory integration (e.g., balance, exploration, eye–hand coordination), strength, endurance, flexibility, and motor ability (e.g., balance, power, coordination, speed, agility, rhythm). The movements related to these skills include balancing, bouncing, catching, hopping, jumping, pushing, running, tagging, twisting, and many others (Eason and Smith, 1976). Games can provide opportunities for children to practice these skills. Teachers can offer children individual assistance as well.

Gymnastics. Gymnastics helps children control their bodies so they can move skillfully, safely, and aesthetically. Gymnastic activities should be related to children's developmental level. The activities should be individualized, with tasks provided to each child that are challenging but not frustrating.

Coordinating Movement Activities. Movement activities should include a balance of games, gymnastics, and dance. Themes can be used that touch on specific concepts and skills. The theme of flying, for example, can incorporate a series of activities to emphasize jumping and landing. They explore basic jumps, such as jumping from one foot to another, on one foot to the same foot, and so on. Using a theme ensures that relationships are clarified and similarities and differences are accentuated (Spodek, Saracho, & Lee, 1984).

The activities for a movement theme can evolve around an obstacle course, a structured arrangement which includes a series of obstacles which are used to develop all the movement attributes. The children must crawl under them, jump over them, climb on them or walk around obstacles. Objects are spaced so that several children can work on them separately but simultaneously. In the obstacle course illustrated in Figure 11-6, a child may move in different ways between the tractor tires on the ground—jump on one foot, jump on two feet, or turn in the air while jumping; another child may balance in the balance walk; still another child may climb or run through the ladder. The obstacle course can be used individually or with a group. It allows children to use the equipment without waiting for or interfering with each other. Children enjoy going over, under, and through the objects.

Movement activities can be coordinated with other areas of the curriculum. In teaching children to follow directions, the teacher can offer instructions for children to perform as follows:

> Clap walk, walk clap
> Clap step, step clap
> Give a little twist
> Then clap, clap, clap.

Teachers and children can change the words and make up songs similar to this with different actions. This activity can be extended, with the instructions becoming more complicated. Young children can be given the following directions:

> Clap, clap your hands
> Pat your knees
> Rub your arms
> Touch your nose
> Crawl around
> Walk on your knees
> Jump up and down
> Jiggle all over
> Turn around
> Jump around
> Jump up and down
> Rub your legs
> Wash your hair
> Jump up and down (again)
> Sit back down

The teacher can also teach counting, asking the children to join her or him in a small circle. They all sit down. Children are asked to count slowly to ten and to clap their hands as they say each number. When they

FIGURE 11-6 Obstacle Course

reach number ten, they get up, jump high into the air, shout their name, and immediately come back to their beginning sitting position with the palms of their hands flat on the floor. This activity can be varied by shouting the name, saying it in a whisper, or saying different words.

Through movement activities children can develop increased skills and control of their muscles. Their bodies become a medium for creative expression as the children learn to use the various parts of their bodies competently. Self-concept becomes more positive as children feel they can do more with their own selves.

Movement activities should be individualized so that children can learn without being pressured. Children should work on their own capabilities at their own rate, disregarding any specified standards. A practical method for individualizing instruction is using learning centers, which can be set up in a gymnasium, a playground, an all-purpose room, or a regular classroom. Figure 11-7 provides an example of three learning centers for skills and activities. An activity sign at each center displays designated skills and tasks. Each child selects an area and takes a skill sheet; since children this age are usually unable to read, the sheets can have pictures instead of words. Students can move to other areas before mastering all levels of a particular skill.

Several learning alternatives should be provided for each skill to be taught, with the activities within each area varying in complexity.

FIGURE 11-7   Learning Centers

Skill: Space Relation

Mats *(for forward and backward roll)*
Tumbling Table
Tire Run
Obstacle Course

Skill: Eye-hand Coordination

Ball on a cone with a bat
(Ball is hit with the bat)
Jacks with ball
Frisbee
Kickballs
Footballs

Skill: Balance

Mats
Hopping on one foot
Tumbling Table
Short stilts

Children can work on the skill they need to develop, following the directions given on the sheet. For example, instructions on developing a skill may consist of a series of pictures illustrating how a specific skill may be mastered and the types of activities that develop these skills.

Learning centers make it easier for the teacher to work with the children on a one-to-one basis without taking time from the class or embarassing them. Elsie C. Burton (1977) identified several steps to implement learning centers: (1) the teacher presents to the children the different types of learning experiences that are available; (2) she or he provides the children with the opportunity to select the skill(s) they wish to pursue; (3) the teacher and the children discuss the process and the performance objectives for each child; (4) the teacher recommends instructions on how the task can be completed, where equipment and supplies are located, and the time limit; and (5) the teacher offers instructions and enrichment materials. Instructional materials and resources help children work toward their own goals independently, with a partner, or in a small group.

Learning centers must be varied to propose a wide range of options. However, learning centers depend on facilities, equipment, instructional materials, and, most important, the teacher's philosophy concerning the students' responsibility and decision making.

SUMMARY

Young children can learn to express themselves through a variety of media. Art, music, and movement all offer opportunities for children to use their imaginations. As they develop skills in each area, the children can become more creative in their productions.

Young children express themselves in a variety of ways. Early childhood programs should support this expression using art, music and movement as forms of expression. A balance of skill development and opportunity for creative expression should characterize these program activities.

REFERENCES

BAYLESS, K. M., AND M. E. RAMSEY (1978). *Music: A way of life for the young child.* Saint Louis: C. V. Mosby.

BURTON, E. C. (1977). *The new physical education for elementary school children.* Boston: Houghton Mifflin.

COPPLE, C., I. SIGEL, AND R. SAUNDERS (1979). *Educating the young thinker.* New York: Van Nostrand.

EASON, R. L., AND T. L. SMITH (1976). A perceptual motor program model for learning-disabled children. *Physical Education Research Journal,* **33**(1), 4.

LABAN, R. (1971). *The mastery of movement.* London: Macdonald and Evans.

LASKY, L., AND R. MUKERJI (1980). *Art: Basic for young children.* Washington, DC: National Association for the Education of Young Children.

LIGON, E. M. (1957). *The growth and development of Christian personality.* Schenectady, NY: The Union College Character Research Project.

LOWENFELD, V., AND W. L. BRITTAIN (1982). *Creative and mental growth* (4th ed.). New York: Macmillan.

MACDONALD, D. T. (1979). *Music in our lives: The early years.* Washington, DC: National Association for the Education of Young Children.

MOOMAW, S. (1984). *Discovering music in early childhood.* Boston: Allyn & Bacon.

PANGRAZI, R. P., AND V. P. DAUER (1981). *Movement in early childhood and primary education.* Minneapolis: Burgess Publishing Co.

SKEEN, P., A. P. GARNER, AND S. CARTWRIGHT (1984). *Woodworking for young children.* Washington, DC: National Association for the Education of Young Children.

SPODEK, B. (1985). *Teaching in the early years* (3rd ed.). Englewood Cliffs, NJ: Prentice-Hall.

SPODEK, B., O. N. SARACHO, AND R. C. LEE (1984). *Mainstreaming young children.* Belmont, CA: Wadsworth Publishing Company.

TORRANCE, E. P. (1962). *Guiding creative talent.* Englewood Cliffs, NJ: Prentice-Hall.

SUGGESTED ACTIVITIES

1. Visit an early childhood school that uses commercially made musical instruments. After practicing on the available instruments, design and implement a musical activity with a group of four children.

2. Create a number of homemade instruments with some of your classmates. Use them to accompany a song.

3. Begin a file of songs that are appropriate for young children.

4. Collect drawings of different age groups and place them in sequence related to the children's ages. Compare the developmental differences reflected in the drawings.

5. Collect a box of scrap materials for use in art activities with young children.

6. Begin a file of art activities for young children.

7. Design and implement an art center for children to use during activity time. Include a wide variety of materials.

8. Observe a young child for at least half an hour during a movement activity. Record the different kinds of movements observed.

9. Go through current catalogs and make up a supply and equipment order for an art program for a particular class. In your order include quantity, quality, colors, and costs.

12

LANGUAGE
AND LITERACY

OBJECTIVES

After completing this chapter on language and literacy, the student will be able to:

1. Identify the components of communication skills in an early childhood language arts program.
2. Describe the goals of a language arts program in early childhood education.
3. Organize expressive language experiences relating to children's literature, poetry, storytelling, puppetry, and creative dramatics.
4. Identify the goals for a literature program in early childhood education.
5. List the criteria for selecting young children's books.
6. Describe several ways to present poetry in the early childhood classroom.
7. Discuss the value of storytelling, puppetry, and creative dramatics.
8. Describe how to prepare to tell a story.
9. Describe the development of young children's written language.

Children differ in their language development. Some start to talk early, others start late; some are highly verbal, others are quiet. Some of these differences are developmental, others are children's reactions to their environments. Research shows that an individual's language development is related to sex, class, position in family, and ethnic group membership.

By the time children enter the preschool, they have learned a language at home. Once in school the children are ready for their language to be extended and enriched. Both teacher and other classmates make language demands to which they must adapt. This chapter will present aspects of the language arts program, including children's literature, poetry, storytelling, puppetry, and creative dramatics. It will also deal with the beginnings of reading and writing.

LANGUAGE ARTS PROGRAMS FOR YOUNG CHILDREN

Language is an important communication tool enabling individuals to develop new means of speaking with, for, and to others about any subject or event. At four or five, young children have mastered the basic grammar of their language and a great deal of vocabulary. They have learned the four rule systems of their language: pronouncing and combining sounds (phonology), constructing grammatical sentences (syntactics), conveying a wide range of meanings as they join words (semantics), and varying speech patterns based on the social interaction and context (pragmatics) (Honig, 1982).

There are two kinds of communication skills in an early childhood language arts program: *receptive* and *expressive* language skills. Listening and reading are used to *receive* communications, while speaking and writing are used to *express* communications. All four of these components—listening, reading, speaking, and writing—have equal importance in the language arts program. A high-quality language arts program for young children needs to provide many opportunities for children to hear, read, speak, and write the language in a flexible way, though reading and writing are usually not part of early childhood programs.

Goals of a Language Arts Program

A language arts program for young children needs to have multiple goals. Spodek, Saracho, and Lee (1984) suggest the following general goals:

1. *Developing basic oral language skills.* Learning to speak in sentences, express ideas in logical sequence, enunciate clearly, and pronounce words correctly.
2. *Developing listening skills.* Learning to attend, increase attention span, and understand what is said.

3. *Building a meaningful vocabulary.* Developing a vocabulary to use in a variety of contexts.
4. *Developing writing skills.* Learning to express thoughts in writing as in speech. (p. 204)

To achieve these goals, the early childhood language arts program needs to integrate the receptive activities of listening and reading and the expressive activities of speaking and writing. For young children, activities are used to develop *preliminary* learnings in the written communication skills, with actual reading and writing skills developed later. Thus, the focus is on oral language experiences. In time, young children will recognize the relationship between the spoken and the written language. They will learn to receive ideas and impressions as they read, just as they learned to listen; they will learn to express ideas, impressions, and feelings as they write, just as they learned to speak. At the preschool level we must offer a wide range of receptive and expressive language experiences with children's literature, poetry, storytelling, puppetry, and creative dramatics.

Children's Literature

Experiences in literature consist of two elements: the book and the reader. Maurice Sendak's (1963) *Where the Wild Things Are* is considered a great book for children. However, before children are capable of experiencing it as literature, they need to understand fantasy, to understand the complexity of the plot (story within a story), and to be able to respond to its emotional appeal through pictures and words. Children need to be able to consider the purpose of the book's words and pictures. They also need to understand how symbols create an aesthetic experience and guide the reader to understand the patterns, relationships, and feelings which are all part of the experience. The aesthetic experience in a book can be seen as a meaningful reconstruction of past experiences, an extension of experiences, or a development of a new experience (Huck, 1979).

Children's literature presents words and illustrations to help the reader/listener recognize an order of events, a unity of action, a balance of occurrences, or a new frame of reference for situations. Children can learn new things that they integrate with what is already known. Literature allows both an intellectual and an emotional response. The reader/listener learns to understand the characters, settings, and problems. He or she can enjoy beauty, wonder, and humor of the story or experience the despair of sorrow, injustice, and ugliness; can have vicarious experiences in other places, times, and lifestyles; can identify with others. The reader/listener can observe nature from a different perspective; can experience risks, mystery, and suffering; can enjoy a sense of achievement or a sense of belonging. Literature allows readers the opportunity to dream, to think, and to ask questions about themselves (Huck, 1979).

Literature experiences for young children should be enjoyable. At the same time they need to be planned in order to promote the children's appreciation of language and literature. Paul M. Williamson (1981) suggests five goals for a literature program in early childhood education:

1. *Many types of literature must be recognized, enjoyed, and valued.* Young children need to know literature well and to enjoy it to the point where they feel it "belongs" to them. Learning to value literature helps them learn to value the worth of learning to read.
2. *A strong sense of story must be developed.* Children need to learn the concept of a story. The younger children will probably be aware of it only when the same story is presented to them repeatedly, even if in a different way, and will remember the sequence of events.
3. *Literature must be actively and appropriately responded to in different ways.* Young children can learn to acquire meaning from literature. This process can be enriched through dramatization, art projects, field trips, cooking, performance, puppetry, and other expressive experiences.
4. *The magic and power of words must be recognized and appreciated.* Words have power, but individuals transmit the power over words. Young children need to be provided with many experiences using words, to develop their language and to help them understand how meaning is conveyed through artful use of language.
5. *Literature must provide identification with characters.* Young children can identify their own lives and experiences and relate them to those of characters in the literature. Many excellent books focus on issues that are important to young children.

The first step in a literature program is to help children enjoy books. Experiences can be provided both before and after reading a book to intensify the children's participation and perception. These literature experiences can be structured to develop understandings and appreciations while maintaining the sense of spontaneity, pleasure, and exuberance. Literature can be shared to enrich the lives of both children and teachers (Williamson, 1981).

Good literature experiences require a careful selection of books. Leland B. Jacobs (1955) developed a set of criteria for selecting young children's books:

1. The story should have a fresh, well-paced plot.
2. It must have unique individuality.
3. It should contain plausible, direct conversation.
4. It must have well-delineated characters.
5. It must have an authentic outcome. (p. 194)

In addition, books must possess a main plot, an arousing climax, and a predictable outcome. Young children also prefer books that have action, conflict, heroic characters, and tongue-teasing language. Illustrations should be synchronized with the text.

Teachers should carefully select books to read to children.

A number of categories of books can be used with young children. A small collection of books from the following categories can provide a balanced literature program (Coody, 1983):

Mother Goose. Mother Goose stories have a strong appeal for the young. Young children find their humanism, nonsense, high adventure, and rhythmic language fascinating. These old folk rhymes are among the best available literature. Several editions of Mother Goose as well as puzzles, art prints, pillows, figurines, filmstrips, and other materials can be provided in the early childhood classroom. Examples of Mother Goose books are:

> *Book of Nursery and Mother Goose Rhymes* compiled and illustrated by Marguerite de Angeli, Garden City, New York: Doubleday and Company, Inc., 1952. This book has a good collection of art work with its soft, delicate black and white drawings interfused with mellow pastel paintings. It has 376 of the most popular rhymes.

> *The Real Mother Goose* illustrated by Blanche Fisher Wright with an introduction by May Hill Arbuthnot, Chicago: Rand McNally and Company, 1944. This edition has been continuously popular with young children for over forty years. It includes an interesting description of the origins of Mother Goose.

Alphabet Books. Children cherish ABC books as they learn the letters and sounds of the alphabet. Photographs, realistic paintings, or semi-abstract art are used to illustrate ABC books. In good alphabet books, meaningful objects are used to represent each letter of the alphabet, not more than two objects are used on each page to introduce each letter, and the letters are projected conspicuously. Examples of ABC books are:

The ABC Bunny by Wanda Gag, New York: Coward-McCann, Inc., 1933. Soft black and white drawings illustrate a small bunny's adventures. Each alphabet letter is printed in bright red.

Peter Piper's Alphabet illustrated by Marcia Brown. New York: Charles Scribner's and Sons, 1959. The sounds of the alphabet are represented through famous old tongue-twisting nonsense rhymes. The pictures are loaded with fun and silliness.

Counting Books. Counting books present single mathematical concepts and their symbols, introducing the language of mathematics in an entertaining way. These books should be chosen much like ABC and other books. Two important criteria are good-quality art and each numeral being located on its own page. Shapes and forms presenting the number must be clearly and simply balanced and spaced on the page. Examples of counting books are:

My First Counting Book written by Lilian Moore and illustrated by Garth Williams. New York: Simon and Schuster, 1956. A sturdy book with each number (one to ten) introduced using a similar plant or animal. A complete review is provided at the end of the book.

The Very Hungry Caterpillar written by Eric Carle. Cleveland: Collins, William and World Publishing Company, Inc., 1972. This colorful book can be used to teach numbers, the days of the week, and the caterpillar's life cycle. A hungry caterpillar eats through an amazing group of foods throughout the book. The holes allow young children to follow the caterpillar's life cycle from egg to butterfly.

Concept Books. Concept books help young children learn specific concepts, such as size, shape, speed, and weight, which are introduced in graphic and artistic form. Examples of concept books are:

Big Ones, Little Ones by Tana Hoban. New York: William Morrow and Company, 1976. This book of black and white photographs depicts large and small zoo animals and domestic animals.

Symbols written and illustrated by Rolf Myller. New York: Atheneum, 1978. This colorful and attractive book shows that a symbol represents something and that symbols communicate a concept. It also shows young children that symbols are everywhere and are an essential component in everyone's life.

Machines Personified. Machines and other inanimate objects are often personified and given human qualities in young children's books. The purpose of these stories is usually to inspire: The plot is constructed around some staggering, overwhelming problem which a machine or inanimate object must overcome. The ending is always successful and happy, providing the reader or listener with a feeling of satisfaction. Examples of books in which machines or inanimate objects are personified are:

> *The Little Engine That Could* by Watty Piper. New York: Platt and Munk Publishers, 1955. A little engine attempts to achieve a difficult task while repeating the phrase, "I think I can, I think I can." This book tells young children they can overcome big obstacles.

> *Mike Mulligan and His Steam Shovel* written and illustrated by Virginia Lee Burton. Boston: Houghton Mifflin Company, 1939. Mary Anne, a steam shovel with personality, digs her way into a deep hole and cannot get out. The story ends in a humorous and satisfying way.

Animal Stories.   Young children like stories in which animals show human qualities. They work, play, laugh, cry, make silly mistakes, and perform kind and wise acts. These stories can be told, read aloud, and dramatized. Examples of books on animal stories are:

> *Curious George* by Hans A. Rey. Boston: Houghton Mifflin Company, 1941. A curious little monkey explores and examines his environment. When his curiosity gets him into trouble, his friend in the yellow hat always helps him.

> *Millions of Cats* by Wanda Gag. New York: Coward-McCann, Inc., 1928. Among millions of cats, only one was humble and modest. This cat is also the most beautiful and lovable. The modern folk tale is illustrated with black and white drawings.

Humorous and Nonsense Books.   Humorous books make children laugh. Children need to understand humor in a book in order to enjoy its wit. Examples of humorous and nonsense books are:

> *Horton Hatches the Egg* by Dr. Seuss (Theodor Seuss Geisel). New York: Random House, 1940. This book has the type of humor that appeals to young children. Horton is an elephant up in a tree. Its ending is happy and surprising.

> *Sylvester and the Magic Pebble* by William Steig. New York: Simon and Schuster, 1969. Sylvester Duncan, a young donkey, lives with his parents at Acorn Road in Oatsdale. Sylvester finds a magic pebble and finds himself in humorous and suspenseful events. The book is illustrated in cartoon style that compliments the witty text.

Picture Books.   In picture books the pictures are essential to the text. Young children often prefer to have pictures transmit the story so they do not have to read the text. Beginning readers can benefit from experiences with these books. Each year the artist with the most distinguished American picture book for children wins the Caldecott Award, presented by the Association for Library Services to Children of the American Library Association. Examples of picture books are:

> *Crow Boy* written and illustrated by Taro Yashima. New York, The Viking Press, 1955. Chibi, a young Japanese boy, really appreciates school. Every day for six years he leaves his home and goes to school at sunrise. At the end of the year, he is the only one in his class who is honored for perfect attendance. Chibi's classmates do not accept him until his schoolmaster finds out that Chibi can imitate crows.

> *Cinderella* illustrated by Marcia Brown. New York: Charles Scribner and Sons, 1954. This is a delightful folk tale with delicate illustrations about rags-to-riches.

Easy-to-Read Books. Easy-to-read books have a controlled number and range of words which are used often throughout the book. The print tends to be large. Pictures assist in telling the story and the text encompasses a large degree of conversation. Examples of easy-to-read books are:

> *Grasshopper on the Road* written and illustrated by Arnold Lobel. New York: Harper and Row Publishers, 1978. A grasshopper journeys on the road, where he interacts with some strange creatures who find it difficult to accept his philosophy.

> *Little Bear's Visit* written by Else Holmelund Miniarik and illustrated by Maurice Sendak. New York: Harper and Row Publishers, 1961. Little Bear visits Grandmother and Grandfather Bear in their little house in the woods.

Participation Books. Participation books provide children with sensory experiences of looking, feeling, patting, and smelling. In addition, they involve children in searching for visual cues, solving problems, and making decisions. These books require some manipulation; therefore, they may seem more like a toy or game than a book. They are fascinating and irresistible to children, especially toddlers, and they are a good way to introduce children to literature. Examples of participation books are:

> *Brian Wildsmith's Puzzles* written and illustrated by Brian Wildsmith. New York: Franklin Watts, Inc., 1970. A colorful illustrated book providing all of the answers to Brian Wildsmith's brain-teasing questions. Its good humor is integrated with beautiful art work to produce an outstanding participation picture book.

> *Zoo City* written and photographed by Stephen Lewis. New York: William Morrow and Company, Inc., 1976. This book is about machines, plumbing, cars, and other city fixtures which are similar to animals. It has

beautiful black and white photographs with pictures of their real-life counterparts. The book has a split-page, puzzle format that allows children to match animals with look-alike objects.

Information Books.   Information books can enhance the young children's inquiring minds. They need to be carefully selected for the knowledge presented and the language used. The language must be understandable to young children without being condescending. Examples of information books are:

> *Kites* written and illustrated by Larry Kettlekamp. New York: William Morrow and Company, 1959. This book describes the basic types of kites and tells how to build and fly them. It provides information about kites in other lands and what their practical uses are.

> *Your Friend, the Tree* written by Florence M. White and illustrated by Alan E. Cober. New York: Alfred A. Knopf, Inc., 1969. This book provides information about the uses of trees. It urges children to be kind to trees. "When a tree is cut down, a new one should always be planted, because we cannot live without trees."

When young children are read to regularly, they can begin to view reading as an important and integral component of their lives. Reading aloud to young children is part of reading readiness and is reading in the fullest sense of the word. The children examine the pictures in the book and follow the story lines as the adult unlocks the printed symbols for them.

Children need opportunities to explore books on their own.

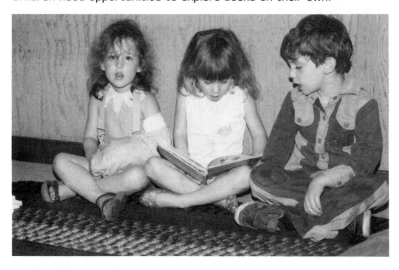

Dealing with Stereotypes in Children's Literature

Unfortunately, among the books that are available to young children are many that portray stereotypes regarding race, sex, age, physical condition, and class. Women may be shown as being dependent on men or serving only in traditionally female roles. The elderly may be pictured as ugly, mean, and incapable. Members of ethnic groups may appear as having limited capacities. The handicapped may be pictured as incapable of doing anything. Some of the stereotypes relate to how society viewed these groups at the time the books were originally written. This is true of many fairy tales and children's classics. In some books stereotyped portrayals appear because the authors did not know enough about members of these groups to provide more distinct characters. Sometimes it is just easier to use stereotypes when picturing people (Chambers, 1983).

It is important for teachers to be aware of stereotypes in the books they use and to be able to identify the stereotypes. A decision might be made not to use a book because of the way it characterizes people in words and pictures. At other times a teacher might feel that a book is good overall and should be read even though it projects a stereotype. In this case the book might be used to start a discussion about similarities and differences among people and how a portrayal in a book is different from how people really are. A good source for teachers to use in choosing books is *Guidelines for Selecting Bias-Free Textbooks and Storybooks,* Council on Interracial Books for Children, 1980. This is available from the Council, 1841 Broadway, New York, NY 10023.

Poetry

Poetry communicates experience by attracting the reader's or listener's thoughts and feelings. Rich sensory reflections and intensive emotional reactions are strongly elicited as one becomes involved in the experience. Poetry requires the listener to respond intellectually, emotionally, and imaginatively. While children's poetry varies slightly from adults', poetry for everybody must be meaningful, must use poetic language, and must have content that is appropriate and fascinating to its audience.

Young children tend to be poetic in nature. They use their senses to enjoy and react to their experiences. Children are like poets who explore and attempt to arrange the elements of their experiences according to facts and emotional symbols. They even coordinate their body in a rhythmic way and are fascinated with the expressive qualities of the time, sight, and sound. They become aware of how persons coordinate their work and play as they adapt to their everyday life situations.

Young children enjoy the language they hear in school. They immediately recite those expressions that are most appealing to them and enjoy new and original ways to use language intellectually and emotionally.

According to Betty Coody (1983), children enjoy poetry that has the following characteristics:

Rhythmic language. Poetry for young children must constantly have words and phrases that sound melodious and harmonious. Lilting language sets poetry aside from other literature. An appropriate poem for young children must have rhythm and melody in its language.

Emotional appeal. Poetry elicits emotional reactions from its listeners: sadness, delight, reflection, empathy, or anger. A poem can stimulate the young children's emotions. Teachers should mirror their feelings about the poem.

Familiar themes. Poetry for young children should be related to children's life experiences. Young children tend to favor poems that tell a story or that are about animals, people, or places or that are fun, humorous, and nonsense.

Sensory appeal. Poetry should provoke the children's senses of touch, taste, smell, sight, and sound.

Good poetry must be shared in the early childhood classroom so children develop a lifelong fondness for many types of poetry. Leland B. Jacobs (1972) suggests several ways to present poetry in the classroom:

- Read poetry to young children regularly enough that children begin to expect and ask for it.
- Read poetry relating to an immediate situation: the season, weather, holiday, or experiences in science, social studies, mathematics, or reading.
- Share poetry with young children, especially original poems that children have written themselves.
- Pantomime and dramatize poetry.
- Use a variety of media including paint, clay, wood, or wire to illustrate poems. Murals of favorite poems are successful with young children.
- Develop poetry anthologies by collecting favorite poems from newspapers, magazines, and books or those composed by the children.
- Schedule poetry reading based on themes relating children's interests and school events.
- Have poetry recordings available to listen to alone or with music.
- Record the children's own interpretations of poetry.

Among the fine anthologies of young children's poetry available are the following (Coody, 1983):

The Complete Nonsense Book by Edward Lear. New York: Dodd, Mead & Company, 1912. This anthology has Edward Lear's nonsense rhymes, his nonsensical drawings, his famous limericks, "The Owl and the Pussy Cat," and other nonsense songs and stories.

Hailstones and Halibut Bones written by Mary O'Neill and illustrated by Leonard Weisgard. Garden City, New York: Doubleday and Company, 1961. This popular anthology is appropriate for all ages. It can be used as a springboard for other activities such as art, creative writing, and dramatization. It describes twelve colors in rhyming verse, naming familiar objects, feelings, and concepts.

Hey Bug! and Other Poems about Little Things selected by Elizabeth M. Itse and illustrated by Susan Carlton Smith. New York: American Heritage, 1972. This anthology consists of poems about beetles, mice, snails, and other small creatures which are fascinating to young children. Its illustrations are scientifically accurate drawings.

Oxford Book of Poetry for Children compiled by Edward Blishen and illustrated by Brian Wildsmith. New York: Franklin Watts, Inc., 1963. This anthology has a variety of poems to introduce young children to poetry and help them to make the transition from nursery rhymes to more serious verse. The illustrations establish the mood for the poems.

Poetry provides a different kind of language experience for young children. They experience the way an artist manipulates words and they hear words in a different arrangement than in conversation. Children usually experience poetry for the first time in school. Teachers should see that these first experiences are as glorious and pleasurable as possible.

Storytelling

The art of storytelling began long before there was written language to record the tales. In ancient times people would gather to share their problems, to discuss natural phenomena, to admire their heroes, to commemorate victories, and to grieve tragic losses. The storyteller was a musician, a newscaster, an actor, and a spinner of tales.

Storytelling provides young children with many values. Betty Coody (1983) suggests that through storytelling:

1. The child is introduced to some of the best literature.
2. The child is acquainted with many cultures from around the world.
3. The child is presented with many characters with whom he or she can identify.
4. A wholesome relationship between the child and the adult is developed.
5. The child is helped to understand life and to develop worthwhile goals.
6. The child is stimulated to want more literary experiences and to develop an interest in reading.
7. The child's vocabulary is enriched and expanded.
8. The child's listening and comprehension skills are improved.
9. The child's creative writing and other creative activities are stimulated.
10. The child is provided with valuable information and knowledge.

Children interpret stories they hear according to their experiences. When they listen to a story, they perceive the characters in relation to people they have known. A story must be read or told with unusual care, and the teacher should learn the story well before telling it.

The following suggestions may prove helpful to a teacher preparing a story to be told (Baker & Greene, 1977; Ward, 1957):

1. *Read the story over and over again.* Read the story several times until you learn it well and have a feeling for the story's rhythm and style. The story should become part of your experience.

2. *Learn the major incidents in sequence.* Learn the story by incidents. Doing this helps to organize the story so that you can remember it easily and tell it in an orderly way. For example, in "Chicken Little," the incidents might be:

   When Chicken Little felt an acorn fall on his tail
   When Chicken Little met Henny Penny
   When Chicken Little and Henny Penny met Cocky Locky
   When Chicken Little, Henny Penny, and Cocky Locky met Ducky Lucky
   When Chicken Little, Henny Penny, Cocky Locky, and Ducky Lucky met Turkey Lurkey
   When Chicken Little, Henny Penny, Cocky Locky, Ducky Lucky, and Turkey Lurkey met Hooty Tooty, the owl, who went to help Chicken Little discover that an acorn had fallen on his tail and not the sky.

3. *Describe the characters in the story.* Use words to draw a picture of the characters, their clothes, their unique characteristics, their personalities, their ways of speaking, and their mannerisms. For example, in "The Little Rabbit Who Wanted Red Wings," Carolyn Sherwin Bailey describes the rabbit in the following way:

   Once upon a time there was a Little White Rabbit with two beautiful pink ears, and two bright eyes and four soft little feet. Such a pretty little white rabbit, but he wasn't happy.

4. *Plan the presentation of the story.* Do not memorize the story. If you do, it can sound formal and forgetting something can leave you helpless in the middle of the story. Some dialogue may need to be memorized, especially in a story that is a well-known classic or with a conversation that is very clever or funny. For example, the dialogue may need to be memorized for better effect in the "Three Little Pigs".

   WOLF: Little pig, little pig, let me in.
   LITTLE PIG: Oh, not by the hair of my chinny chin chin.
   WOLF: Then I'll huff and I'll puff 'til I blow your house in.

   Picturesque or humorous words, phrases, or sentences may also be memorized in telling the story.

5. *Tell the story.* Have a relaxed and intimate atmosphere in an informal setting. Sit the children facing you in a semicircle that is not too wide. Children should sit in several rows of not more than eight children each, with no child directly behind another. Children need to sit facing away from the sunlight or from any distractions which can divert their interest.

Before settling them down, ask the children to put everything they are carrying (such as books, marbles, purses, dolls) on a separate table or under their chairs. These can easily distract other listeners.

Use a warm, friendly manner in telling the story. At the same time be direct, including all the children. Consider the children's point of view, their understanding, and their interest. Make the story simple enough for the children to understand but do not talk down to them. The setting, the presentation, the plot, and the characters must be clear to the children. Tell the story in such a way that the children see pictures vividly. Good action words are valuable in helping children picture the story.

Experience in telling stories will sharpen your storytelling skills. Remember, a story that is presented well will be remembered and dramatized by the children.

Some books that have good stories for telling are the following:

Merry Tales for Children by Carolyn Sherwin Bailey. New York: Platt and Munk Publishers, 1943. This contains a series of humorous short stories about home, stories about animals, folk tales, and holiday stories which can be read and told to young children.

Stories for Little Children by Pearl S. Buck. New York: The John Day Company, Inc., 1940. Short stories based on the lives of five young children who strive to understand such phenomena as daylight, darkness, and the seasons of the year.

Tales from Grimm by Wanda Gag. Eau Claire, Wisconsin: E. M. Hale and Company, 1936. (Translated from German.) Her interpretations of Grimm in both text and the small black and white sketches are delightful.

Puppetry

Puppetry is an old art form. Puppets provide children with a disguise as they become active in manipulating strings, paper bags, or their fists. This activity eases their self-consciousness and allows them to express their feelings more freely.

Puppets also make it easy for children to penetrate a magic world of fantasy. In this world children are able to solve all of their problems. They give evidence of their inner world through puppets (Jenkins, 1981). The use of puppetry can accomplish the following:

- Develops children's creative thinking and imagination.
- Provides children with the opportunity to test life circumstances.
- Helps children become aware of their own behavior.
- Allows children to expose their anxieties and release their tensions.

Puppets help children explore the world of fantasy.

- Develops communication skills.
- Promotes critical listening skills and critical thinking.
- Expands children's attention span.
- Assists children in acquiring knowledge.
- Offers children opportunities to work cooperatively and share ideas.
- Develops problem-solving skills.

Young children can make many kinds of puppets including hand puppets, head puppets, and body puppets (see Figure 12-1) (Hennings, 1982). Following are some suggestions:

Hand Puppets

1. Felt tip pens, crayons, construction paper, yarn, or colored pictures clipped from magazines can add characteristics to puppets made out of hand-sized paper bags.
2. Buttons, yarn, scraps of material, twine, and glitter can add characteristics to puppets made out of socks, stockings, or white work gloves.
3. Faces can be drawn on the balls of each finger.
4. Styrofoam or ping-pong balls can be taped to the ends of fingers or to the ends of ice cream bar sticks, or the sticks can be inserted into them for support. The puppets can be elaborated with glitter, tinsel, buttons, and yarn.

Head Puppets

1. Crayon and felt tip pens can be used to add characteristics to paper plates; holes are cut for children to see through.

2. Eyes, nose, and mouth openings can be cut in a full-sized paper bag. Carpet fringe can be stapled across the top of the bag for curly hair, long lashes can be drawn around the eye openings, and a nose can be stapled above the nose opening.

Body Puppets

1. Large-sized cartons can be colorfully painted; one side is removed and a head hole is cut in the opposite side.
2. Children's bodies can be traced on heavy cardboard to make people-shaped and sized cut-outs. The children can cut on the line and color the body.

Figure 12-1

Hand Puppets

Head Puppets

Body Puppets

Shadow puppets can also be used for creative drama. Puppets are held behind a thin curtain with a strong beam of light shining from behind the puppets through the curtain. In a darkened room, the puppets look like silhouettes. A puppet can represent a person, an object, or any shape.

Children can make their own simple puppets to share a story. Provide materials such as ribbons, bows, twine, scraps of fabric, lengths of old yarn, paper bags, worn-out but clean socks, gloves, paper plates, buttons, and other odds and ends to allow children to make puppets with which to share their stories.

Puppets can be characters in a story, which can be read or told by one child while the other children manipulate the puppets according to the plot. Or children can manipulate and talk for their own puppets to share a personal story.

Creative Dramatics

Creative dramatics is informal drama. In creative dramatics a story may be dramatized. Ideas and feelings may be explored, developed, and expressed through dramatic enactment as the players create the dialogue.

According to McCaslin (1984), creative dramatics is valuable for young children because it:

- Develops the imagination.
- Develops independent thinking.
- Develops one's own ideas.
- Provides an opportunity for cooperation.
- Builds social awareness.
- Releases emotion.
- Develops speech habits.
- Provides experiences with good literature.
- Introduces the theater arts.
- Provides a form of recreation.

Dramatization helps children to interpret and understand literature. In creative dramatics there is no script, lines are not memorized, and few, if any, properties or costumes are required. Although the drama is unstructured, young children take their roles very seriously.

Selections from children's literature often serve as vehicles for dramatization. If used skillfully, creative dramatics can add to literary understanding and provide an opportunity to use language skills.

Creative drama can be introduced for the first time with simple activities, such as finger plays, single action poetry, action songs, and simple pantomimes. Later, when drama periods are longer, these simpler activities can be used for warm-up (Heining & Stillwell, 1981).

LESSON PLAN FOR CREATIVE DRAMATICS

Story:

Goldilocks and the Three Bears

Goal:

To identify and describe the characters who help develop the story and the main character (Goldilocks).

Materials:

Book, pictures, flannel board characters, and puppets of Goldilocks and the Three Bears.

Arrangement:

Children sit on the carpet in a semicricle.

Prerequisites:

1. Children know the story.
2. Children can place the pictures in sequence.
3. Children can tell the story using flannel board pictures.
4. Children can tell the story using puppets.

Procedures:

After the children have achieved the prerequisites, the teacher explains the purpose of the activity. The teacher then guides the discussion by asking questions such as:

— Who is the story about?
— What is her name?
— Can you describe Goldilocks?
— Who else was in the story?
— Can you describe Baby Bear?
— Can you describe Mama Bear?
— Can you describe Papa Bear?
— If Baby Bear were bigger and fatter, how would the story be different?
— What could Mama Bear and Papa Bear have done to change the story?

The number and types of questions asked depend on the children's interests and developmental level.

Follow-up-Activities:

— Children can dramatize the story according to the book.
— Children can dramatize the story by changing the characters and discussing how the characters changed the story.
— Children can illustrate the characters.

Children's language can be developed through creative dramatics. Creative dramatics also increases children's understanding and frees their responses to literature. It helps children to respond to experiences and to interpret the printed page in spoken word and gesture.

Finger Plays

Finger plays—little rhymes, songs, or chants—can be acted out as young children recite them. Some examples are "Eensy Weensy Spider" and "Hickory, Dickory Dock" (see Figures 12-2 and 12-3). There are many

Eensy, Weensy Spider

Eensy, weensy spider
  (Let opposite thumbs and index fingers climb up each other.)
Climbed up the waterspout.
Down came the rain
  (Let hands sweep down and open wide.)
And washed the spider out.
Out came the sun
  (Form circle over head with arms.)
And dried up all the rain.
So the eensy, weensy spider,
  (Let opposite thumbs and fingers climb up each other again.)
Climbed up the spout again.

Figure 12-2 Eensy, Weensy Spider

Figure 12-3 Hickory, Dickory, Dock

Hickory, Dickory, Dock

Hickory, dickory, dock,
  (Bend arm at elbow; hop up, palm open.)
The mouse ran up the clock,
  (Run fingers up arm.)
The clock struck one,
  (Point to "one o'clock.")
The mouse ran down,
  (Run fingers down arm.)
Hickory, dickory, dock.

sources for finger plays, such as *Let's Do Fingerplays* by Marion F. Grayson (1962). Teachers can also make them up from favorite nursery rhymes. A variety of anthologies of nursery rhymes are available that can be helpful.

Action Stories

Some stories have actions which children can perform. Someone tells the story and does the actions. Then the children imitate the actions. "Bear Hunt," in which children can use actions to describe the hunter going through grass, mud, hills, and so on, is an example of an action story.

Original stories can be made up, with actions being assigned to story characters or to frequently used words. Children act out each word, or specific words can be assigned to rows or groups. Original action stories based on the children's experiences or field trips can also be made up, with actions or words assigned in the same way. The children can also change posts.

Actions can be added to popular stories such as *The Hare and the Tortoise* (Galdone, 1962). Children can agree on a dialogue to act out the story such as the following:

> *Characters:* hare, tortoise, fox
> *Setting:* woods
>
> *Story:*

HARE:	Good morning, Mr. Tortoise. Ha! Ha! Ha! Ha!
TORTOISE:	What's so funny?
HARE:	Ha! Ha! Ha! Ha!
TORTOISE:	What's so funny!!!
HARE:	Your little legs. Ha! Ha! How can you walk?
TORTOISE:	I can walk and even run faster than you.
HARE:	What?

The dialogue continues throughout the story. This story can be acted out by three children or three groups of children. With groups, when the Hare speaks, for example, the group of children who have selected that character will speak and act in unison on the agreed-upon dialogue.

TEACHING READING AND WRITING

Readiness is a stage when children are ready to learn something without intellectual or emotional stress and when they can feel the satisfaction of having achieved that learning. Generally, reading readiness refers to the ability of a child to profit from reading instruction. Readiness can be conceived of for many learning stages of reading from beginning to mature reading in adulthood (Downing & Thackeray, 1978). Many use the term readiness to refer to the child's maturational state. If readiness depended only on maturation, then teachers could wait until each child matures. However, there is more than maturation involved in reading readiness, and a purely maturational approach to reading readiness is simply not effective. A reading readiness program must teach the pre-requisite skills for reading.

Designing a Reading Readiness Program

A reading readiness program for young children must integrate expressive and receptive oral and written language. It must help children achieve fluency in speaking and listening abilities. An emphasis on oral language helps children develop an extensive speaking and listening vocabulary, an asset to developing a reading vocabulary. Listening to stories provides them with the opportunity to manipulate books and to become aware that information is found on the printed page, even in pictures. Children acquire simple skills like holding a book, opening it, turning its pages, and caring for it. These experiences also make children aware of the rela-

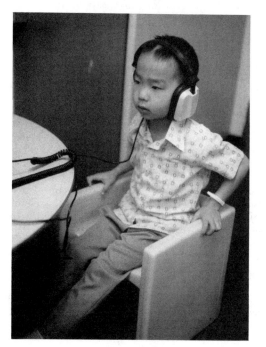

A listening station allows the child to control the number of times he or she hears a story read.

tionship between the written and oral language. As a result of this awareness, they establish the concept that the written word has the same power to communicate meaning as the spoken word. They also need to be provided with many opportunities to dictate personal stories to the teacher, and these stories can be read repeatedly. Both informal and formal language experiences guide children into making the transition to actual reading.

In addition, a reading readiness program must provide learning activities that help children acquire competencies in the specific skills required for reading. Hillerich (1977) recommends the following progression in developing reading readiness skills:

> *Auditory discrimination.* Children need to hear the difference between phonemes in words, such as "book" or "look."
>
> *Listening comprehension.* Young children need to expand their understanding of what they hear. Children must learn to understand conversational, informal oral language in order to comprehend written language.
>
> *Recalling sequence of events.* Young children need to be able to remember events as they occur in order.
>
> *Language development.* Children need to be capable of using the spoken language before beginning reading. Oral language can be developed through experiences that stimulate language.
>
> *Oral language development—basic vocabulary.* Young children need to learn to understand and use a vocabulary of common words. An effective technique to develop vocabulary is through direct and personal experiences. If direct experiences are not feasible, good pictures or models can be provided.
>
> *Following spoken directions.* Listening comprehension should be initiated by the teacher's giving simple one-step oral directions. Playing a game like Simon Says or Hokey Pokey provides practice in following oral directions.
>
> *Using oral context.* Most four-year-olds intuitively know how to use oral context. A four-year-old can easily provide a missing word to complete a sentence. Children can also develop their own incomplete sentences for the class to provide the missing words. This activity can be varied with riddles, which also help develop skills that employ oral context.

Teaching about the Written Language

Writing experiences help young children to read. When children try to copy letters, they become aware of the distinctive shapes of letters and words. Many young children write by themselves, and some early writers become quite independent.

Young children's writing involves more than just print markings on a page. They know that writing communicates ideas. Several research studies (e.g., Clay, 1975; DeFord, 1980; Hildreth, 1936) show that children progress in a series of sequential stages as they gain writing skills.

Marie Clay describes how children explore the variation in their early writing efforts. She has identified principles that can guide teachers in understanding young children's writing efforts. Teachers can observe the children's written responses in order to identify each child's perception of written language. They can collect a large number of writing samples and the necessary information to develop an appropriate writing program for young children. Vukelich and Golden (1984) suggest that the following activities and opportunities be included:

- Daily opportunities to write
- A writing center where children record on paper their thoughts and words
- Writing materials such as pencils (both regular and primary size), pens, magic markers, and paper (with and without lines)
- Other materials that promote writing, such as a typewriter, magnetic letters, wooden letters, and blocks with letters

For some children, writing is a forerunner of reading. They copy signs, labels, or letters. They are intrigued with using pencils, crayons, and paper. Many researchers provide evidence that young children are interested in learning to write in the early years. Marie Clay (1977) observed that three- to five-year-old children recognize that people write for a purpose, and they are therefore motivated to express their ideas in written form.

The "language experience approach" is a way for children to express their ideas through written language. Children dictate individual or group stories to a teacher or other adult. The teacher may set up a field trip or other exciting activity to motivate the children's thinking. A discussion follows in which children share their experience and the teacher clarifies concepts. The children then dictate a story which is written on a chart or chalkboard. Each child may contribute a sentence. The teacher uses the child's exact words and reads it back immediately, emphasizing left to right progression. The teacher then asks the children to read the line and simultaneously moves his or her arm from left to right. The children then agree on a title for the story.

The children read and reread the story many times and work on reading skills appropriate to each child's developmental level. These skills can include rhyming words and identifying words with the same meaning, words with opposite meaning, words that sound the same but have different meaning, and vocabulary words. The chart is displayed where children can read it on their own. Copies of the story can also be duplicated for children to take home.

Teachers should use many opportunities to help children become writers.

After a field trip, the children dictate a letter of thanks to the teacher, which they can all sign before mailing.

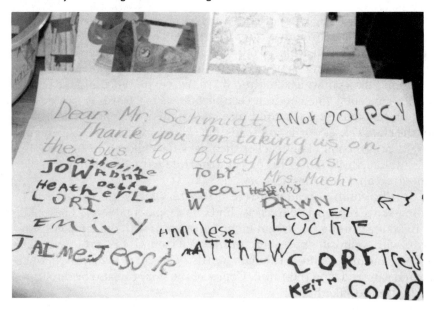

The individual experience story is similar to the group experience story. A child may be more interested in the individual experience story because of personal involvement. Any language experience story is personally meaningful to children because they are the authors. They use their own experiences and their own language to communicate their thoughts in written language.

In a writing program for young children, many children will learn to write their names and others will go beyond that. Pushing children who do not have the skill needed to write discourages them and develops poor writing habits which are later difficult to overcome (Lamme, 1983).

Barbe and Lucas (1974) suggest there should be handwriting readiness programs which cover prerequisite skill areas:

> *Small muscle development.* Many young children cannot hold a pencil adequately because they lack the small muscle control. Small muscle skills can be developed through manipulative tasks such as completing jigsaw puzzles.
>
> *Eye–hand coordination.* One has to have the muscle control to have the hand do what the eye and brain want it to do. Most small muscle activities also develop eye–hand coordination.
>
> *Holding utensils or tools.* Children enjoy playing with writing materials. Before young children write, they need many experiences with drawing; in painting with paint brushes, markers, sponges, chalk, and crayons; and in writing with pencils. Pencils are very difficult tools to manipulate and should be the last material children learn to hold.
>
> *Letter perception.* Children should be taught to recognize form, notice likenesses and differences, infer the necessary movement in producing forms, and verbally describe letters.

Marie Clay (1975) also recommends that children learn:

- To attend and orient themselves to written language,
- to organize their exploratory investigation of printed forms,
- to tell left from right, and
- to visually analyze letters and words.

It is important that children see written language as a way to communicate so that they see the importance of handwriting skills. Young children need to be provided with the appropriate opportunities of writing books, greeting cards, or letters.

Skills in written language include determining the difference between print and nonprint, learning specific characteristics of print, learning to write, knowing and understanding the letters of the alphabet, and learning conventions of print including left to right, top to bottom, upper- and lower-case letters, and punctuation. Young children need to learn about the purposes and types of written language and ways to communicate through writing.

SUMMARY

Early childhood language arts programs include learning both receptive and expressive language skills. When children read and listen, they receive communications; when they speak and write, they express communications. These four areas—reading, listening, speaking, and writing—are all important in any language arts program and need to be integrated through a variety of experiences. These experiences include children's literature, poetry, storytelling, puppetry, and creative dramatics.

The emphasis in preschool should be on oral language experiences. Experiences for young children are planned to develop preliminary learnings in the written communication skills, although the more sophisticated reading and writing skills are usually developed after six years of age. A good foundation in oral language helps young children to recognize the relationship between spoken and written words. Then they can learn to read to receive ideas and impressions just as they are able to listen; they can express ideas, impressions, and feelings in writing just as they are able to speak.

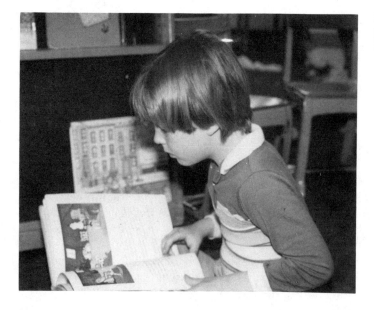

Children can be encouraged to read and reread a story they have heard.

REFERENCES

BAKER, A. AND E. GREENE (1977). *Storytelling: Art and techinque.* New York: R. R. Bowker.

BARBE, W. B. AND V. H. LUCAS (1974). Instruction in handwriting: A new look. *Childhood Education,* **50,** 207-209.

CHAMBERS, B. (1983). Counteracting racism and sexism in children's books. In O. N. Saracho and B. Spodek (Eds.), *Understanding the multicultural experience in early childhood education.* Washington, DC: National Association for the Education of Young Children.

CLAY, M. M. (1977). Exploring with a pencil. *Theory into Practice,* **16,** 334-335.

———— (1975). *What did I write?* Aukland, New Zealand: Heinemann Educational Books.

COODY, B. (1983). *Using literature with young children.* Dubuque, IA: Wm. C. Brown Company.

DEFORD, D. (1980). Young children and their writing. *Theory into Practice,* **19,** 157-162.

DOWNING, J. AND D. THACKERAY (1978). *Reading readiness.* London: Hodder & Stoughton.

GALDONE, P. (1962). *The hare and the tortoise.* New York: McGraw-Hill.

GRAYSON, M. F. (1962). *Let's do fingerplays,* illustrated by Nancy Weyl. New York: Van Rees Press.

HEINING, R. B. AND L. STILLWELL (1981). *Creative drama for the classroom teacher.* Englewood Cliffs, NJ: Prentice-Hall.

HENNINGS, D. G. (1982). *Communication in action teaching the language arts.* Boston: Houghton Mifflin.

HILDRETH, G. (1936). Developmental sequences in name writing. *Child Development,* **7,** 291-303.

HILLERICH, R. L. (1977). *Reading fundamentals for preschool and primary children.* Columbus, OH: Charles E. Merrill.

HONIG, A. S. (1982). Language environments for young children. *Young Children,* **38**(1), 56-67.

HUCK, C. S. (1979). *Children's literature in the elementary school.* New York: Holt, Rinehart & Winston.

JACOBS, L. B. (1955). Children's experiences in literature. In V. E. Herrick and L. B. Jacobs (Eds.), *Children and the language arts,* pp. 192-218. Englewood Cliffs, NJ: Prentice-Hall.

———— (1972). Enjoying poetry with children. In M. D. Cohen (Ed.), *Literature with children,* pp. 32-38. Washington, DC: Association for Childhood Educational International.

JENKINS, P. D. (1981). *The magic of puppetry: A guide for those working with young children.* Englewood Cliffs, NJ: Prentice-Hall.

LAMME, L. L. (1983). Handwriting in an early childhood curriculum. In J. F. Brown (Ed.), *Curriculum planning for young children,* pp. 109-116. Washington, DC: National Association for the Education of Young Children.

MASON, G. E. (1981). *Primer on teaching reading: Basic concepts and skills of the early elementary years.* Itasca, IL: F. E. Peacock Publishers.

McCaslin, N. (1984). *Creative dramatics in the classroom* (4th ed.). New York: Longman.

Ross, R. R. (1980). *Storyteller.* Columbus, OH: Charles E. Merrill.

Sendak, M. (1963). *Where the wild things are.* New York: Harper & Row.

Spodek, B. (1985). *Teaching in the early years* (3rd ed.). Englewood Cliffs, NJ: Prentice-Hall.

Spodek, B., O. N. Saracho, and R. C. Lee (1984). *Mainstreaming young children.* Belmont, CA: Wadsworth.

Vukelich, C., and J. Golden (1984). Early writing: Developmental teaching strategies. *Young Children,* **39**(2), 3-10.

Ward, W. (1957). *Playmaking with children* (2nd ed.). New York: Appleton-Century-Crofts.

Williamson, P. M. (1981). Literature goals and activities for young children. *Young Children,* **36**(4), 24-30.

SUGGESTED ACTIVITIES

1. Begin a file of language activities for young children using categories such as children's literature, poetry, storytelling, puppetry, creative dramatics, and action plays.

2. Read a story to a three-, four-, and five-year-old child. Describe the changes in the story form as you prepare for different age groups.

3. Record on tape some children's conversations at snack time, story time, play time, or other similar activities. Compare the different types of conversations.

4. Collect a set of poems appropriate for use with young children. Cut pictures from magazines or find other appropriate pictures to be used with the poems.

5. Develop a lesson plan for a week of reading readiness activities for a group of three-year-olds.

6. Observe a teacher of two- to five-year-old children teaching a language experience. Determine whether the teacher is teaching early listening, speaking, reading, or writing.

13

COGNITIVELY ORIENTED LEARNING
Science and Mathematics

OBJECTIVES

After completing this chapter on cognitively oriented learning, the student should be able to:

1. Explain the scientific processes of observing, classifying, predicting, and communicating.
2. Describe a developmentally appropriate science program for young children.
3. Describe a developmentally appropriate mathematics program for young children.
4. Identify the goals of nutrition education for young children.
5. Explain the relationship between cognitive development and the science and mathematics curriculum.
6. Discuss why environmental education is an appropriate part of science for young children.

Children are active learners—both in and out of the classroom, by themselves and with others, and with objects and materials of every conceivable size and shape. Physical activity puts children into contact with the world and enables them to develop a sense of the world. Mental activity enables children to understand their world—in their own way and at their own level.

Firsthand, direct experience with real things helps give children a deeper sense of the world. While we all know what a dog is, those who have a dog for a pet or have similar contact with dogs know more about dogs than those who have gained their knowledge of dogs through being told, or being shown a book or a picture, or watching a television program. Both groups may be able to describe a dog, but what they describe—what they know and feel—will be significantly different.

In a very real sense, experience is the basis for children's knowledge, including knowledge about mathematics and science. Young children learn mathematical and scientific concepts as they interact with objects that are a part of their everyday world. Children learn about quantity, size, shape, order, number, classes, and many other concepts through their everyday experiences.

This chapter will explore the child's developing cognitive ability and its relationship to the mathematics and science program. It will also provide examples of activities to help young children develop science and mathematics concepts.

COGNITIVE THEORY

One of the theories of knowledge upon which many early childhood programs are built is *constructivist theory*. This theory states that humans construct their own understanding of the world by acting on their experiences. Jean Piaget is best known for his constructivist theory. According to Piaget, children develop *schema*, or conceptual systems, through the process of *equilibration* as they construct their knowledge. This process of equilibration is made up of two complementary processes: *assimilation* and *accommodation*. In assimilation children acquire information from the environment and incorporate it into their existing schema or systems of knowledge. Children revise their existing system of knowledge through accommodation when the information they gather cannot fit within the system. The result is a balance of existing and new knowledge: an *equilibrium*.

Assimilation and accommodation complement one another and operate together. A child who knows that a car has four wheels may call every four-wheeled object a car. However, when the child learns that trucks also have four wheels and are different from cars in that they can carry large objects, he or she can assimilate this new information, but he or she must accommodate it into his or her existing knowledge by creating a new category of wheeled vehicles: trucks. Thus a new balance, or equilibrium, is established that will be modified again and again. It is the schema that is modified as the child assimilates and accommodates information. Another way of looking at a schema is as the organized, personalized information system that an individual uses to understand the world.

Piaget, as was noted in Chapter 5, theorized that children go through a series of stages in intellectual development relating to how they process information. Most three- to five-year-old children are in the *preoperational* stage. They have not yet developed the ability to think logically or abstractly about the world. Their thinking is unsystematic and intuitive, bound by their perceptions as they focus on one attribute of an object at a time. Children who are playing with colored blocks of different shapes, for example, may focus only on color and not on shape, or only on shape disregarding color, but they can't consider both attributes at the same time.

Children at this stage focus on the beginning or end state of a transformation rather than on the process of transformation itself. Thus, if a child is given two equal-sized balls of clay and then one is rolled out while the other is left alone, the child might say that the rolled-out one is bigger. The child does not keep in mind that initially they were of equal size and that no clay was added or taken away. Similarly, these children are not aware that pouring water from a tall, thin cylinder into a short, fat one does not change the amount of water. In each of these cases, focusing on only one attribute, length or thickness, and being perceptually bound, limits children's understanding.

The ability to conserve develops between five and eight years of age, as children mature, gain experience, and learn from others. The more opportunities children have to play with objects and the more they are confronted with other children's ideas, the sooner they are likely to develop the ability to think logically.

The science and the mathematics programs in an early childhood class should give children firsthand experiences with objects that allow them to observe, manipulate, and describe them. It should also provide opportunities for children to create and test their schema about these objects, and opportunities to interact with other children who are also developing schema, in this way becoming more mature intellectually as they learn about the physical world.

SCIENCE FOR YOUNG CHILDREN

Science is concerned with the physical properties of the world. Science orders properties, identifies relationships among properties, and attempts to establish theories that can be tested to validate the relationships found in these theories. Science may also be seen as a set of organized concepts and generalizations. By organizing information into systematic sets of concepts knowledge of the world can be scientifically ordered (Spodek, 1985).

Science is a system of knowledge about the physical world. It includes ideas about processes, objects, and the relationship among them. In developing concepts, scientists involve themselves in the process of creating knowledge. The American Association for the Advancement of Science (1967) identified the processes of science as including:

- observing
- using space-time relationships
- using numbers
- measuring
- classifying
- communicating
- predicting
- inferring

Many of these processes are the same ones young children use when they act on the physical world, discovering attributes, organizing schema, and representing the world. Thus, at the early childhood level the science curriculum can provide opportunities to learn some of the processes of science as they observe and describe *attributes* and observe and describe *actions*. Concepts about animals, plants, weather, water, and food are appropriate for young children to develop as a way of learning about science. Children can be helped to organize the information they gather related to these concepts. Creating and testing scientific concepts can become the basis for the science curriculum. In order to do this, children must have access to materials that will help them to understand objects and their actions and interactions in the world.

TOPICS FOR EARLY CHILDHOOD SCIENCE

There are a number of topics in the area of science that interest most young children. Plants, animals, sound, light, water, seasons, and simple machines are all a part of the young child's experiences and are topics that can be approached first-hand. Topics that are particularly appropriate for young children—physics, animals, plants, nutrition, and ecology—are discussed here.

Physics

Young children can approach physics in relation to what is called physical knowledge: knowledge of the physical attributes of things. They learn about objects by acting on them and observing reactions.

Constance Kamii and Rheta DeVries (1978a) suggest that two kinds of activities are important for generating physical knowledge in young children. The first involves the movement of objects where the action is primary and the role of observation is secondary. In the second kind, the role of observation is primary and the child's action is secondary because the object observed actually changes. Kamii and DeVries suggest the following criteria for selecting phenomena involving the movement of objects:

1. The child must be able to produce the movement by his or her own action.
2. The child must be able to vary the action.
3. The reaction of the object must be observable.
4. The reaction of the object must be immediate. (p. 8-9)

These criteria reflect the importance of equilibration in the child's construction of knowledge of the physical world. As children deal with objects within their experience, the actions they perform are based on what they already know. As they vary their actions and observe the changing reactions, they not only assimilate new information, but they must accommodate into their existing cognitive structures the information they gather.

Constance Kamii and Lucinda Lee-Katz (1979) offer a number of suggestions for activities that enable children to actually move an object. Table 13-1 describes some of those activities.

Activities for children that involve objects changing their status include:

- Melting ice
- Juicing an orange
- Boiling water to make steam

TABLE 13-1 Physics Activities for Young Children that Stress Movement

Rolling on rollers. Place a board on a set of rolling cylinders and use it to move objects or children across the room.

Jumping. Use a cylinder and plank to make a teeterboard. When someone jumps on one end, an object can be propelled into the air.

Tilting. Place a ball bearing in a maze and then tilt the maze to allow the ball to roll freely.

Dropping. Objects such as clothespins or buttons are dropped into a plastic bottle. The child stands up straight and attempts to drop the object into the bottle.

Blowing. Use a straw to blow on an object and propel it toward a goal.

Sucking. Use a straw to lift an object such as a piece of paper and move it from one box to another.

Pulling. Have children run around the play area while holding up streamers.

Swinging. Let the children swing a pendulum and attempt to hit a stationary object with it.

C. Kamii and L. Lee-Katz, "Physics in Preschool Education: A Piagetian Approach." *Young Children,* 34(4), 1979, 4-9.

- Making applesauce out of real apples
- Cooking raw potatoes and mashing them
- Leaving wax to melt in the hot sun
- Painting with plain water, then allowing it to evaporate

Children can see the changes take place. They can then describe these changes, discuss them with others, and record them in a picture or an experience chart.

Animals

Living things in the classroom seem to provide children with a feeling of wonder and excitement that cannot be generated by inanimate objects. Things that grow, breathe, move, change, and need care cause children not only to sharpen their observation skills but also to ask questions, generate hypotheses, record data, and solve problems. Caring for plants and animals helps to give children a sense of responsibility as well.

Among the concepts that children can learn from animals are:

- Animals are living things.
- Animals need appropriate food.
- Animals need water.
- Animals need safe places to sleep and live.
- Animals may bite when hurt or frightened.
- Animals need activity and rest.

Fish make fine classroom pets.

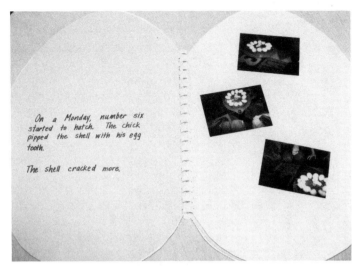

On a Monday, number six started to hatch. The chick pipped the shell with his egg tooth.

The shell cracked more.

The children carefully watched chicken eggs hatch.

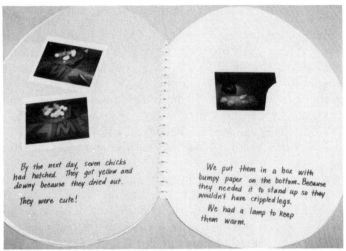

By the next day, seven chicks had hatched. They got yellow and downy because they dried out.

They were cute!

We put them in a box with bumpy paper on the bottom. Because they needed it to stand up so they wouldn't have crippled legs.

We had a lamp to keep them warm.

They regularly took pictures of the process with an instant camera. Along with their verbal descriptions, these made an excellent "egg book."

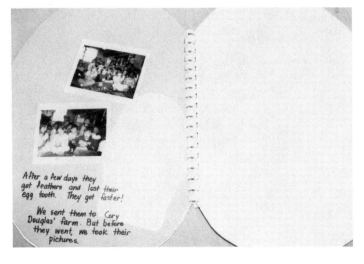

After a few days they got feathers and lost their egg tooth. They got faster!

We sent them to Cory Douglas' farm. But before they went, we took their pictures.

These concepts are not generated in a single experience but evolve out of experiences over a long period of time with classroom pets.

Baby chicks, ducks, guinea pigs, hamsters, rabbits, fish, turtles, snakes, worms, and ants can all be classroom pets if proper care is taken. In each case an appropriate environment, such as a cage, box, or ant farm, must be provided. Additionally, the pet must have adequate food, a source of water, and opportunities to exercise.

Before choosing a classroom pet, the teacher should review different animals that are available. Once an animal is selected, the teacher should be willing to accept the responsibility that comes with bringing a living thing into the classroom. Although children should share this responsibility, the final obligation is the teacher's. In addition to providing a proper home, food, and water, the teacher must see that the cage is cleaned at regular intervals, that new bedding is provided, and that children learn how to care for and treat the animal.

The children must learn that animals are living and feeling creatures, not toys. They must learn about the animal's behavior patterns, what it eats, and how it acts. They must also learn that there are limits on when, how, and where the pet should be handled. Instruction should be given in proper methods of handling animals.

Activities that can be generated from interactions with classroom animals include weighing, measuring, and recording growth, discussions about comparisons of animals, observing the animal and keeping a log of daily habits, and learning adjectives that describe the animal's behavior, coat, and temperament.

Even when pets are not kept in the room, children can benefit from animal visitors. Their home pets—cats, dogs, sheep, or goats—can be brought into school for a short time as guests. Children take pride in sharing their pets with others, and the class benefits from the comparisons that are made and the language that is generated.

Plants

Although plants are not as cuddly as a rabbit or hamster, they do provide children with a living thing in the classroom. The growth of roots, leaves, stems, and flowers provides many opportunities to observe, describe, classify, measure, and communicate.

Plants require little care and very little expense compared with animals. Also their death or destruction causes less trauma. Often vegetables from home can start a plant collection. An onion placed in a clear glass of water will let children observe white roots growing out of the bottom and green leaves out of the top. A sweet potato in a jar of water placed in the sunlight will also put out roots and stems. Carrot tops, seed potatoes and many other vegetables work well, too.

Cuttings, pieces of big plants that have stems and leaves but no

Experiments with vegetables from home provide opportunities for observation, description, and discussion.

roots, can also be started in water. Place the cutting in water and watch the roots grow over time. When the root system is large enough, the cutting can be planted in soil. Sometimes a root hormone is helpful to promote growth.

Children can grow grass, flowers, and some vegetables in the classroom using topsoil or potting soil. A flower pot, a pie pan, or a milk carton can be filled with soil, then seeds planted, watered, and placed in the sun to grow. Children can measure the plant weekly and record its growth on a wall chart. Flowers grown this way make fine Mother's Day gifts, especially if children have decorated the homemade planter.

Schools with large, grassy play areas should consider putting in a garden. A section of the yard that gets enough sun can be set aside and fenced off. Once the soil is turned over, the children can rake, make rows, plant seeds, weed, and record the growth of plants. Leaf lettuce, radishes, and beans are all vegetables that grow in a reasonably short time. Children can eat the vegetables they have grown as part of their lunch or snack. The garden can also serve as a springboard to a unit on cooking, nutrition, or ecology.

A word of caution; plants need to be watered regularly, but they can be destroyed by overwatering. Adequate sunlight is also necessary once the seedlings have started to grow.

Nutrition

Good nutrition is essential for good health and proper growth. Children can be helped to understand that they should eat a variety of foods. They can learn to appreciate different foods and to make wise choices in selecting what to eat. Breakfast, lunch, and snacks are part of many early childhood programs. Teachers can use these opportunities to help children learn about good nutrition.

In planning a unit on nutrition, teachers must be sensitive to the family patterns and cultural backgrounds of the children. Not all families eat the same kinds of food, although their meals may be highly nutritious. Other families may not practice good nutrition. Criticizing a family's practices can make a child angry or defensive, and the criticism may not always be valid.

Herr and Morse (1982) use ten categories of foods to help children select a variety of foods rather than the usual basic four food groups of milk, protein, bread and cereal, and vegetable and fruit. They feel that teaching about only four food groups requires children to make difficult generalizations in regard to foods. They feel that with ten groups it is easier for children to fit specifics into the given categories. The food and nutrition concepts Herr and Morse identify are presented in Table 13-2. These concepts are not taught to children directly but should underly the activities teachers provide.

Cooking is an enjoyable and useful activity to include as part of a nutrition unit. Cooking can support language development, help children develop mathematics and science concepts, and present social knowledge. Children can follow recipes using basic ingredients and can go through the process of food preparation, watching the ingredients merge, change their appearance, and finally emerge as a tasty snack.

In planning a cooking experience, teachers should make sure that there are enough utensils and enough ingredients for the number of children who will participate. Cooking experiences are best done with small groups. Care should be taken that the cooking activity is a safe one. If a heat source is to be used, such as an oven or a hot plate, the children should be aware of the dangers of being burned and adequate insulated pads and pot holders should be available. Electric appliances must be treated with respect. Children should be expected to wash and dry their hands before preparing food and to treat ingredients with care. Aprons are helpful in protecting clothing. The children should know what will be happening and what they will be able to do.

It is a good idea to write the recipe on a chart. Pictures as well as words can be used to designate ingredients and amounts. The recipe can be discussed at the beginning, then referred to regularly as the group follows each step in sequence. The teacher can ask the children to describe what is taking place, what changes they see happening, what ingredients they are using, or any thoughts they may have as the activity evolves.

Children should help clean up the area after cooking is done, washing the surfaces of tables, sweeping the floor, and scrubbing the utensils. Whatever is cooked may be eaten by the group itself or by the entire class. This is an important part of the lesson and deserves attention.

TABLE 13-2 Food and Nutrition Concepts for Young Children

1. There is a wide variety of food.
2. Plants and animals are sources of food.
3. Foods vary in color, flavor, texture, smell, size, shape, and sound.
4. A food may be prepared and eaten in many different ways—raw, cooked, dried, frozen, or canned.
5. Good foods are important to health, growth, and energy.
6. Nutrition is how our bodies use the foods we eat for health, growth, and energy.
7. Food may be classified according to the following categories:

   a. milk
   b. meat
   c. dried peas and beans
   d. eggs
   e. fruits
   f. vegetables
   g. breads
   h. pastas
   i. cereals, grains, and seeds
   j. nuts

8. A good diet includes a wide variety of foods from each of the food categories.
9. There are many factors that influence eating:

   a. attractiveness of food
   b. method of preparation
   c. cleanliness/manners
   d. environment/atmosphere
   e. celebrations

10. We choose the foods we eat for many reasons:

    a. availability and cost
    b. family and individual habits
    c. aesthetics
    d. social and cultural customs
    e. mass media influence

J. Heer, and W. Morse, "Food for Thought: Nutrition Education for Young Children." *Young Children*, **38**(1), 1982, 5-6.

Eating can be a social occasion, one in which the activity is discussed and the experience is shared.

There are a number of foods that can be prepared without a heat source. The following are suggestions for cooking experiences that do not require heat:

- Make butter either by churning the cream or shaking it in a jar. The children can then spread the butter with tongue depressors on crackers or bread.
- Make ice cream with a hand-cranked freezer.
- Prepare fresh fruit—apples can be cored and sliced, oranges peeled and sectioned.
- Squeeze oranges or lemons to make a juice drink; add water and sugar if necessary.
- Peel carrots or cucumbers with a hand-peeler; slice for snack.
- Make applesauce by putting peeled and cored apples through a food mill or potato ricer.

Children can be encouraged to share nutritious snacks brought from home.

Both in cooking and in serving meals and snacks, good nutrition practices should be followed. Snacks need not be high in sugar and salt. Fruits, vegetables, and other snacks that are high in protein, fiber, and complex carbohydrates serve nutritional needs better. Teachers might wish to have "tasting parties" for children to try out different foods. Various raw fruits and vegetables can be offered in small quantities, including those foods that children might not normally encounter. The children might also be offered the same foods in different forms:

- A fresh pineapple and cans of pineapple could be put out one day to be examined by children and to build interest. All preparation, such as cutting the fresh pineapple, should be done in front of the children. Serve the fresh pineapple one day, the canned pineapple another.
- On another day, let the children have a choice of sliced pineapple or crushed pineapple. The crushed pineapple can be spread on crackers for ease in eating. Encourage the children to say what they want. On another day, serve pineapple juice.
- Serve raw apples, canned apple slices, applesauce, apple butter on crackers, and apple juice.
- For variety, cut the apples crosswise to show the "star" in the center. Another time, give each child a choice of an apple with a red skin or a yellow skin. Draw attention to the shape, smell, and texture or "crunch" of the apple.
- Different varieties and colors of grapes can be eaten. (Be careful with seeds.)
- Other possibilities are fresh peas, peas in a can, and frozen peas; fresh carrots and canned carrots; fresh tomatoes, canned tomatoes, and tomato juice.

Nutrition education helps open up children to new eating patterns that will lead them to a healthy life. It is a part of the curriculum that can be integrated into the daily lives of the class.

ECOLOGY AND THE ENVIRONMENT

One purpose of science for young children is to teach them the importance of conserving natural resources and taking care of the environment. Young children may not be old enough to understand why they should be concerned with environmental neglect, but they are old enough to appreciate the beauty of the world and to begin developing good habits. They can learn simple rules like these:

- Do not pull leaves off trees, break branches, or otherwise harm plant life.
- Do not dirty the air, the water, or the earth.
- Respect the lives of animals and humans alike.
- Do not take more than you need of anything. Do not be wasteful.
- Actively work to improve the environment by leaving food for birds and animals, planting flowers, and picking up trash.

They can also be involved in class activities that help them learn the proper uses of the environment. For example, the class could be taken on a trip to a local park to pick up trash and deposit it into trash containers. Simple bird or animal feeders can be made to be placed in the playground in the winter. Peanut butter spread on pine cones and hung on a tree or spread on an ear of corn nailed to a board and left on the ground can attract winter birds and squirrels. Different birds and different climates and terrains have their particular requirements. Often local park

A trip to a local ecological center is followed by the opportunity for each child to categorize his or her personal sensory experiences.

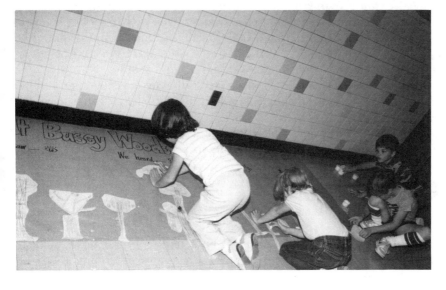

employees can be invited to the school to talk with children about ecology and to suggest projects that children can do and that serve a real purpose in the community.

Concern for the environment should not just be a special project, however. Teachers should continuously model good environmental habits for children. Regular attention to conservation is most likely to help children develop a positive environmental orientation.

MATERIALS AND EXPERIENCES FOR EARLY CHILDHOOD SCIENCE

Children need to be provided with adequate tools and opportunities to "do science" to get the most out of the science curriculum. The materials of science include such things as animals, plants, stones, seeds, leaves, sand, water, snow, and other things from the world at large. While children are familiar with these, they may never have carefully studied them. Children can observe these materials singly and together to generate hyptheses and make predictions. Placing seeds in dirt and in sand may generate ideas about whether the seeds will grow better in one or the other. Similarly, adding water to one pot of planted seeds and not to the other, or putting one pot on a windowsill and the other in a closet, can lead to similar predictions. Placing live plants alongside artificial ones may lead to comparisons of likeness and differences.

The tools for science include magnifying glasses, simple microscopes, tweezers, magnets, pan balances, timers, basins, funnels, cups, clear plastic hoses, collection boxes, eye droppers, clear plastic containers with covers, sieves, pulleys, ramps, rollers, boards, wheels, and labels. Such tools help children to act on the materials of science and make their observations. Different stones can be placed on the two pans of a balance to compare weights. Magnifying glasses or simple microscopes allow for closer observation of objects. But children should also use direct observation, seeing, hearing, and touching things around them.

The materials and tools of science should be kept together and be kept accessible by children. There should be open shelves for storage and a display area for ongoing projects. Plants should be placed in an area of the room that gets adequate sunlight. The kinds of materials and tools available should be changed periodically to keep children's interest high.

MATHEMATICS FOR YOUNG CHILDREN

Many adults shy away from mathematics as being too difficult. Somehow the way they were taught led them to be afraid of it. Yet mathematical concepts are a part of everyone's normal activities, including those of young children. Mathematics is rooted in the concrete experiences that children have with quantitative qualities of objects—the size of things, their shapes, their numbers.

As children develop logico-mathematical knowledge, they organize and make sense of information that is abstracted from activities. Classifying, seriating, quantifying, and placing things in time and space relationships are examples of how logico-mathematical knowledge is developed. In helping young children learn mathematics, the teacher can focus on classification, seriation, and number. For instance, if children are given three balls, they can learn to recognize the relationship of "three" among the balls. In classifying, children can sort objects by some common attribute, such as shape or color. A child might place crayons in order from the shortest to the longest to seriate them.

The way young children develop logico-mathematical knowledge is through activity with the quantitative qualities of objects. Many areas of the early childhood classroom provide opportunities for grouping and counting objects. Counting blocks, buttons, beads, and dolls and sorting pegs, dress-up clothes, stones, and leaves can give children practice in understanding quantity.

According to Bernard Spodek, Olivia N. Saracho, and Richard Lee (1984), early childhood education mathematics programs must do the following:

1. Provide a rich environment in which children can accumulate sensory data about quantity.
2. Use a range of teaching techniques that will help children develop mathematical concepts.
3. Demonstrate the relationship between mathematical experiences and mathematical language.
4. Present problems that require children to understand the meaning of situations and to apply their mathematical knowledge.
5. Focus on methods that promote both computational skills and problem-solving ability. (p. 239)

A good mathematics program is one in which children collect information, learn the appropriate terms to describe the new information, and learn to apply the information in problem-solving situations.

TOPICS FOR EARLY CHILDHOOD MATHEMATICS

There are a great many topics that can be part of a mathematics program for young children and that build on their daily experiences. Jean Shaw (1981) suggests that these activities include:

- Describing—noticing one or more characteristics of an object.
- Ordering—arranging objects in order according to some quality such as length, shade of color, or weight.
- Classifying—putting objects in sets or groups according to a characteristic such as color, texture, or shape.
- Patterning—creating, reproducing, varying, and describing arrangements of objects.
- Comparing—making direct side-by-side comparisons; using one-to-one correspondence to see if sets are equivalent.
- Joining and separating sets—making larger or smaller sets by adding or taking away members.
- Equalizing—making sets have the same number of objects; teaching equality by using one-to-one correspondence.
- Experiencing symbols and concepts—tallying and graphing information; recognizing and writing numerals.
- Experiencing geometry—understanding concepts such as open and closed, inside and outside, flat and solid geometric shapes.

These activities can become part of the daily classroom routine. Teachers should recognize their potential to generate mathematic concepts and to help children learn the appropriate language to describe their learning. Included here are suggestions for presenting three mathematics concepts to young children: number, seriation, and set.

Number

Number is the synthesis of two kinds of relationships that children create: ordering and class inclusion (Kamii & DeVries, 1978b). Because a number is an abstract idea, children need many experiences with related activities that help them to move toward the conservation of conversation. To *conserve* number is to realize that the quantity remains the same even when the spatial arrangement of the objects has been changed (Kamii, 1982).

Some experiences that are appropriate before counting are:

- Making complimentary sets—set of dolls to set of dresses; set of napkins to set of children; pencil for each child.
- Matching one-to-one correspondence—matching objects that are not usually found together: flower petals to plants; bottle caps to sticks.
- Ordering elements in a set of physical objects (copying a pattern)— arranging a set of objects such as knife, fork, spoon from left to right and then reverse order; doll clothes; colored beads; geometric shapes.
- Ordering sets of objects in which a relation has been imposed: shortest to tallest; lightest to darkest; fattest to thinnest.

After the child has such experiences, it is helpful to provide counting opportunities throughout the day. Children can count aloud, use counting rhymes and songs, use finger games requiring counting, bounce

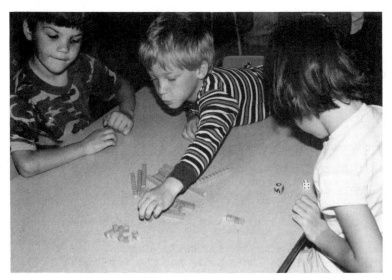

Concrete manipulative materials allow children to explore number concepts.

balls and chant numbers, count the steps of a slide, count children by touching heads, or count cups, cookies, or forks.

Children can be provided with materials to develop the idea of more than one, such as counting cubes, hundred board, number rods with lines indented, Cuisenaire rods, abacus, and charts on which objects can be placed. Kamii and DeVries (1978b) suggest the following situations that are conducive to the development of the concept of number: distributing materials, dividing objects, collecting things, keeping records, cleanup tasks, voting, group games, board games, hiding games, music, movement, and art.

Teachers should teach number concepts when these are useful and meaningful to the child. Children should be encouraged to think about numbers when they feel a need and interest. Teachers also need to figure out how children think. It is more important to learn why an error was made than to correct it.

Seriation

In seriation a relationship is formed when two or more separate objects are arranged, one before the other, on the basis of one distinguishable characteristic. The child is asked to compare one object with another in arranging a group of objects.

According to Piaget there are generally three phases a child passes through in developing the concept of seriation.

1. The child succeeds in constructing fragments of a series in terms of isolated pairs.
2. Then the child can form a series through a trial-and-error process, picking randomly one object at a time.
3. Finally, either the shortest or tallest object is chosen to start and the rest of the series is built systematically.

Table 13-3 presents a list of activities for developing seriation.

TABLE 13-3   Seriation Activities for Young Children

1. Ordering objects in a series according to one property:
   a. Arranging materials from roughest to smoothest.
   b. Arranging objects or materials from hardest to softest—styrofoam, erasers, rocks, pencils, cloth, rubber, cotton, sponges.
   c. Seriating shades in color from lightest to darkest—shaded wood grains, homemade color cards.
   d. Arranging groups of miscellaneous objects from smallest to largest.
   e. Arranging things from shortest to tallest (or longest)—making a Family Graph, using an abacus with removable seriated rods, using a hundred board and seriating by number of blocks in a column, using counting blocks, counting rods or other objects (twigs, combs, pencils, dowel rods, etc.). Arranging things from thinnest to thickest—counting blocks, dowel rods, etc.
   f. Ordering a set of Cuisenaire rods from the shortest to the longest.
   g. Ordering boxed sets of beads or objects (ranged from a set of 1 to a set of 5).
   h. Seriating objects on the basis of weight.
   i. Nesting toys, ordering on the basis of base area.
   j. Pink Tower (Montessori), ordering on the basis of size.
   k. Ordering sounds on the basis of pitch (lowest to highest) and intensity (softest to loudest).
2. Ordering objects in two series inversely related to one another. Referring to the activities in 1 above, take the last item of a completed series and ask the child to use that item as the first in a series.
3. Using pictoral representation in seriation. The flannel board may be used with flannel pieces ranging in size (height, length, width) and color (shades) to help the children order pictures of objects.
4. Seriation of geometric shapes. Ordering two-dimensional figures on the basis of number of sides and three-dimensional shapes on the basis of number of faces. Ordering a group of like shapes (for example, all squares) varying in area.

Sets

Organizing things into sets is a basic part of a child's activity with objects. A set is a well-defined collection of objects, ideas, or symbols. In order to recognize a set, a child must know what things are its elements or members. Children can compare two sets either visibly or by counting the elements. The teacher's role in developing the concept of sets is to provide children with opportunities for manipulating objects into sets, to supply vocabulary at appropriate times, and to structure needed learning experiences for individual and small groups. Table 13-4 presents activities that are appropriate for learning sets.

TABLE 13-4   Activities for Learning Sets

PLAY AND MANIPULATION

—Many things can be put into sets:

dishes	flowers in a vase
silverware	clothespins in a bag
clothes	pins in a pin cushion
family (dolls, doll clothes)	tongue depressor sticks in juice cans
crayons	balls
books	cooking equipment (spoons, utensils cookie
checkers	cutters, pans, beaters)

—Display on the mathematics table "sets" that are not usual to classroom. Talk informally with individuals about these.

A set of golf clubs in a bag
A can of tennis balls
The objects in a pocketbook
Coins in a coin purse

—Introduce new types of materials for making sets. Display them and watch what children do with them. Talk informally with the children about them.

keys	shoes and socks
coins	buttons
beads	matching cards
rocks	bottle caps
clothespins (colored)	spools (different sizes)
balls	bolts, washers
bowls	boxes (different sizes)

Containers for sets:

muffin tins	
ice cube trays	jars
divided boxes	pie pans (various sizes)
milk cartons with tops cut off	paper cups (assorted sizes)
	egg cartons

—Display sets that are pairs of objects:

a pair of shoes, boots, rubbers
a pair of gloves, mittens
a pair of socks
a pair of earrings

pictures—a pair of eyes, ears, feet, hands
walk in pairs

—Make sets (and subsets) of objects collected on nature walks.

seeds	nuts
leaves	rocks
acorns	shells
	feathers

—Provide models (miniature toys) and pictures for arranging sets. Talk with children about what they are doing, their reasons for grouping the materials into sets.

—Provide hoops (embroidery hoops, wire hoops, hula hoops) and strips of yarn for children to use in defining sets.

TABLE 13-4, continued

—Provide children with objects that can be ordered (buttons, leaves, counting cubes, beads). Watch for seriation.

COMPARISON

—Use day-to-day activities. Children discover "not enough" crackers, straws, etc.

—Have children make comparisons in play—enough cups for the saucers, carriages or chairs for the dolls, etc.

—Look for comparison in room equipment—lockers to children, etc.

—Snack time presents opportunities for matching:
cups on a tray, cups per person (one-to-one)
cookies on a plate, crackers per person (many-to-one)
napkins, straws (one-to-one)
other snack items—pieces of fruit, sandwich, etc. (one-to-one or many--to-one)

—Structure problems of correspondence (equivalent, greater than, less than) for individuals or small groups.
flowers to vases
paint brushes to cans
dresses to dolls or paper dolls
miniature cups to saucers, etc.
eggs to egg carton holes
shoes to socks

—Provide more astract problems—sets of objects to put into one-to-one correspondence
cubes to cubes
sticks to sticks of another color or size
cubes to sticks
rocks to cubes

—Provide games that use one-to-one correspondence.
cherries to holes
lotto card pictures to cover other pictures
bingo-type games
parquetry blocks and design cubes to 2-d patterns
simple card games

MATERIALS FOR EARLY CHILDHOOD MATHEMATICS

Manipulative materials are commonly found in early childhood classes. These materials can be acted on by children using their own hands and their own imaginations.

Both Froebel and Montessori made wide use of manipulative materials in their programs, but they used them in different ways than we do now. Today we have a more sophisticated understanding of what children learn when they manipulate objects and how their actions lead to learning.

Many things can be manipulated to develop mathematical under-standings. Beads, buttons, blocks, geo boards, zipping frames, sewing cards, Lincoln Logs, and Cuisenaire rods are examples of good manipu-lated materials. The characteristics of worthy manipulative materials are:

- The materials should be easy to use and familiar to the children.
- The materials should be brightly colored and pleasing to the eye.
- It should be possible to classify the materials in more than one way. For example, a bead can be classified as wooden, round, or red.
- The materials should be of varied sizes, shapes, and textures.
- The materials should have a variety of uses.
- The materials should be safe for children to use.

These materials should be available on an open shelf so that children can easily make choices.

USING EVERYDAY EVENTS TO TEACH ABOUT MATHEMATICS

The daily activity of the early childhood class is full of opportunities to teach children about mathematics. Children can help record attendance, matching a mark or symbol to each boy or girl who comes. Preparing for the snack allows children to match one cup or one napkin to one child and to count how many are needed for each table. Music, dance, and games all offer children opportunities to count. Dramatic play, where children might, for example, play "supermarket" or "bus driver," allows children to use play money, count, and measure. Work in the block-building area and at the woodwork bench also provides children with the chance to develop a sense of mathematics.

One way for children to gain an understanding of number and the different forms of quantity and space is by measuring. Young children approach measuring simply and intuitively. They first compare things with one another directly; later they learn to compare things to an established standard or unit of measurement.

Young children can be seen dealing with the problem of measur-ing length as they try to match the height of two sides of a block structure or search for a piece of wood the right size for their wood construction. As they deal with these problems, they learn the words "short," "shorter," "long," "longer," "tall," and "taller." They can soon begin to match the length of objects that are far from one another by making a mark showing the object's length on a piece of paper or cardboard, then taking the paper or cardboard to a second object and comparing its length to the mark, making a judgment from that. Words like "foot" and "inch" can be introduced as kindergarten children use rulers.

Weight is harder for children to perceive than is length. A pound of foam plastic feels lighter than a pound of iron. A simple balance scale can help children see whether one thing is heavier than another. Teachers can make a simple balance scale with a short wooden stick, two pie tins, and some string, being sure that the two tins balance when empty. The children can then compare things around the room, using words like "heavier," "lighter," and "the same weight" to describe their comparisons. Later a teacher might provide different kinds of scales along with standard weights for the balance scale.

Time is much more difficult for children to measure and understand. We cannot see time, and our perception of the passage of time is

Learning to read a clock is often an extension of early childhood number work. Discussions and demonstrations can be followed by opportunities for children to practice their developing understanding.

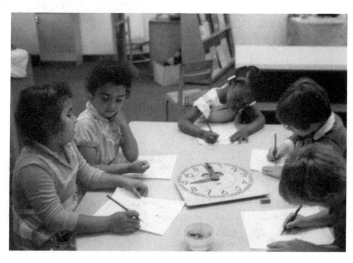

influenced by many things. We measure time indirectly using what seem to be arbitrary units. What passes for learning to "tell" time is more a matter of learning to read instruments for measuring or keeping track of time: clocks and calendars. Kindergarten children can learn to read an analog clock, understanding the meaning of the hands and the numerals on its face. They can learn to mark a calendar and read it as they read numerals. Using a clock and calendar in the classroom gives children a better sense of the passage of time and the weekly order of the days.

Using everyday occurrences helps children see that mathematics is not an abstract, isolated subject but a way of thinking about elements in our actual life. As a result, mathematics can become a much more meaningful and less fearful subject.

SUMMARY

Children must construct their understanding of the world. Mathematics and science are learned as young children create their understandings. This understanding is based on physical knowledge and on the construction of logical-mathematical knowledge.

The science curriculum should be built around the active involvement of children with their world. The approach should stress children's learning more about the physical world while developing a positive value orientation toward the environment.

A good program should offer mathematics and science experiences in a variety of contexts. Many kinds of materials should be used to present the concepts and many opportunities provided to practice their use. Each child's understanding and progress in mathematics and science should be recorded by the teacher. Open-ended questions should be used to extend children's learning.

If teachers have a clear understanding of what they wish children to learn, and if a rich environment is provided in an open setting, exciting discoveries can be made by children who are relating to the physical world. This is the stuff of which science and mathematics are made.

REFERENCES

AMERICAN ASSOCIATION FOR THE ADVANCEMENT OF SCIENCE (1967), *Description of program—Science: A process approach*. New York: Xerox Educational Division.

AUSTIN AEYC (1973). *Ideas for teaching with nature*. Washington, DC: National Association for the Education of Young Children.

GINSBURG, H., AND S. OPPER (1979). *Piaget's theory of intellectual development*. Englewood Cliffs, NJ: Prentice-Hall.

HERR, J., AND W. MORSE (1982). Food for thought: Nutrition education for young children. *Young Children,* **38**(1), 3-11.

KAMII, C. (1982). *Number in preschool and kindergarten: Educational implementation of Piaget's theory.* Washington, DC: National Association for the Education of Young Children.

KAMII, C., AND R. DEVRIES (1978a). *Physical knowledge in preschool education.* Englewood Cliffs, NJ: Prentice-Hall.

————, (1978b). *Piaget, children, and number.* Washington, DC: National Association for the Education of Young Children.

KAMII, C., AND L. LEE-KATZ (1979). Physics in preschool education: A Piagetian approach. *Young Children,* **34**(4), 4-9.

SHAW, J. M. (1981). IDEAS: Math for young children. *Dimensions,* **10**(1), 15-16.

SPODEK, B. (1985). *Teaching in the early years* (3rd ed.). Englewood Cliffs, NJ: Prentice-Hall.

SPODEK, B., O. N. SARACHO, AND R. C. LEE (1984). *Mainstreaming young children.* Belmont, CA: Wadsworth Publishing Co.

SUGGESTED ACTIVITIES

1. Collect a set of buttons, beads, bottle caps, and other things that can be sorted, ordered, weighed, or otherwise manipulated.

2. Start a recipe collection for young children. Pay particular attention to the nutritional value of the foods, avoiding those that have empty calories.

3. Design, develop, and implement a no-heat cooking experience for a group of young children. At the end of the experience make a list of concepts in various content areas (social studies, mathematics, science, etc.) that evolved from the activity.

4. Interview a teacher of young children about the mathematics and science programs in his or her class. Pay particular attention to any suggestions about methods or materials.

14

SOCIAL-PERSONAL LEARNING The Social Studies and Beyond

OBJECTIVES

After completing this chapter on social-personal learning, the students should be able to:

1. Define physical knowledge, social knowledge, logico-mathematical knowledge, school-appropriate behavior, prosocial behavior, and multicultural education.

2. Identify the difference between content and socialization in a social studies program for young children.

3. Identify the attributes of a good social studies program for young children.

4. Describe the three elements in planning for a field trip.

5. Explain why mapping activities are appropriate for young children.

6. Discuss how representational activities allow children to refine what they know.

No single subject in early childhood education encompasses more of the child's day than do the social studies. Social studies is both a content area that can be studied separately and a set of skills, knowledge, and values that pervade all other activities in the early childhood classroom.

There are two components of any good social studies program for young children: *social science content* and *socialization skills.* The content component of social studies is made up of elements taken from the scholarly fields of history, geography, economics, political science, anthropology, sociology, philosophy, and psychology. Knowledge from all of these social sciences may be a part of the child's curriculum. The second component, socialization skills, helps a child to learn how to work with others within the intimate environment of the school and the larger environment of the community. Children without adequate social skills have trouble interacting with peers and adults. Because of this, they may not participate fully in the learning opportunities offered.

The social studies help children to understand the world and to understand themselves. They learn to make sense of the world as known through personal experience and action. Children also come to know about themselves and to develop a self-concept that is strong, confident, and supportive of trying new things.

The social studies can also be used as an organizer for the other areas of curriculum. The themes, activities, skills, knowledge, values, and materials that are part of any good social studies program can serve as the basis for all of the subjects that are presented in a classroom for young children.

This chapter will present the social studies as an integral part of the young child's day. It will offer ideas relating to social studies content as well as to concerns about socialization.

DEVELOPING AND UNDERSTANDING THE SOCIAL WORLD

All of the goals of early childhood education have also been the goals for social studies education. Because of the concern of social studies for both the child's world and the child herself or himself, the goals for a social studies program should be closely related to the overall goals of early childhood education. That is not always the case, however.

There is a lack of agreement among educators on the definition and priorities of social studies education. R. D. Barr, T. L. Barth, and S. S. Shermis (cited in Price, 1982) suggest that three contending views of social studies exist: (1) citizenship transmission, (2) age-appropriate exposure to the methods used by the social sciences, and (3) an exposure to reflective inquiry that will help children to arrive at reasoned decisions. Most current early childhood social studies programs tend to emphasize the development of social skills and socially desirable behavior. This approach is a mixture of concern for citizenship transmission and reflective inquiry.

One of the best ways to come to understand what appropriate social studies programs are possible for young children is to look back at two experts, Patty Smith Hill and Lucy Sprague Mitchell. Each was a pioneer in early childhood education who many years ago developed innovative approaches to teaching social studies. Hill (1913) suggested that the child's social experience was the basis for knowledge and that themes reflected in child's play should be the basis for a social studies program. Children tended to play out what they knew best, and their experiences with family, peers, and community provided them with a wealth of information that could be replicated, refined, and understood.

Mitchell (1971), who wrote originally in 1934, believed that the "here and now" approach to social studies was the most appropriate for young children. Concrete, familiar, everyday experiences should provide the basis for social studies. Mitchell took children on field trips into the community to help them understand the neighborhood and their relationship to it. According to Bernard Spodek (1974), children who use the "here and now" approach act as laboratory scientists, abstracting information from what they know and applying it with new information to solve new problems. Although Mitchell initially provided children with concrete materials and activities, she felt that older children could function with more abstract, theoretical information.

Both Hill and Mitchell believed in using the real experiences of children to help them develop social studies concepts. While Hill focused on social activity and Mitchell on the social environment, both recognized the importance of beginning with what was real and accessible to children. Both Hill and Mitchell seem quite contemporary in their ideas about social studies education. Social studies programs with similar intellectual goals can be developed in early childhood classes and can serve to integrate the curriculum (Spodek, 1974).

Jean Piaget has posited that children develop three types of knowledge as they come to understand their world: physical knowledge, social knowledge, and logico-mathematical knowledge. Children act on their world and abstract information from it. *Physical knowledge* is knowledge of the physical attributes of things. Through field trips, observations, and interviews children experience firsthand how things smell, feel, look, and taste and, in general, what the world is about. Physical knowledge is directly derived from these experiences. The child's senses are important in gathering the bases for this knowledge.

Social knowledge is knowledge of social rules, conventions, symbols, and values. Social knowledge tells children what things are called. It helps children to understand appropriate and inappropriate social behavior. Social knowledge is arbitrary; it is validated by authority. Unlike physical knowledge, social knowledge cannot be discovered. It must be taught to children, either directly or indirectly.

Logico-mathematical knowledge is the intellectual processes that are used to organize and make sense of information that children are abstracting from activities. Classifying, ordering, quantifying, and putting things in space and time relationships are examples of logico-mathematical knowledge. These are internal processes that are developed through self-regulation.

All three forms of knowledge are present in the social studies and all three need to be acquired by young children. Physical knowledge of places and things can be discovered by children and social knowledge can be told to them. Logico-mathematical knowledge requires that children act on the information they receive to make sense of it.

A fourth element in social learning is that children need to represent what they know. In early childhood programs, children represent things through dramatic play, stories, paintings, block buildings, or other constructions. These activities help children refine their understanding of newly learned information.

When we substitute secondhand and thirdhand information for real experiences from the children's world, we deny them the opportunity to gain a variety of forms of knowledge. Children become "information receivers" rather than "information generators." We have limited their opportunities to know.

An appropriate approach to social studies should (1) reflect the child's real experiences, (2) show a concern for children's gaining physical knowledge, social knowledge, and logico-mathematical knowledge, and (3) value a child's efforts at representing what he or she knows. It should also be inquiry oriented. In an inquiry program children gather social data, organize that data, interpret it, and represent what they come to know (Spodek, Saracho, & Lee, 1984). An inquiry approach views the child as both the receiver and generator of knowledge. Such an approach can be related to social science content and to the development of socialization skills by young children.

A SOCIAL STUDIES PROGRAM FOR YOUNG CHILDREN: CONTENT

A good social studies program should reflect the following goals:

- Children should learn social studies concepts and knowledge.
- Children should have an opportunity to apply that knowledge to problems.
- Children should learn physical knowledge from the real world.
- Children should learn to understand the world and their relationship to it.

- Children should be able to learn social science concepts as long as they are presented in a developmentally appropriate manner and are arranged so that children can reflect and act on their learning.
- Children should have access to a wealth of materials.
- Children should have an opportunity to represent their knowledge in many and varied ways.
- Children should become socialized into both the school and community.

All children come to school with some knowledge of the social world. They know about their family and they know about their immediate surroundings. It's important to remember, however, that each child's understanding of the world is unique. No two children have had the same set of experiences and, unless there are siblings in a class, they have not grown up with the same set of family values.

Initially, the teacher's role is to provide children with opportunities to share ideas and to learn from each other. As children discuss their families, pets, homes, and neighborhoods, the teacher learns about their perceptions of the world. When children play together, they hear other views and begin to incorporate new vocabulary and ideas into their previous conception of the world. Dramatic play is a particularly rich vehicle in which children learn from others.

After teachers develop an understanding of what their children already know, they can begin to present new ideas to enhance the children's understanding of the social world. Social studies activities can be organized around significant social studies concepts acquired through personal experiences in acting on physical and social information.

Concepts

A concept helps children to establish a framework upon which to understand and process information. Huber Walsh (1980) refers to a concept as a word or short phrase that represents a key idea.

He suggests three points to consider in choosing concepts:

1. A high priority should be given to concepts like helping, sharing, rules, values, family, safety, and home, and these concepts should be repeated throughout the social studies program.
2. Concepts need to be carefully screened so that they are appropriate for children and not intellectually confusing.
3. In selecting concepts, preference should be given to those that can be learned through the use of concrete materials.

Young children's concepts include such things as *family, dog, car, store,* and *home.* Children who have learned the concept of car can construct a class of objects which have the attributes of a car, such as wheels, engine, and passenger compartment. Those who have not learned the concept may assign the label "car" to trucks, buses, vans, or campers, vehicles which have some but not all of the attributes of "cars." Concepts lead to efficient use of new information. A child who knows that *McDonald's* is a "restaurant" will have little problem putting other fast-food places in the same category. It is important that teachers be aware of which concepts are developmentally appropriate for young children and which might be beyond their ability to grasp.

There are two levels of meaning that children develop in understanding concepts. The first is the *classification* level, where a child decides which object or event fits into a given category. The second level is *association.* At the association level the child is developing a set of understandings about a given concept (Walsh 1980). When a child categorizes a chair as a type of furniture, she or he operates on the classification level. When she or he explains that furniture is generally found in homes and makes living more comfortable, she or he is dealing with association.

Concepts are not learned in an all-or-none fashion. They are developed slowly through experiences with examples of the concept as well as with nonexamples. Language is important in labeling concepts, but the word cannot stand for the class of objects initially.

Field Trips

Field trips are one of the best ways for children to begin to acquire new social studies concepts. A field trip enables a child to learn firsthand what a neighborhood, a post office, a grocery store, a gas station, or a firehouse is like. Many children have never walked through their own neighborhood or visited a firehouse. Time constraints may not allow some families to take children on errands and, as a result, they do not have firsthand knowledge of their own immediate community. Even when they do have the experience, the child's perceptions may not have focused on critical elements. Teachers should approach each field trip as if it is a new and unique experience for each of the children.

Field trips do not have to be big productions, such as trips to the zoo, circus, or other major attractions. Often important trips are simple, such as a walk through the neighborhood, or to a store to shop in preparation for a cooking activity. Even taking repeated trips to the same place can provide children with new learnings each time.

Many field trips fail because of a lack of preparation. Teachers must focus on three distinct elements as they prepare for a trip. First, they have to decide how to get the children ready for a trip. Talking about the destination, reading books, generating questions to be answered or hypotheses about what will be seen are all ways to set the stage. A pretrip visit to the site is a good way for the teacher to learn about any safety concerns or other problems that may take special arrangements.

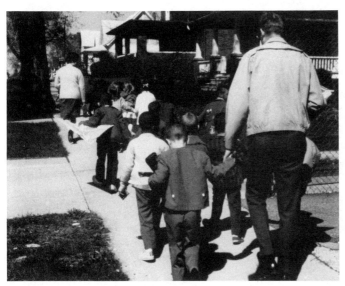

Field trips can often be walks around the neighborhood.

Second, the teacher must decide what types of activities will be provided on the trip. It is impossible to take a group of young children anywhere without prior thought of what they will do while there. Giving children things to look for, questions to answer, discussing what has been seen, and taking pictures while on the trip will help children to focus their attention and keep them involved during the trip.

Finally, after the trip children need opportunities to discuss what they have seen and to work through new ideas in their play. For instance, simple still photographs can be used for stimulating discussions as well as for providing information. They should be large enough so that they can be seen by a group of children and be relatively free of clutter. Projected slides can work well, too. Pictures taken on the trip can provide a good way to review. This is the time when children begin to make sense of the new concepts. Do not expect all children to learn the same thing while on a field trip. Each will focus on the aspects of the experience that most interest them (Spodek, 1968).

As a follow-up to a field trip, an exhibit can be set up in the room. It could include pictures, props, and photographs from the trip presented in an aesthetically pleasing way. As children explore the exhibit, new concepts are further reinforced. Other follow-ups can be putting on a play, dictating a group story, or any activity that will allow children to recall and reflect on their experience. Figure 14-1 presents an example of plans for a field trip to the supermarket.

Figure 14-1

A FIELD TRIP TO THE SUPERMARKET

I. Preparation
  A. Supermarket
     1. Contact the manager requesting permission to visit and set a date.
     2. a. Make a pretrip visit, noting special areas that you particularly want the children to see.
        b. Pay particular attention to any safety hazards and any barriers that may inhibit a handicapped child, if one is in your class.
     3. Discuss the trip with the store manager. Explain what the children are like, how many there will be in the group, and how long you will stay.
  B. Children
     1. Arrange for transportation, extra adults, and parental permission.
     2. Bring books, filmstrips, props, and other materials related to the grocery store into class. Set up a grocery display.
     3. Discuss with children what they think they will see on the field trip. This is a good time to generate questions that can be answered on the trip.
     4. The day before the trip and again on the day of the trip, remind children about appropriate behavior and the rules they must follow.

II. At the supermarket
  A. Use the questions generated in class as a way for children to learn about the store. Tell children particular things to look for.
  B. Make sure each child has an opportunity to see everything.
  C. Take photographs of the experience.
  D. Purchase some foods that can be used to make a soup or salad back at school
  E. Periodically check that children are not lost.

III. After the trip
  A. Prepare a snack with the ingredients purchased on the trip. Discuss the trip in the process.
  B. Review the questions that the children asked on the trip.
  C. Set-up a "supermarket" in the dramatic play area of the room.
  D. Display pictures taken on the supermarket trip. Children may want to discuss or write about their pictures. A class book can be made of the stories.
  E. Additional books, filmstrips, and recipes can be used as appropriate.
  F. Write a thank you note to the grocery store manager. Have all the children sign their names as best they can.

Resource Persons

In many early childhood programs resource persons are invited to the class to provide firsthand information similar to what can be gained in a field trip. Fathers, mothers, siblings, community members, and retirees are all good resources for social studies. Inviting a police officer to the classroom allows children to interact with a new figure and to understand better what police officers are like. Anyone who can tell a story, play an instrument, cook a special dish, do arts and crafts, perform a dance, or simply be with the children can provide new, real information.

Planning for having a resource person in class is similar to planning for a field trip. Thought must be given to preparation, the visit itself, and the follow-up. It is important to contact the visitor and to discuss your expectations prior to the visit. The visitor needs to know how many children will be present and what their ages are, how the visit fits into the program and how much time there will be for the visit. The children should have an opportunity to generate questions they want to ask and to review the rules for behavior before the visitor arrives.

During the visit it is important to allow each child to talk and ask questions. There should be a two-way interaction between children and guest. Opportunities for dramatic play as well as for writing language experience stories, painting, viewing pictures, and otherwise representing what has been learned should follow the visit. These can continue until the children begin to lose interest.

Artifacts

Many times artifacts can be interesting and informative. Items from other cultures or from another era, such as toys, clothes, shoes, eating and cooking utensils, and musical instruments, allow children to make comparisons with what they know from their own experiences and can begin to understand that different people see the world in different ways.

Children need to try on, feel, and smell objects in order to learn about them. The artifacts provided should be those that can be handled. Fragile, priceless, or dangerous artifacts have no place in a classroom.

One good way to present artifacts is to show and discuss them in a large group. They can then be placed on a display table for children to handle and explore on their own. Ideally, the artifacts should be on display long enough for all children to explore. They can also be used as parts of learning centers. Old clothes or jewelry can be placed in the housekeeping corner. Beaters, bowls, spoons, cups, and other utensils can be used in cooking. Musical instruments can be played. The use of artifacts is limited only by the teacher's willingness to incorporate them into the classroom experiences.

Mapping

Many young children have experiences with maps before they learn anything about map keys, distance, or direction. Children may lay out streets with blocks, pretend to read a road map in dramatic play, or talk about the shortest way to get to a friend's house. These represent a good introduction to mapping.

Young children can do maps (or floor plans) of their classroom, of their school center, of their bedroom at home, or of the playground. At first these maps may be no more than lines drawn on a page; later they will become representations that attempt to show objects in relation to one another. Children may have all the furniture strung out on the bottom edge, or they may show a table with legs sticking out in all four directions. These are all good beginnings.

A good way to begin mapping is to place an outline of the classroom on the floor and let children place blocks or boxes on the outline to indicate the position of desks, tables, or activity centers. The same process can be used to present the playground or a child's bedroom. Using familiar places helps the child refer to reality as the representation is developed.

Later activities can be based on maps of the neighborhood, a local store, or the route from school to home. Children can walk around these areas before representing them. The process allows the child to move from real objects in space to three-dimensional representations to two-dimensional representations.

The best mapping experiences are those that children choose to do. Once they have the basic idea that a map indicates how to get somewhere, they can work on their own maps. The important element that children will learn is that the maps are representations of places in the children's world and that these representations show distance, direction, and the relation of elements to one another.

Using Audiovisual Materials

A number of audiovisual materials can be used to provide children with information about their world. Picture sets can be obtained from many libraries and are available for purchase. Picture sets on families, pets, transportation, holidays, careers, and many other subjects that are developmentally appropriate provide children with the opportunity to increase their knowledge through careful observation and discussion. They can be particularly useful as discussion starters before or after field trips.

Sound filmstrips and films are also available on a wide range of social studies topics. The sound and action in a film are particularly attractive to children, but a sound filmstrip has the advantage of allowing frame-by-frame discussions. Many local libraries have catalogs of available films and filmstrips that can be obtained either free or for a small fee.

Portable video cassette recorders can be used to record day-to-day classroom experiences as well as field trips and presentations by resource people. Young children (or adults) love to see themselves and their friends on television. Videotape can also convey to children the excitement and involvement of classroom experiences.

A particularly useful machine is the audio cassette recorder. Many of them can be operated by children and can be used to record stories, neighborhood sounds, rhymes, and anything else that intrigues children.

While media can provide children with a wealth of information, teachers must choose wisely and use only those things that are appropriate for children. Of particular concern is selecting appropriate television programs for children. Teachers should select programs according to the developmental appropriateness of the material for young children and to its relation to the instructional program. Television should not be used to fill time that could be used for other kinds of learning.

Acting on Acquired Knowledge

The first step in a social studies program is providing children with information to generate new knowledge. The second is allowing them to act on the knowledge, play with it, refine it, and come to understand it fully.

Children apply their newly acquired information through the use of sand, water, blocks, the housekeeping area, dramatic play materials, art, and dance. For example, after a trip to the firehouse the teacher can add fire hats and trucks, a length of hose, and some small ladders to the block area. These additional props will motivate the children to "play firehouse" and to build structures and play out themes that are representative of what they have learned.

While the class is studying about cars, traffic signs can be placed on the outdoor wheel toy path so children can stop, go, and practice their knowledge of cars in other ways. They may also build superhighways in the block area or act out the mechanic repairing a car in a service station. In these ways they will refine their understanding of cars and rules relating to cars.

A grocery store can be set up with workers and shoppers so the children can experiment with different roles. Stocking shelves, checking groceries, making decisions on food, purchasing groceries, and ultimately bringing the parcels home to the housekeeping area are all valuable learning experiences that enable children to represent their knowledge about grocery stores. Additionally, while children play grocery they are refining their logico-mathematical knowledge by sorting, classifying, organizing, and comparing the items in the store.

Tempera paint, fingerpaint, clay, collage, junk sculpture, chalk, and crayons are media that children can use to represent knowledge. Often a child will draw many different pictures of a trip, each one a further refinement of a new concept. As the drawings are completed and discussed, the teacher gains insight into the child's thinking and understanding.

A field trip to a barber shop is followed up by children's playing barber in the classroom.

Children play through the new information they receive in the dress-up area also. Items from the real world support children's play as a way to advance their understanding. For example, after a visit to the post office a prop box containing stamps, envelopes, junk mail, a scale, mailbag, shirts, rubber stamps, and other postal artifacts could be set up in the classroom. A limited number of children can use the props to play post office and refine what they've learned.

Materials are a critical part of the social studies program. They provide both new information and an opportunity to refine knowledge that was previously acquired. Materials are an extension of the teacher in that they become significant in the framework of goal-oriented activities. Their worth is in how well they advance a child's understanding of a concept (Spodek, 1968).

The inquiry approach to social studies enables children to generate information, act on it, and represent the information in a reasonable way. Children are both consumers and producers of knowledge.

A SOCIAL STUDIES PROGRAM FOR YOUNG CHILDREN: SOCIALIZATION

The second part of a social studies program for young children relates to socialization. Socialization refers to children becoming functioning members of a community, such as the school or the classroom. Children must obey rules, following directions and accepting the fact that sharing, taking turns, and assertive, but not aggressive, behavior is suitable. They also learn that they fit into a role which is related to other roles in the community. In social studies, socialization also refers to children learning the rules, values, history, and expectations of the community at large.

In socializing it is necessary for children to develop a sense of school and community expectations. They must also develop a sense of what they are like. Their self-image, social behavior, value system, and cultural view are all variables that affect the way they respond to socialization efforts.

This section will focus on socialization and ways to socialize children to school and community expectations.

Learning School and Community Roles

As children study topics such as the neighborhood, the grocery store, or community helpers, they begin to understand how society is organized and how each person contributes to the well-being of a community. While knowledge of society is important, perhaps more important is the fact that children learn to value the way society works. Such a value is based not on a sophisticated understanding, but rather on the child's modeling of values that are important to adults.

Children also become socialized to the larger community through listening to stories about historic figures, participating in holiday celebrations, singing traditional songs, learning traditional dances, and interacting with special guests. As children hear about and participate in the traditions of society, they learn to enjoy them and to value them, accepting the traditions of the community as their own.

Holidays are particularly important to children. Celebrations are fun and help to transmit traditions. They are also social events that help form a special bond between child, family, and community. Teachers must plan holiday celebrations that reflect the cultural backgrounds and experiences of the children. Hanukkah, Christmas, and similar holidays can be celebrated during the winter holiday season. Children should understand the significance of the holiday symbols and learn the games, stories, and foods related to the celebrations.

New Year's Day is widely celebrated throughout the world, but not always on January 1. A New Year's unit should help children to learn about the different ways and times of the year that the day is celebrated. For example, the Jewish New Year, Rosh Hashanah, is a two-day fall celebration (in September or October), whereas the Chinese New Year is celebrated on the full moon some time between January 21 and February 19. UNICEF's *Festival Book*, published by the U.S. Committee for UNICEF, is a useful resource.

It is seldom easy to socialize children to the rules, expectations, values and appropriate behaviors that ensure smooth functioning in the classroom environment so they can become successful learners. Children differ in their developmental readiness and their willingness to work for the good of others. Teachers must begin with the needs of the individual child before proceeding to the needs of the group.

Developing School-Appropriate Behavior

When children first enter school at any level, teachers must help them understand what behaviors are appropriate for school. Many have learned the proper way to behave at home and believe this is the way they should behave at school. However, while fighting may be acceptable at home, it is out of place in a classroom. In this instance, children must learn how to influence other children in a nonaggressive manner that avoids the use of force.

There are a number of school-appropriate behaviors that children must learn. Independence, assertiveness, sensitivity to others, and the willingness to participate in social problem solving are traits that help a child have successful social experiences (Walsh, 1980). Children who are pro-social, who show a degree of sociableness, and who are socially competent are more likely to have positive social experiences (Price, 1982). *Pro-social* behavior refers to helping others without anticipation of a personal reward. *Sociableness* is willingness to be part of a group and interacting with others rather than being an isolate and working and playing alone. A *socially competent* child is one whose behavior and thought processes result in effective interpersonal relationships. Asa Hilliard III

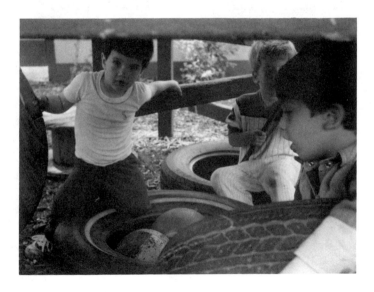

Children need opportunities to develop social competence in school.

TABLE 14-1   Social Competencies for Young Children

1. One of the domains for assessment of social competence should be the child's attitude. A healthy learning pattern that produces healthy development is dependent upon a set of attitudes in the child which lead that child toward less fear of the environment and interest in and willingness to take risks with the personal and physical environment.
2. Every child, at every stage of life, has a world view that is the product of his or her own unique interaction with the world. That world view has an integrity and can be understood only as a reflection of that child's special environment. The socially competent child's view of the world has a contextual integrity.
3. Social competence would be reflected by the child's increasing acquisition of social skills and school skills. Social competencies have been assessed primarily in relation to "school skills." These are an important element of social competence but only a fraction of the total. The child's relationship to adults and other children, and the ability to negotiate successfully in those relationships, is another aspect of social competence.
4. In order for a child to be successful socially, it is necessary to have an appropriate amount of socially and contextually relevant information. That information is specific to the environment within which the child is growing and learning.
5. The socially competent child is an active learner, displaying a curiosity to use and transform experiences.
6. The socially competent child accurately perceives his or her environment. Distortion and perception of the environment will be reflected in inappropriate responses to that environment.
7. The socially competent child experiences a sense of continuity in growth.
8. The socially competent child has a growing sense of personal and group identity.
9. The child becomes more socially competent when the range of objects and experiences encountered expands at a rapid rate.

A. G. Hilliard, "How Should We Assess Children's Social Competence?" *Young Children, 33*(5), 1978, 12-13.

(1978) has generated a list of nine social competencies he considers to be appropriate for young children (see Table 14-1). The competencies are based on the child's internal processes rather than on external norms.

Skills that lead to social competence can be taught either directly or indirectly (Price, 1982). In direct teaching the teacher tells or show children how to behave. A teacher might explain the importance of taking turns or sharing, then demonstrate sharing or organize a method of taking turns. Three indirect ways of teaching can be successfully used to teach social skills: modeling, shaping, and planning (Ladd, 1984). In *modeling*, teachers demonstrate pro-social behaviors as they interact with children. Teachers *shape* behavior by helping children achieve a series of successive approximations toward proper behavior. They need to reward acceptable behavior so these behaviors will be shown more frequently. In *planning*, teachers structure both the interpersonal and physical environments to enhance children's social interaction and allow them to develop relationships with others. Most teachers use all four approaches—direct teaching, modeling, shaping, and planning—as they assist children in developing social competence.

Building Self-Awareness

To some extent, socialization is a function of getting individual children to conform to the expectation of the group. However, children first need to be ready to work with others, and part of that readiness is having a positive self-image. Children need to be aware of themselves and feel good about who they are, what they are, and how they interact with others. Many children come to school feeling inadequate. Supportive teachers can help them feel more adequate by reflecting positively to the child and increasing each child's competency.

Teachers should be positive and caring. They can compliment children on new and attractive clothes. They can welcome children when they return after a sickness or after a trip. They can praise children for completing a block structure. They can hug children or simply sit and talk with them, affirming each child's worth as an individual. Teachers can also provide opportunities to explore new materials and to participate in problem-solving situations. The completion of a task leads to feelings of accomplishment and self-worth.

These opportunities for children to learn more about themselves are critical. It is helpful to provide mirrors for children to see themselves in and opportunities to discuss what they see, or to outline the child's body on butcher paper and color it in, or to place photographs of children in the classroom; however, these activities provide limited meaning. It is more important for teachers to provide activities that offer feedback to children relating to their worth and that increases a child's understanding of self as viewed by others.

As children interact successfully with others and with the physical world, their self-image will improve. Teachers must carefully structure initial attempts at group activities. All children should come away from such activities feeling successful and having positive feelings about school. A child who is bullied, belittled, or ignored in a social situation will most likely develop a negative self-image.

Young Children and Values

Values are inherent in everything we say or do. When we make a decision to attend a concert rather than go to a movie, we are valuing the concert over the movie at that time. Teachers demonstrate their values in the classroom decisions they make and in the way they govern their lives. Either intentionally or not, teachers transmit their values to children. While teachers have a right to their personal values, they need to be aware of the impact these values might have on children and how they relate to family and community values.

Huber Walsh (1980) defines a value as a principle or standard that is made a part of a person's code for living. Transmitting values is a critical part of the socialization process. It helps a person learn how to act in any given situation. According to Bernard Spodek, Olivia N. Saracho, and Richard C. Lee (1984), values that are basic to early childhood education include the worth of the individual, concepts of freedom and responsibility, the importance of democratic decision making, and concern for the safety of persons and property. While young children would not be expected to understand each of these values or their sources, they would be expected to make them a part of their "code of living."

Teachers can help children to develop values by modeling appropriate values, by using role playing and creative dramatics to clarify and transmit values, by using stories that present value dilemmas, or by reading unfinished stories that require children to provide an ending to a difficult situation. Carolyn Pope Edwards, Mary Ellen Logue, and Anna Sargent Russell (1983) suggest providing three kinds of learning encounters to expose children to social ideas. First, a dramatic skit can be presented to a group of children and the teacher can then allow children to offer opinions on ways to resolve the situations. Through the discussions, children begin to realize there is more than one way to solve a problem. The second type of learning encounter is the "thinking game," in which individuals or small groups of children have a private conversation with the teacher. The thinking game is an open-ended interview about the same problem that was used in the dramatic skit. A third encounter consists of spontaneous discussions as a way to understand further what the child is thinking and why.

Edwards, Logue, and Russell offer five rules for teachers who are interviewing children:

1. Do not assume too soon that you understand what the child is saying.
2. Never ask rhetorical or leading questions.
3. Do not reinforce children's answers with evaluative terms like "good" or "that's right."
4. Do not race ahead of yourself in your pacing of the discussion.
5. Phrase questions simply. Avoid hypothetical questions with younger children. (pp. 17-18)

These five rules can help teachers to talk with children about value-laden situations without influencing their answers.

Levels of Moral Thought

Every teacher who has taught young children has run into problems such as lying and stealing. There is no situation that is more difficult to handle than a child's being accused of taking someone else's toy. While the teacher has to see that the rightful owner receives his or her toy back, the action of "stealing" also requires a response.

Young children do not act out of a sense of what is morally right. Rather, they tend to make judgments on a much more pragmatic basis.

E. Turiel, "Stage Transitions in Moral Development." In R. M. W. Travers (Ed.), *Second Handbook of Research on Teaching* (Chicago: Rand McNally, 1973), pp. 732-758.

FIGURE 14-2

Lawrence Kohlberg, building on the work of Piaget, has developed an approach to the study of moral thought and action that can help to explain how children base their moral decisions (Turiel, 1973). Kohlberg views moral development as moving through a universal sequence of stages which represent ways of thinking and interacting with the environment. There are six stages to Kohlberg's theory of moral development (see Figure 14-2). Each stage represents a way of making moral judgments that is the result of an individual's actions in the social world.

When children arrive at preschool, most are at stage 1 or 2. For stage 1 children, those with a punishment and obedience orientation, the physical consequence of an action determines whether it is good or bad. A child in this stage does the right thing because of a fear of punishment. In stage 2, the instrumental-relativist orientation, right action consists of behavior that satisfies one's own needs and occasionally those of the other child. A stage 2 child will do the right thing to earn an ice cream cone or a ride on a pony.

Kohlberg has demonstrated that children's thinking about right and wrong and their ways of making moral decisions form organized patterns that vary as the child develops. His studies indicate that children generate their values and conceptions out of efforts to understand the world around them and to organize their social experiences.

Young children can come to grips with moral dilemmas that are much the same as those that adults experience. However, children view these dilemmas and cope with them differently. They are not able to understand adult morality, nor can they understand reasoning more than two stages above their own.

Children need the opportunity to explore moral dilemmas, to hear ethical reasoning different from their own, and to decide on the relative worth of various solutions. The use of unfinished stories, filmstrips, small debates, and discussion groups can give children an opportunity to grow when topics are both relevant and developmentally appropriate. With most groups of young children, however, the teacher does not need to look far to find situations that present moral dilemmas. Not sharing toys, breaking rules, lying, taking the property of others, and telling on others are everyday occurrences. The sensitive teacher can use these situations as opportunities for learning.

If lying becomes a problem, a group discussion can be used to talk about why people tell the truth and why they lie, who is hurt by lies, and who is helped. Children can learn from each other's reasoning in these discussions. The teachers should be careful to see that no child becomes the focus of a dilemma discussion. The purpose is not to punish someone, but to help children learn through reasoning.

Susan Stengel (1982) suggests that there are a number of ways for teachers to facilitate moral development. The first is to create a moral atmosphere in the classroom so children can see examples of fair treatment with everyone getting a chance and everyone sharing materials. The second is to have a limited number of meaningful rules that are enforced. Reasoning with children to help them understand the importance of the rules should be part of the enforcement process and is the third suggestion. Teachers who understand that values and moral reasoning are part of the developmental process are in a position to plan for the inclusion of values clarification activities as a part of the social studies curriculum.

Developing Cultural Awareness

The purpose of socialization is to help children attain the values and expectations of the school and community. While children who are "socialized" are more likely to be comfortable and successful than those who are not, they are also likely to experience a conflict between values held at home and those taught at school.

For many children the move to school represents a major break from the home. The values, culture, language patterns, and forms of social interactions may all be different. Children who are forced to use a new language and style of behaving may have difficulty accommodating to the school. The school may reject the child's language and culture, leaving the child feeling strange and bewildered. When a child does succeed in accommodating to the school values, there is a price that is paid in feelings of self-worth and the valuing of traditions (Saracho & Spodek, 1983).

Most communities (and most classrooms) include people from a wide range of cultural, social, ethnic, and religious backgrounds. It is easy for teachers to lose sight of the rich heritage children bring to school. Cultural awareness can help a classroom reflect the values and heritage of everyone in the class. Differences among people can be accepted and valued rather than ignored.

Teaching that everyone is the same is denying children the right to be proud of who they are. It is difficult to build a positive image of one's culture if that is denied or demeaned. Teachers who prize the differences in children are those who reinforce a feeling of self-worth.

Cultural awareness should be concerned with more than cultural differences. Patricia G. Ramsey (1982) points out that there are three common misconceptions about multicultural education: (1) such programs should focus only on information about other countries and cultures and not on our own, (2) that it is relevant only in classrooms that contain students who are members of the racial or cultural group to be studied rather than for all classrooms, and (3) that there should be a unified set of goals and a standard curriculum for multicultural education. In order to design effective multicultural programs, teachers must first understand the backgrounds of the children in the classroom. The foundation should be the children and not a preconceived notion of content. Further, multicultural education should not be a set of activities added to the

Children learn about another culture as the librarian tells a story using a Japanese *Kamishibaye*, or picture story box.

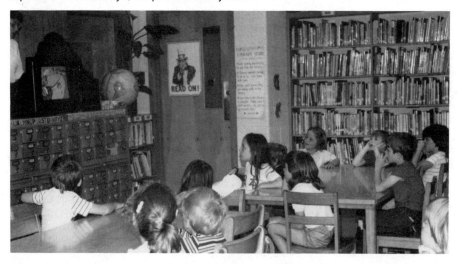

program but should be a value that is pervasive in all parts of the curriculum.

From a social studies perspective, cultural awareness requires teachers to present an accurate, honest presentation of events, groups, or people (Walsh, 1980). It also demands that teachers be open to differences, reject stereotypes, and be aware of any personal prejudices.

Many cultures have contributed to the American heritage. We should praise and celebrate the contributions of each and build upon the varied backgrounds children bring to the school. The multicultural life of children should enrich rather than diminish the curriculum. Cultural awareness is a prerequisite for a truly humanistic approach to the needs of the children, parents, and community. Social studies should reflect who children are rather than to try to make them into someone else.

SUMMARY

A good early childhood social studies program is both a separate subject area and a subject that is intertwined with all other areas of the curriculum. It focuses both on content and socialization. It can provide a framework for instruction in math, science, and language arts and it can provide children with the social skills necessary to be successful in school and in the community. It can serve as the center of the educational program.

Each new day brings many opportunities for providing children with real experiences within the classroom. Taking care of animals, cooking, planting gardens, experimenting with water and sand, playing musical instruments, working with others or alone, and just being a member of a group enable children to acquire a wealth of new information.

These experiences are just the first step. Children must have opportunities to represent what they have learned, to apply their developing understandings, and to refine their understanding. Caring for classroom animals, for example, can generate a wide range of information for children. Children can (1) discuss their experience with the teacher, (2) write about their experience, (3) listen to stories about similar or other animals, (4) tell their parents about what they have learned, (5) collect data on the animal's growth and graph it, or (6) begin to study other living things. The activities help children to make the best possible use of the real experiences.

REFERENCES

EDWARDS, C. P., M. E. LOGUE, AND A. S. RUSSELL (1983). Talking with young children about social ideas. *Young Children,* **39**(1), 12-20.

HILL, P. S. (1913). Second report. In Committee of Nineteen, *The Kindergarten.* Boston: Houghton-Mifflin.

HILLIARD, A. G. (1978). How should we assess children's social compentence? *Young Children,* **33**(5), 12-13.

LADD, G. W. (1984). Promoting children's prosocial behavior and peer relations in early childhood classrooms: A look at four teacher roles. *Dimensions,* **12**(4), 6-10.

MITCHELL, L. S. (1971). *Young geographers.* New York: Agathon Press (originally issued in 1934).

PRICE, G. G. (1982). Cognitive learning in early childhood education: Mathematics, science and social studies. In B. Spodek (Ed.), *Handbook of research in early childhood education,* pp. 264-294. New York: Free Press.

RAMSEY, P. G. (1982). Multicultural education in early childhood. *Young Children,* **37**(2), 13-23.

SARACHO, O. N., AND B. SPODEK (1983). *Understanding the multicultural experience in early childhood education.* Washington, DC: National Association for the Education of Young Children.

SPODEK, B. (1974). Social studies for young children: Identifying intellectual goals. *Social Education,* **38**(1), 40-45.

—— (1985). *Teaching in the early years* (3rd ed.). Englewood Cliffs, NJ: Prentice-Hall.

—— (1968). *The role of materials in teaching social studies to young children.* Paper presented at a conference for teachers on the child and the real world. University of British Columbia, Vancouver, B. C., October 4-5, 1968.

SPODEK, B., O. N. SARACHO, AND R. C. LEE (1984). *Mainstreaming young children.* Belmont, CA: Wadsworth.

STENGEL, S. R. (1982). Moral education for young children. *Young Children,* **37**(6), 23-31.

TURIEL, E. (1973). Stage transitions in moral development. In R. M. W. Travers (Ed.), *Second handbook of research on teaching,* pp. 732-758. Chicago: Rand McNally.

WALSH, H. M. (1980). *Introducing the young child to the social world.* New York: Macmillan.

SUGGESTED ACTIVITIES

1. Develop a teaching unit with a holiday theme lasting at least four or five days and containing at least one cooking activity.

2. Plan and implement a mapping activity for a small group of young children. Be sure to focus the activity on an area the children know.

3. Plan a post office field trip for a group of 15 four-year-old children. Describe what you would do at each of the three stages of taking a field trip.

4. Visit your local resource center and review/preview audiovisual materials that are designed to advance moral development. Start a file of those that are appropriate for young children.

5. Begin a file of books, songs, poetry, and the like that have multicultural themes. Be sure to include materials that reflect the geographic area where you hope to teach.

15

TOWARD PROFESSIONALISM

OBJECTIVES

After completing this chapter on professionalism, the student should be able to:

1. Describe ways that teachers can pursue their professional development.
2. Identify and describe several types of in-service programs.
3. List the important professional associations in early chiidhood education.
4. Compare the different professional organizations and journals in early childhood education.
5. Identify several resources which provide information on various topics in early childhood education.

The previous chapters have focused on providing the foundation knowledge for becoming an early childhood teacher. It included knowledge of the history of the field, its institutions, the range of practitioners that work in the field, and the child itself. This knowledge must be integrated with conceptions of curriculum, methods of organizing the physical and social resources, and methods of teaching. Ways of evaluating the program and working with parents are also important.

This text has presented foundational knowledge, just the beginning of what anyone should know to be a good teacher of young children. Just as in building a home, a foundation is important but it is not sufficient in itself. There is more that must be built upon that foundation. Preparing to teach at any level is a long-term process that should extend over a person's entire career. Continued professional development is critical for early childhood teachers.

Even though early childhood teachers have a major impact on young children's lives, they do not enjoy high status as professionals (Spodek, Saracho, & Davis, in press). There is considerable concern today that teaching standards need to be raised. If perceptions of teachers are to change, teachers themselves need to assume responsibility for becoming better prepared (Saracho, 1984; Saracho & Spodek, 1983). Teacher preparation that includes both personal development and professional development can be meaningful and practical.

TEACHERS' PERSONAL DEVELOPMENT

What teachers do and what they think about what they do are affected by their own values, attitudes, and perspectives. Teachers with a low self-concept might feel threatened and attempt to control children to show their superiority. Teachers with positive self-concept are able to share their concerns for their classroom children and transcend their personal needs.

According to Arthur Combs (1965), effective teachers have positive attitudes toward themselves and others. Similarly, research shows that teachers who have positive attitudes toward themselves foster a positive classroom environment; in contrast, teachers who have negative attitudes toward themselves foster negative feelings among their classroom students (Hart, Allen, Buell, Harris, & Wolf, 1964). Teachers with favorable attitudes toward themselves are better able to develop a supportive learning atmosphere. Teachers who feel inferior may put others down to make themselves look better. A child who constantly seeks a teacher's approval usually satisfies the teacher's nurturant instincts, but those actions may prevent the child from becoming independent.

Self-knowledge is important. It helps teachers sense when their own needs and concerns affect their judgment. Teachers need to be able to control their reactions toward their children in relation to their own personal needs and their own emotional structure. Self-understanding can guide teachers in reacting positively to their children and lead to understanding of others.

TEACHERS' PROFESSIONAL DEVELOPMENT

Teachers need a considerable amount of practical knowledge to function well in a classroom. This is usually gained through some form of systematic preparation. All teachers possess strengths and weaknesses. Strengths can be built upon, and weaknesses can be overcome through professional development.

Often beginning teachers discover that there is much they still need to learn. They often express the need to learn more about discipline, curriculum ideas, learning centers, early literacy training, language development, and dealing with transitions.

Ms. Rocha discovered that one of her classroom children was mentally retarded. While Ms. Rocha had learned something about special education, she did not know enough to work on a day-to-day basis with a mentally retarded child. She felt the need to gain new knowledge. She visited with the resource room teacher in the local elementary school who served as a consultant to her.

Teachers need to seek out many sources of information to extend their knowledge and skills.

The professional development of the entire staff (including teach-ers, aides, cooks, and others) can improve the children's educational program. Schools should invest a portion of their resources in some form of staff development. Some schools organize their own in-service training program; others rely on professional organizations that provide con-ferences and publications. Some schools require their teachers to enroll in college or community courses; others leave teachers to their own resources. Whether schools provide the means for staff development or not, teachers ultimately must become responsible for their own professional improve-ment. Teachers can engage in in-service training, continue their formal education, participate in professional organizations, or independently use the range of educational resources available.

In-service Programs

In-service programs may include workshops to deal with resource mate-rials, viewing films or videotapes, attending lectures, classes, or study groups, or observing other teachers.

In-service meetings should be based on what teachers feel they need to know. Teachers can assess their strengths and needs, then develop their own in-service remedial activities. Specialists might be called in to identify the resources that could be used to meet those needs.

> Mr. Slater was uncomfortable with transitions in his class. After reading about strategies for transitions in an early childhood textbook, he decided it would be helpful to observe good transitions being implemented. He arranged to observe a teacher who was good at transitions. He also had the school director observe his performance during transitions. They then jointly worked out new strategies to be used in transitions.

Each school differs in its educational needs. It is essential to match particular in-service programs to the staff's needs and interests. Early childhood staff members who have the maturity to discuss problems openly and to provide helpful feedback to each other are developing competence and creating a more productive school. Continual feedback and evaluation of the in-service training can provide insightful informa-tion to administrators so that future in-service training will meet the teachers' needs and make their attendance worthwhile.

Teacher-directed in-service. Some early childhood schools do not provide in-service teacher training. In such situations, a meaningful and systematic in-service program can still be developed by teachers them-selves using a team approach. If teachers and aides have a good rela-tionship, they can share ideas and coordinate activities. An in-service program that is jointly planned and implemented has the capacity to develop esprit de corps in a center as well as help the teachers grow. The major goal of such meetings is to create an environment where staff members can share and learn together and allow teachers to assume responsibility for their own professional development.

> Ms. Klein was concerned that her arts and crafts projects were quite limited. She felt that she was using the same material in the same way over and over again. After talking with her colleagues in the school, she realized that her concerns were shared by others. Ms. Klein invited teachers from two neighboring centers for a series of Saturday morning sessions in which each teacher would share favorite activities. The group also began searching through activities books in the local library for other projects to share.

It is best to excuse from the program individuals who have strong reservations. If there is a core of teachers who have an interest in their own professional development as well as that of their fellow teachers, other teachers will join the in-service activities when they are ready. Those who benefit from these sessions will spread the word to other teachers, who will become interested and join in.

Teacher-directed in-service education is based on the belief that a group can provide support for individual efforts in exploring new ideas and testing a variety of teaching strategies. Teachers who isolate themselves professionally do not benefit from the sharing of ideas, the encouragement, and the support that a group offers. Teachers can share and learn from each other if they are motivated to exchange ideas.

Teacher Study Group. Individuals who participate in a teacher study group should work on one small manageable set of problems (such as transitions, flexibility, or short-term planning) at a time. Once the group is established, the participants identify an area of study, assess themselves in the area, develop specific learning plans to improve themselves, and establish a system for acquiring feedback.

> Mr. Oliver and his colleagues in the child care center were beginning to feel that the knowledge of child development they had gained in their preservice training was not enough to help them understand the characteristics and behavior of the children in their classes. They arranged to have a local community college loan them a series of video tapes on child growth and development. The college also loaned them a videotape player and small television set. The teachers would gather once a week during the rest period to view and discuss the tapes while a teacher's aide supervised the children.

A teacher study group serves the interests of the members of the group. Together teachers study, discuss, share, and acquire knowledge that is particularly relevant to each individual. Participants may view vid-

Teachers' study groups can work on common problems.

eotapes, focusing on questioning techniques or pacing skills, or they can observe other teachers' practices. Participants in the group will remain involved as long as they are satisfied. Once teachers have lost interest, the group will fall apart.

A study group promotes objectivity in the individual's own behavior by sharing it with others. Teacher study groups also offer their members emotional support. Like any in-service program, these groups must be regularly evaluated to determine their worth.

Observing Other Teachers.   Teachers can observe other teachers as a way of improving their own teaching. They will gain a more objective view of teacher behavior and its effects on children. When teachers are actively engaged in their own teaching, they are so involved in responding and managing the class that it is hard to be aware of many classroom events and behaviors around them.

There are a variety of ways that observations can be scheduled. Two teachers can be paired to observe each other, or teachers can visit another school. Some teachers are fearful of being observed. They may become anxious about what others might think about them. They may be concerned that an observer does not share the same educational philosophy and that they will be demeaned. Visiting teachers can be helpful, however. They can share their view of incidents that the classroom teacher may not have noticed. At the same time visitors can learn new instructional techniques, expanding their repertoire of teaching skills.

A teacher and an aide in the same class can also observe each other. This pairing may be unbalanced, because the aide is usually not as qualified as the teacher. However, since the two work together as a team, they know their classroom situation and may share a similar educational philosophy. They should be able to provide each other with useful feedback. A teaching team can schedule occasional observations where the teacher (or aide) only observes and is freed from other responsibilities for a short period, possibly only fifteen or twenty minutes. The teacher can observe the class more intensely, thereby obtaining important information about individual children that can guide the teacher to respond to their unique developmental levels instead of to some stereotyped characteristics or group norms.

Teachers and aides may not be aware of everything they do or of their influence on their class. Their expectations about children and their ideas about the way specific lessons should be taught may influence what they see. Thus, seeing the classroom from the observer's point of view can be useful in eliminating some of the personal biases we all have.

Mentoring and Networking.   Mentoring and networking are two informal but important techniques teachers use to improve their knowledge of practice. Often a new teacher hired in a school is taken under the wing of a more experienced teacher. Standard procedures will be shown, help will be given in organizing the room, and information will be shared about the staff, the children, the parents, and the community. In addition the senior teacher will often share accumulated knowledge of practice, providing support for the novice teacher who might feel somewhat unsure of what is happening or why.

This help, or *mentoring*, may continue for a while. It eases the transition into the profession and is important for the development of both the novice and the experienced teacher. As a matter of fact, being able to serve as a mentor is an indication of personal maturity, as is noted in Eric Erikson's stages of development (see Chapter 5).

When teachers leave college and move into professional positions, they often promise to keep in touch with their fellow students. Usually one loses touch with those students who do not enter the profession or who move some distance away. However, others can develop a *network* of relationships, communicating with one another, sharing ideas, and providing emotional support when it is needed. Teachers find that networking serves many purposes in their professional development. They also seek or establish new networks as their maturity leads them to find new challenges and accept new roles.

Using Technology.   Recent developments in communications technology have provided other means to promote teachers' professional development. Video recordings are being used more widely for in-service training, evaluating teachers, and conducting research. Teachers can use video cameras and video cassette recorders to observe themselves. Self-viewing can provide teachers with information for self-improvement. Not all teachers accept self-viewing, however. Many are concerned that their spontaneity will suffer or that their rights might be violated. Nevertheless, teachers are learning to use these techniques and precautions are being taken to protect teachers' rights. Teachers' permission should be received before their videotapes are made available to anyone. The teacher should also have the right to limit the viewing of the tape and to request that the videotape be erased. The use of videotapes to analyze teachers' classroom instruction will probably not be accepted until teachers are fully protected and do not feel threatened.

College or University Courses.   Another alternative to in-servie training is college or university courses. Some institutions offer programs leading to various certificates or advanced degrees. For many early childhood programs, teachers are required to take college courses regularly as a way to keep abreast of the field. Tuition might be paid or salaries adjusted to the amount of advanced education a teacher has. Schools may modify a teachers' work schedule to facilitate college or university attendance.

College teachers can serve as consultants beyond the classroom.

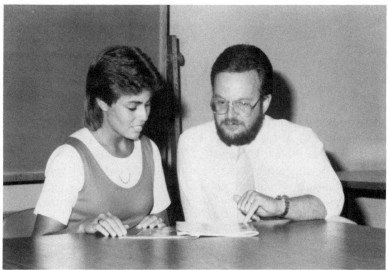

Professional Organizations

Professional organizations provide many resources to help teachers' self-development. A brief description of some of the major professional organizations in early childhood education follows.

National Association for the Education of Young Children (NAEYC). 1834 Connecticut Avenue N.W., Washington, DC, 20009. In 1926 a Committee on Nursery Education met, and the predecessor to NAEYC, the National Association for Nursery Education, was established. It has become one of the strongest and largest organizations in early childhood education, with over 43,000 members in almost 300 affiliate groups. Membership is open to those who are concerned with the education and well-being of children. The major goal of NAEYC is to facilitate the advancement and development of early childhood education. NAEYC provides professional development opportunities to early childhood educators to help them improve the quality of services for children ages birth to eight. NAEYC publishes a journal, *Young Children,* along with other publications, and organizes an annual conference. Its affiliates also hold conferences and workshops and publish and distribute a range of printed material.

Association for Childhood International (ACEI). 11141 Georgia Avenue, Suite 200, Wheaton, MD 20902. This organization grew out of the International Kindergarten Union and works for children's education, fostering appropriate educational conditions, programs, and practices through the elementary grades. It is concerned with teachers' professional growth and shares information with the public about school programs. ACEI is composed of individuals, local affiliate groups, and state and provincial associations. It publishes a journal, *Childhood Education,* as well as other publications, and holds an annual conference.

World Organization for Early Education (OMEP). OMEP, Organisation Mondial pour l'Education Prescolaire (French), was founded in 1948. Its major goals are to foster the study and education of young children and assist all of those working with young children to become aware of young children's needs. It shares information among early childhood educators throughout the world on education, development, health and nutrition, playgrounds, and toys. OMEP holds an international assembly every second year. OMEP and UNESCO have combined their efforts to work on projects of mutual concern. OMEP publishes a journal titled *The International Journal of Early Childhood Education.* There is an active U.S. Committee for OMEP.

Other Professional Associations

Other organizations related to the education of young children include the following:

> *American Montessori Society, Inc.* 150 Fifth Avenue, New York, NY 10010.
> *Child Welfare League of America, Inc.* 67 Irving Place, New York, NY 10010.
> *Council for Exceptional Children.* 1920 Association Drive, Reston, VA 22091.
> *National Committee on Education of Migrant Children.* 1501 Broadway, New York, NY 10016.
> *Parent Cooperative Preschool International.* 9111 Alton Parkway, Silver Spring, MD 20910.
> *Southern Association for Children Under Six (SACUS).* Box 5403 Brady Station, Little Rock, AR 72205.
> *United States National Committee for Early Childhood Education.* A unit of World Organization for Early Childhood Education (OMEP). 2400 Lahser Road, Southfield, MI 48034.

ERIC Clearinghouses

Teachers can also promote their own professional development by obtaining information from a variety of resources. The most widely available print resources are those of the Educational Resource Information Centers (ERIC). This resource, funded by the U.S. Office of Education, provides information upon request on various educational topics. Teachers can request the information they need from the appropriate ERIC clearinghouse, which taps a national data base. Their documents are also available in microfiche collections in many libraries. The following are current ERIC clearinghouses:

> *Adult, Career, and Vocational Education,* Center for Vocational Education, Ohio State University, 1960 Kenny Road, Columbus, OH 43210.
> *Counseling and Personnel Services.* 2108 School of Education Building, The University of Michigan, School of Education Building, East University and South University Streets, Ann Arbor, MI 48109.
> *Early Childhood and Elementary Education (ERIC/EECE).* University of Illinois, 804 West Pennsylvania Avenue, Urbana, IL 61801.
> *Educational Management.* University of Oregon, Eugene, OR 97403.
> *Handicapped and Gifted Children.* Council on Exceptional Children, 1920 Association Drive, Reston, VA 22091.
> *Higher Education.* George Washington University, One Dupont Circle, Suite 630, Washington, DC 20036.
> *Information Resources.* School of Education, SCRDT, Stanford University, Stanford, CA 94305.

ERIC clearinghouses provide a wealth of resource materials on microfiche.

Junior Colleges. University of California, 96 Powell Library, Los Angeles, CA 90024.

Language and Linguistics. Center for Applied Linguistics, 1611 North Kent Street, Arlington, VA 22209.

Reading and Communication Skills. National Council of Teachers of English, 1111 Kenyon Road, Urbana, IL 61801.

Rural Education and Small Schools. New Mexico State University, Box 3AP, Las Cruces, NM 88003.

Science, Mathematics, and Environmental Education. Ohio State University, 1800 Cannon Drive, 400 Lincoln Tower, Columbus, OH 43210.

Social Studies/Social Science Education. 855 Broadway, Boulder, CO 80302.

Teacher Education. American Association of Colleges of Teacher Education, One Dupont Circle, N.W., Suite 610, Washington, DC 20036.

Tests, Measurement, and Evaluation. Educational Testing Service, Rosedale Rd., Princeton, NJ 08540.

Urban Education. Teacher College, Box 40, Columbia Unversity, 525 West 120th Street, New York, NY 10027.

Journals

Publications are available from a number of organizations and agencies that are concerned with the education and well-being of young children. Private publishers also issue journals related to early childhood education. These include:

American Education. Superintendent of Documents, U.S. Government Printing Office, Washington, DC 20402.

Child Care Information Exchange. C-44, Redmond, WA 98052.

Child Care Quarterly. Human Sciences Press, 72 Fifth Avenue, New York, NY 10011.

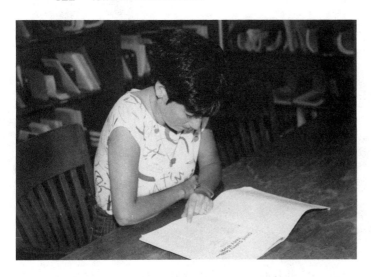

Early childhood educational journals offer much useful information for teachers.

Child Development. Child Development Abstracts and *Child Development Monographs.* Society for Research and Child Development, University of Chicago Press, Chicago, IL 60637.

Child Welfare. Child Welfare League of America, Inc., 44 East 23rd Street, New York, NY 10010.

Childhood Education. Association for Childhood Education International, 11141 Georgia Avenue, Suite 200, Wheaton, MD. Bulletins, leaflets and books are also published.

Children Today. Office of Human Development Services, Department of Health and Human Services, Room 356-G, 200 Independence Ave., S.W., Washington, DC 20201.

Day Care and Early Education. Human Sciences Press, 72 Fifth Avenue, New York, NY 10011.

Dimensions. Southern Association for Children Under Six, Box 5403, Brady Station, Little Rock, AR 72215.

Early Years. Allen Raymond, Inc., P.O. Box 1266, Darien, CT 06826.

Instructor. 545 Fifth Avenue, New York, NY 10017.

Journal of Home Economics. American Home Economics Association, 2010 Massachusetts Avenue, N.W., Washington, D.C. 20036.

National Parent-Teacher. National Congress of Parents and Teachers, 700 North Rush Street, Chicago, IL 60511. Study guides are also available.

Young Children. National Association for the Education of Young Children, 1834 Connecticut Avenue, N.W. Washington, DC 20009. Bulletins, materials, and books are also published.

SUMMARY

There are a variety of ways that teachers can learn more about themselves and their teaching. Staff meetings can be used to upgrade the quality of teaching. Speakers can be invited, films shown, or workshops held. Teachers can also share craft activities, songs, or action plays.

Teachers who are interested in improving themselves profession-ally can do so in several ways. They can learn through their own experience, from the experiences of their fellow teachers, and from a number of resources outside the school. Some schools support staff members' attendance at community workshops, at local, regional, and national conferences, and in college and university courses, so they may keep abreast in the field.

A number of professional associations also provide resources. Staff members may belong to one or more of these professional organizations, may attend conferences, workshops, and meetings, and may read early childhood publications and resource materials to keep up-to-date in the early childhood field. Professional journals are also helpful.

Early childhood education is growing rapidly. Educators must continue their self-education throughout their career.

REFERENCES

COMBS, A. W. (1965). *The professional education of teachers: A perceptual view of teacher preparation.* Boston: Allyn & Bacon.

HART, B. M., K. E. ALLEN, J. S. BUELL, J. R. HARRIS, AND M. M. WOLF (1964). Effects of social reinforcement on operant crying. *Journal of Experimental Child Psychology,* **1,** 145-153.

SARACHO, O. N. (1984). Perception of the teaching process in early childhood education through role analysis. *Journal of the Association for the Study of Perception,* **19** (1), 26-39.

SARACHO, O. N. AND B. SPODEK (1983). Preparing teachers for multicultural classrooms. In O. N. Saracho and B. Spodek (Eds.), *Understanding the multicultural experience in early childhood education,* pp. 125-146. Washington, DC: National Association for the Education of Young Children.

SPODEK, B., O. N. SARACHO, AND M. D. DAVIS (IN PRESS). Professionalism and the preparation of early childhood practitioners. In S. Kilmer (Ed.), *Advances in early education and day care,* Vol. 5. Greenwich, CT: JAI Press.

SUGGESTED ACTIVITIES

1. Interview a successful teacher to find out the aspects of teaching that are most challenging and least challenging. Ask the teacher for advice to those considering the teaching profession.

2. Review issues of *Young Children,* the journal of the National Association for the Education of Young Children, for a recent six-month period of publication. Report the main themes and points of view evident in these issues. Do the same for *Childhood Education,*

the publication of the Association of Childhood Education International. Share the reports with a small group or the whole class.

3. Attend a professional conference, meeting, or workshop for teachers of young children.

4. Interview a local officer of a professional organization. If possible, invite the officer to speak to the class on the way the organization improves the teachers' personal and professional development.

INDEX